*The Public Life
of the Arts
in America*

Rutgers Series on the Public Life of the Arts

A series edited by:

Ruth Ann Stewart
Margaret J. Wyszomirski
Joni M. Cherbo

The Public Life of the Arts in America

JONI M. CHERBO
MARGARET J. WYSZOMIRSKI
EDITORS

RUTGERS UNIVERSITY PRESS
New Brunswick, New Jersey, and London

Library of Congress Cataloging-in-Publication Data

The public life of the arts in America / Joni M. Cherbo and Margaret
    J. Wyszomirski, editors.
        p. cm.—(Rutgers series on the public life of the arts)
    Includes bibliographical references and index.
    ISBN 0-8135-2767-8 (cloth : alk. paper)—ISBN 0-8135-2768-6 (pbk. :
alk. paper)
        1. Arts and society—United States—History—20th century.   I. Series.
    II. Cherbo, Joni Maya, 1941–   III. Wyszomirski, Margaret Jane.
    NX180.S6 P83 2000
    700'.973 21—dc21

                                                                99-042390

British Cataloging-in-Publication data for this book is available from the
British Library

Manufactured in the United States of America

Contents

JONI M. CHERBO

MARGARET J. WYSZOMIRSKI

Introduction: The Public Life of the Arts in America

In 1997, the American Assembly, a nonpartisan think tank based at Columbia University, convened "The Arts and the Public Purpose" at the Arden House in Harriman, New York. From May 29 through June 1, 1997, a diverse group of seventy-eight participants met to examine a wide range of issues regarding the arts in America. A report based on the discussions and background materials was drawn up at the conclusion of the meeting. *The Arts and the Public Purpose* was widely disseminated and has stimulated extensive follow-up meetings and activities.

This volume includes chapters based on the background papers that were commissioned in advance of the American Assembly meeting. The papers have been extensively revised and updated, incorporating discussion points that arose at the meeting and ideas that evolved from the deliberations. An additional chapter has been written by the coeditors, articulating the significant ways in which arts and culture policy is changing at the end of the millennium.

The chairpersons of the 1997 American Assembly meeting were Alberta Arthurs, the former director for Arts and Humanities at the Rockefeller Foundation, and Frank Hodsoll, the chairperson of the National Endowment for the Arts from 1981 to 1988. The Steering Committee was headed by Margaret J. Wyszomirski, then professor of political science and director of the Arts Management Program at Case Western Reserve University. The project director was Daniel Ritter, former counsel to the U.S. Senate Subcommittee on Education, Arts, and Humanities.

Joni M. Cherbo, a sociologist, educator, and independent researcher, was the project research director.

The 1997 meeting "The Arts and the Public Purpose" was guided by the belief that reexamination of the structures and support for the arts in America was timely. Two concerns were uppermost: to better articulate the public purposes that the arts serve, in order to formulate more effective public policies that pertain to the public life of the arts in America; and to understand all of the arts—commercial, nonprofit, and unincorporated (avocational, hobbies, community based)—as part of an interrelated arts sector or industry.

An examination of the arts as a sector with interrelated components was long overdue. American arts had become an enormous, important, global industry. Art and entertainment constitutes our second largest export after defense. Domestically, most Americans are engaged in the arts, whether as live audience participants, as hobbyists, or via the media of broadcasting, recording, video, or the Internet. Despite its size and impact, public funding for the arts has persistently met with resistance, and a broad notion of cultural policy has gone virtually unrecognized. An understanding of what the arts include, what public issues they address, and how they serve public purposes presages consideration of their policy presence and public support.

A comprehension of the interconnectedness of the various components that constitute an arts sector can facilitate our ability to see the scale and impact of the arts in ways not possible when we focused on separate artistic disciplines. The nonprofit arts and the unincorporated arts have been given separate and marginal consideration, while the commercial arts are viewed as entertainment. Yet they interact and are interdependent in important ways and areas that pertain to all and face similar policy issues, such as copyright and trade agreements. Taken as a whole, the arts in America constitute a significant sector or industry; their domestic economic impact is substantial, as they make noteworthy contributions to the GNP, employment, and the tax base.

Exploring and advancing our understanding of these two basic concerns—identifying and articulating the public purposes of the arts and the interconnectedness of the broad arts sector—was the task for the contributors of this volume. Each chapter addresses a piece of these larger concerns. This book represents a new thrust in our thinking about the arts and cultural policy in America, and is a contribution to the growing scholarship in the field of cultural policy studies.

The volume is divided into three parts. The first part, "Exploring a Changing Landscape," includes three chapters, each of which advances a new, organic framework for thinking about the arts sector and public policy. The lead chapter, by the editors, Joni M. Cherbo and Margaret J. Wyszomirski, takes a broad overview of the state of the arts and arts policy in America. It focuses on the old policy paradigm that has governed public arts support since the 1960s, changing conditions prompting a paradigm shift, and the possible dimensions of an emerging policy paradigm. The second chapter, by Harry Hillman Chartrand, sketches the dimensions of what he sees as a holistic American arts industry. Using an industrial organization model drawn from mainstream economics, Chartrand identifies the major components and interrelations of a broad inclusive arts industry. Next, Margaret J. Wyszomirski discusses a range of constitutionally rooted public purposes that the arts in America have addressed and the connections between values, purposes, issues, and the programs that have characterized America's cultural policies.

The second part, "The Public and the Arts," also includes three chapters. First, Judith Balfe and Monnie Peters explore the many ways Americans are involved in the arts. They present data on American participation in the nonprofit arts as audiences, amateur practitioners, and media participants. The authors reflect on the limits of past thinking and data collection on arts participation, advocating expansion of our concept of involvement from a relatively passive notion of audience participation to a more inclusive and active one. John P. Robinson and Therese Filicko review survey data on American attitudes toward art and culture. They note serious limits in our knowledge of American opinion on this topic and suggest further research that would improve our understanding of how Americans think about arts and cultural issues and how such public opinion information can inform and influence policy. The final chapter in this part is Kevin V. Mulcahy's comparative survey of public support for the arts in the United States, Canada, Norway, and France. A comparative focus highlights and contrasts our system of support with others and illuminates new possibilities for the organization and support of the arts and culture, many of which are discussed by Mulcahy.

The third part, "Perspectives from Arts Subsectors," presents three examples of areas that are germane to understanding the arts sector. Ann M. Galligan and Neil O. Alper review data on the careers of a variety of artistic professions in America. They look at such issues as early education, training, remuneration, multiple job holding, union and service organization membership, retirement, and benefits, noting problems that are unique to distinctive arts professions. They remind us that artistic careers and creativity are socially embedded—that is, enhanced or impeded by any number of institutional practices and public policies. Charles M. Gray and James Heilbrun provide an economic overview of the nonprofit arts sector—its overall performance, unique organization, and market structures. They note that the nonprofit arts represent a tiny portion of the American economy, a fact that belies the overall importance of the arts in America. Finally, Harold L. Vogel reviews our nation's most important commercial art form—the movies. He covers the historical evolution of the film industry, the continuing impact of technology on the industry, the constant need for capital, key government regulations, markets, recent mergers between the communication and entertainment fields, and the growth of independent production and cinema complexes.

*The Public Life
of the Arts
in America*

PART

I

Exploring a Changing Landscape

JONI M. CHERBO
MARGARET J. WYSZOMIRSKI

1

Mapping the Public
Life of the Arts
in America

The Arts and Society

The artifacts that have endured from the dawn of human existence remind us that the arts have been a ubiquitous part of human life from its inception. So evident are its manifestations from our early history—cave paintings, pictographs, petroglyphs, simple carvings; body painting, adornments of dress, tools, weapons, housing; musical sounds from early instruments, chanting, and songs; ceremonial movements or dance—it is tempting to speak about an aesthetic dimension that is generic to the human species.

In all likelihood, it is the same forces that drove our ancestors throughout history to paint, sing, dance, and act that are the same rudimentary motives that drive us to artistic expression today: the need to celebrate the unknown, mystical aspects of being; to indicate social distinctions; to establish and honor power; to document affiliation; to educate, decorate, entertain, serve as a mode of self-expression; and to solve social problems. Art serves countless purposes, both social and personal.

The fascination of the arts' universality, however, resides in their extraordinary historical diversity. Tribes, towns, nations, civilizations, eras have produced a wide, variable, and rich array of artistic expressions and products ranging from the glorious to the mundane. And the social context of the arts has been organized in different ways in various times and places. Certain art forms take precedence in each era; the functions art serves will vary along with the meanings and valuation associated with them; the arts are produced, supported, and distributed in various ways; the range of artistic activities and their stratification among the population differ according to time and place as well as in the ways they are linked to power and government, and the ways they are taught.

The limitations of historical data often fail to provide us with an in-depth look at how the arts were practiced in different historical contexts, especially in the case of those artistic practices not of the dominant classes. We know little about the practices of the multitude of court painters, craftspersons such as glassmakers and metalworkers; fashion designers, furniture makers, and a multiplicity of other artists whose work didn't find its way into the historical record. We know little about the arts of the lower classes and the peasantry. In effect, it has rarely been topical among those vocations vested with the task of understanding the social context of the arts to research the full range of artistic practices and their relationship to society in different historical settings (inquiries usually vested in art historians or cultural social scientists). We primarily know the dominant art historical themes.

For instance, sculpture and architecture dominated artistic forms in ancient Greece and Rome. Architecture, in the form of cathedrals, marked the Christian Middle Ages. Large-scale historical and mythological paintings were esteemed in nineteenth-century France, while music proliferated in eighteenth-century Germany. In China, for over two thousand years, calligraphy and painting were considered major art forms; Japanese screen paintings, used as wall separations in elite homes, lasted as significant artistic expressions for over two millennia. Indigenous arts, painting, weavings, and sculptures are dominant art forms in present-day Haiti. In twentieth-century America, an enormous range of artistic expression prevails with film being our most frequented art form, largest capitalized arts industry, and second largest export.

Arts patronage too has taken many forms and mixes, ranging from the coffers of nobility, monarchs, popes, and the wealthy to federal, state, and local government agencies, quasi-municipal agencies; religious institutions, foundations, business entities; guilds, associations, and the marketplace. Different arts connect with different patrons. European governments have historically subsidized a variety of traditional arts and heritage. A wealthy bourgeoisie underwrote the portraiture and association paintings of seventeenth-century Netherlands. Present-day Haitian art is tourist driven. Contemporary American art is supported primarily in the marketplace as private and public subsidies provide only a small portion of total arts support.

Artists themselves have been treated as craftspersons, professionals, or as special creative people, and their training has varied from apprenticeships to formal academic training to self-taught. In some places artists are revered; in others they are treated as simply another type of worker. Ancient Greece and the Roman Empire considered the arts and humanities as means of illuminating themes central to sustaining and embellishing civil society. Ideas arising from the Enlightenment and Romanticism produced the twentieth-century vision of the artist as a creative genius and the notion of art for art's sake.

Clearly, while the arts are an integral part of human life, their expressions and organization within the social fabric are highly variable. There is no standard; each society treats its arts and artists differently.

According to Joseph Alsop in "The Rare Art Traditions" (1982), among the vast number of visual art traditions, five times in the whole of human history the artistic enterprise blossomed into a full-scale industry, one that included not simply the production and patronage of the arts, but also art collecting, art history, an active art market, the existence of art museums, art forgeries, revaluation of artworks, a focus on antiques, and inflated prices for works of art—all practices we take for granted today.

In present-day America, such an arts industry is flourishing. By a number of measures, both objective and subjective, the arts can and should be seen as a defining aspect of contemporary American existence.

According to a variety of public and industry sources, the nonprofit arts industry generates $36.8 billion in economic activity annually.

- Nonprofit arts support 1.3 million jobs.
- Nonprofit arts return $3.4 billion in federal income taxes; spur $1.2 billion in state government revenues; and bring in $790 million in local government revenues.
- The overall economic impact of the nonprofit arts industry in terms of expenditures, full-time jobs, personal income generated, and public revenues was estimated as over $857 million in 1994.

Nonprofit arts institutions have experienced a dramatic growth over the last thirty-five years, spurred in part by the establishment of the National Endowment for the Arts in 1965.

- Dance troops have grown from 28 in 1958 to over 400.
- Opera companies with budgets of over $100,000 have grown from 29 in 1964 to 209 by 1989.
- Chamber-music groups, most formed in the last twenty years, now number around 1,120.

- Half of America's eighty-two hundred museums have come into existence since the 1970s.
- The nonprofit regional theater movement, begun in the 1960s, now consists of more than nine hundred theater groups.
- At least thirty-seven mixed-arts complexes have sprung up nationally in various urban centers in the last twenty years.

America's combined cultural industries (the output of artists and other creative workers in entertainment, publishing, audiovisual, music, and recording) are 5.68 percent of GDP, generating $443.9 billion in annual revenues.

- The combined culture industries are our nation's leading export, generating more than $60 billion annually in overseas sales.
- The entertainment industry generates about $270 billion in revenues annually, over half the revenue of the cultural industries.
- Movie multiplexes are growing in every corner of the country, and top film stars command millions of dollars per picture.

People have a significant interest in the arts and culture.

- Ninety-six percent of the U.S. population is engaged in some aspect of the arts, from attending a film, to listening to CDs, to engaging in an artistic hobby or attending live art performances.
- A 1997 National Endowment for the Arts study found that among adult Americans, attendance at seven of the "higher arts" (symphony, plays, musicals, ballet, jazz, opera, museums) grew from 41 percent in 1992 to 50 percent in 1997, while participation via the media (CDs, TV, videotapes, radio) for the same art forms engaged 75 percent of the population.
- About 46 percent of U.S. travelers include a visit to cultural institutions or sites as part of their vacation.
- America is considered a leader in many of the arts and the premier nation that nurtures creative exploration, drawing a number of artists to our shores. The value America places on innovation is reflected in the 550,000 copyrights for music, art, manuscripts, and software registered per year.
- American openness and cultural diversity continue to produce internationally recognized, innovative artistic expressions such as jazz, American musical theater, and modern dance.
- Many American celebrities hail from the arts and entertainment field. Their performance histories and private lives dominate the media, popular magazines, and conversation.
- A handful of artists, both contemporary and deceased, in various artistic disciplines, command astronomical prices for their artworks.

Reflecting the scope of the American artistic enterprise, cultural policy issues are attracting greater attention and import both at home and abroad.

- Approximately 200 federal programs, 50 state arts agencies, and nearly 4,000 local arts agencies are engaged in dealing with cultural policy issues ranging from funding concerns to regulatory issues to public/private partnerships and investment incentives.
- Overall, public support for the arts (federal, state, local) continues to increase. In 1983, public support was approximately $500 million; in 1998 it amounted to over 1 billion.
- A growing number of organizations such as policy think tanks, foundations, service and advocacy organizations, and research institutions are also involved with, and support, arts and cultural policy initiatives.
- The attention garnered by the culture wars far surpassed the minuscule NEA budget; it was a flash point for competing visions of America.
- So pervasive is the American movie industry abroad, that it is often accused of cultural imperialism, prompting a number of Western nations to convene in an effort to protect themselves from this perceived takeover.

Although we are surrounded by this plethora of artistic activity, we take it for granted, failing to recognize the arts as an extraordinary and defining aspect of contemporary American life. Reflecting on our present-day artistic Renaissance, Tyler Cowen (1998) commented: "Mid-to-late twentieth-century Western culture, although a favorite target of many critics, will go down in history as a fabulously creative and fertile epoch. The culture of our era has produced lasting achievements in cinema, rhythm, dance, graphic and commercial design, fashion, jazz, the proliferation of classical, early music, and 'original instrument' recordings, the short story, Latin American fiction, genre fiction, and the biography, to name but a few examples."

Field Building

Despite the extraordinary growth of American arts activity, their popular involvement, and domestic and international esteem, it appears that most Americans view the arts as marginal activities. As a consequence, educators and lawmakers often fail to recognize the embeddedness of the arts in American life—their economic value, symbolic importance, and benefits for individual communities and personal well being. The aesthetic dimension needs consciousness raising.

In many disparate corners of the arts community, the realization is taking hold that there is virtue and advantage to thinking in terms of an arts sector or arts industry. We have entered into a period of field building—an accelerated and concerted thrust to define this field, its boundaries and players; to document its facts and figures; to relate its importance to life and American society; and to institutionalize an informed arts policy into the polity.

One might suspect that the arts and cultural community is at a similar point to that of the environmental movement in the 1960s. The conservation movement, formed at the turn of the twentieth century, was originally a collection of citizen groups dedicated to saving America's natural sites. Over time this movement became an identifiable, proactive community concerned with a number of issues: preserving national parkland, wildlife habitats, and ecological systems; saving endangered species; maintaining clean air and water; and beautifying roads and highways.

Similarly, we are now engaged in constructing a new policy paradigm for the arts and culture. Once distinct cultural issue areas, arts interest groups and disciplines are beginning to find kindredness and to rally around both the concept and potential of delineating an arts sector or industry. Changing social, economic, and political circumstances and an evolving arts infrastructure, not simply controversy over the fate of the NEA, have brought us face-to-face with the necessity to redefine and update our aging arts and cultural policy paradigm.

These changing circumstances both spurred and shaped the 1997 American Assembly, "The Arts and the Public Purpose." The background materials and final report of that meeting, together with the 1997 report of the President's Committee on the Arts and Humanities (PCAH), *Creative America*, addressed issues related to the changing arts and cultural paradigm. Currently, the establishment of the Arts and Culture Center in Washington, D.C., the growing interest among foundations in cultural policy, and the development of various academic programs and institutes concerned with cultural policy are all evidence of a dynamic field building.

Our Evolving Arts and Cultural Paradigm: Maps and Paradigms

What is a policy paradigm? We can think of it as a multidimensional map that organizes a complex of information into an understandable, coherent format. It does so by identifying key features and concerns and laying them out in relation to one another so that we can understand what is likely to be encountered between different points.

There are many different kinds of maps: geological maps that detail the underlying strata; topographical maps that identify major ground features and landmarks; road maps that sketch our routes, distances, and road conditions; weather maps that track changing environmental conditions; and distribution maps that illustrate how the incidence and intensity of a specific commodity or characteristic varies from place to place. If all these maps for a particular area were overlaid, they would provide rich and coherent information to assist potential travelers as well as regional planners. If the maps were accompanied by an explanation of their relationship and influence upon one another, then this collection of information would constitute the basic ingredients of an empirical theory explaining how existing features interrelate in a defined area of concern. While creating complete maps of any terrain may be an ideal, the attempt to do so for a specific policy area is a necessary and justifiable effort in the process of making informed policy decisions.

Policy, then, might be thought of as an empirical theory that has been politically validated and thus justifies collective action. Once enacted, policy sets into action a number of political processes and activities, and becomes fixed in particular organizational structures and administrative procedures. Over time, a policy construct acquires a normative quality in that it embodies a belief or preference about how things should be. These empirical and normative factors constitute a policy paradigm, a generally accepted understanding of how select assumptions, conditions, values, interests, and processes are interrelated; what goals are desirable and feasible; and what outcomes are expected.

Accumulated change is normally slow, sometimes almost imperceptible, requiring a modest realignment of the empirical maps. On occasion, however, significant changes can require the entire realignment of a conceptual paradigm. The last few years have been such an instance for the arts policy community; we are adrift between a dysfunctional old paradigm and a protean new paradigm. During such periods of change, it can be difficult to get our bearings and reorient our thinking. Yet, the effort must be made; identifying essential issues and elements helps us understand how the previous arts funding paradigm has fallen out of sync with current conditions, what form an emerging paradigm is likely to take, and where its construction could be assisted.

Public Leveraging Arts Paradigm

In 1965, nearly two centuries after the birth of the nation, Congress created the first federal agency in U.S. history dedicated to the ongoing and direct support of the arts. This model, the Public Leveraging Arts (PLA) policy, was centered on the National Endowment for the Arts (NEA) and entailed many aspects and assumptions.

The PLA paradigm was primarily concerned with professional non-profit arts organizations; was organized, in the main, around discrete arts disciplines; and worked largely by awarding matching grants and grants-in-aid to the states. The federal government, according to this paradigm, was to be responsive to the needs of the arts community and specific arts fields rather than to the larger populace, and to catalyze support from other patrons, both local and private. Other issues, such as regulatory policies affecting the commercial arts, were outside the boundaries of the PLA paradigm.

The arts were seen at that time as an asset for diplomacy. The political environment of the times trusted the capacity and accountability of government. Parity with federal support for the sciences was claimed for the arts and humanities.

The PLA paradigm presumed that the so-called high arts were socially valuable and deserved assistance, as they could not be sustained by the marketplace. It regarded the popular arts as entertainment, commercially self-sufficient, and mundane, and therefore in need of being counterbalanced by government assistance to the more worthy, but financially precarious high arts. It also sought to provide greater individual access to the nonprofit arts, especially to those who were disadvantaged, whether by reason of geography, economic means, or cultural heritage. A supply-side strategy was adopted to address these twin problems— the financial instability of nonprofit arts organizations and the inequitable access of the public to these arts. The strategy involved subsidizing an increase in nonprofit artistic production and distribution and encouraging greater financial contributions from private foundations and corporations as well as from state and local governments. The strategy presumed an expanding base of artistic and managerial talent and a large, untapped populace likely to have the time, money, and interest needed to join the nonprofit arts audience if given the opportunity.

The arts funding paradigm gave great credence to artistic excellence and was based on the belief that quality should be determined by professional peer panels entrusted with reviewing grant applications. In the name of artistic freedom, it assumed that creative artists and nonprofit arts organizations should enjoy considerable autonomy from government intrusion and, thus, that public funding judgments should be aesthetically based and not influenced by political, social, or ideological considerations.

In the thirty years of its dominance, the public leveraging policy succeeded in three important regards: (1) It expanded artistic access for citizens throughout the country and dramatically increased the number, variety, dispersion, and professionalism of nonprofit arts organizations.

(2) It cultivated both an intergovernmental and a mixed public-private financial support system for the nonprofit arts. (3) It institutionalized the arts as an area of valid public policy concern at all levels of government. In realizing these accomplishments, the PLA policy paradigm significantly changed the public stature and face of the nonprofit arts in the United States.

Ingredients of a New Paradigm

Times change. During the reigning years of the PLA paradigm, especially in the past decade, many of its assumptions, conditions and procedures have either changed or been challenged. Some of these changes were imperceptibly slow. Some related to specific paradigm elements (such as peer review) but not others (like mixed funding). Some were overt, such as with the culture wars. Yet cumulatively, time and circumstances have shifted the very foundations of federal arts policy.

Three new topographical features presently seem to characterize the emerging cultural policy paradigm:

1. Blurring and enlarging of the boundaries of inclusion and concern, which, in turn, has led to a focus on redefining key policy terms and assumptions
2. The adoption of a systems approach rather than a focus on individual artists, specific arts organizations, particular disciplinary fields, or distinct cultural communities
3. The development of a more complex and diversified approach to all aspects of the policymaking process. This includes giving more explicit attention to what the public purposes of federal arts and cultural policies; developing more ongoing coalitions and advocacy strategies; and developing a repertoire of policy strategies and administrative mechanisms for effecting and supporting arts and cultural policy.

Blurring and Enlarging Boundaries of Inclusion

Significant tectonic shifts occurred within the arts themselves. The long-standing arts hierarchy lost its inviolable status. The evaluative distinction between the high and popular arts became blurred. Rather than being perceived as virtuous, the high arts were negatively characterized by some as elitist. The notion that we could objectively identify artistic excellence came to be thought of as discriminatory by those both within and outside the high arts. Although the popular arts were still criticized for a tendency to be common, vulgar, and violent, they were no longer dismissed as mere entertainment. American commercial arts had become an essential producer of local mass culture, a dynamic export industry, and a pervasive aspect of American life. Furthermore, entertainment often commingled with high art, blurring the boundaries between them.

Unlike the PLA paradigm, the current discussion is no longer exclusively focused on the professional, nonprofit arts. It has expanded to also include the commercial as well as the unincorporated arts (avocational, hobbies, and community-based arts)—exploring the intersections between them as well as shared interests and concerns, programs, and goals. Crossovers, transfers, and collaborations (both actual and potential) among the nonprofit and commercial arts and unincorporated arts are proliferating and garnering attention.

Though policy concerns related to the nonprofit arts and commercial arts remain distinguishable, they have begun to overlap. Issues such as copyright, intellectual property, trade agreements, preservation, and heritage increasingly affect both commercial and nonprofit arts. Both encountered controversy over content control and standards in the form of television rating systems, the V-chip, decency in programming on networks and public television, or the political correctness of certain museum exhibitions. Furthermore, the balance of public costs and benefits came under scrutiny with regard, for example, to broadcast spectrum allocation, public television funding and programming, and computer software marketing.

Recent regulatory changes are affecting the arts and arts-related enterprises. These include the first major reform of telecommunications policy in fifty years; an extension of copyright terms; antitrust action against Microsoft; megamergers in the entertainment field; a more entrepreneurial Corporation for Public Broadcasting; and a number of international trade agreements that affect global traffic in cultural goods, personnel, and services.

While it used to be customary to treat nonprofit issues such as arts funding, humanities support, and broadcast regulation as operating within separate policy arenas, the emerging paradigm seems to be based on the perception that each of these is part of a segmented but interconnected cultural policy framework. It is also now more generally recognized that policies that concern the arts and culture emanate from many federal departments and agencies operating in a variety of policy areas, such as education, taxes, communications, immigration, trade, charitable and business incentives, international cultural exchanges, trade regulations, broadcast licenses, copyrights, and grant making.

In sum, the policy arena is broadening to encompass the high, popular, and unincorporated arts, whether nonprofit or commercial, and deepening to include a number of issues that touch upon the activities of many arts disciplines and are invested in many federal departments and agencies and levels of government.

Along with this widening of perspective came a heightened awareness that the goals of arts policy are not confined to funding issues or to annual appropriations. Funding concerns become subservient to larger goals. Today, a different perspective animates arts policy discussions, one that focuses on how the arts can and do meet public purposes, the needs of the nation, and its citizens. The 1997 American Assembly, "The Arts and Public Purpose," identified four such purposes: (1) helping to define American identity, (2) contributing to the quality of life and to economic prosperity, (3) helping to form an educated and aware citizenry, and (4) enhancing individual life.

There is even some discussion that the term "policy" should be extended to cover the public goals of private, nonprofit institutions such as foundations, service and professional organizations, and arts and entertainment organizations. For example, the acquisition of the ABC television network by Disney recently gave rise to questions about how such business arrangements might affect freedom of the press: an unfavorable investigative story done by ABC about the Disney Corporation was squelched. In such a case, the policy decision of a private corporation has public implications.

Furthermore, it is argued that a more inclusive notion of policy would be justifiable because arts and cultural activity is predominantly a private sector phenomenon. In addition, the NEA relies on nonprofit arts organizations to actually provide cultural activities for nontraditional audiences and arts education programming for children. The agency may help fund such services but does not directly provide them.

The blurring and enlarging of many boundaries embodies reconsideration and reconfiguration of key values and goals with potentially profound implications for the policy topography and construction of public programs. For example, the core value of artistic excellence, originally a guiding principle for public subsidies, seems to be transforming into a focus on creativity. Artistic excellence was associated with elitism and tended to focus attention on artistic products; creativity, however, can more easily accommodate cultural pluralism and tends to focus attention on the artistic process.

The core value of artistic access seems to have migrated from a concern with unequal availability of the nonprofit arts based on geography and economic condition to one based on inclusion of a wide range of artistic expressions of multiculturalism. Thus, access is being transformed to a value that highlights multiple choices. Also, the concept of participation in the arts is changing from a presumption of passive spectatorship into a wider notion that includes active and interactive modes. It is expanding from being synonymous with audience attendance to encompass a broader range of artistic involvement including arts instruction, personal creative pursuits, media consumption, Internet usage, arts collecting, and volunteering.

Adopting a Systems Approach

This is perhaps a subtle yet potentially far-reaching aspect of the emerging cultural policy paradigm. One might describe it as a shift in the "unit of attention" from the individual artist, a particular public art commission, a specific arts organization, a distinctive project, or a particular arts discipline to a reconceptualization of larger policy concerns that cut across and can relate to many of these entities. It could be argued that a systems perspective is a mark of maturity in the evolution of a policy or sector. Certainly, we can discuss a systems approach in cultural policy today in large part because the substantial infrastructure built during the last thirty years under the old arts funding paradigm now allows us to envision its greater potential.

Today, many nonprofit arts organizations are more financially sophisticated and sustainable, less threatened with insolvency than before, and Americans have more cultural opportunities. The successful expansion of artistic production and public access has diminished the necessity for public intervention in these regards. Similarly, the successful cultivation of a multifaceted support system for the arts has diminished the urgency for direct federal subsidy.

The old arts policy paradigm succeeded in establishing arts policy as a valid area of concern. The fact that arts policy survived the criticism and opposition of the past decade is itself a demonstration of the degree to which it has been legitimated in the federal arena. Indeed, the level of political attention directed to the arts and federal cultural policies far surpassed the federal financial commitment. A corollary was that this institutionalization of the arts policymaking system impeded its ability to adapt to changing circumstances including increased scrutiny of federal agencies.

Although systems thinking is relatively new to arts and cultural policy, it is common in other areas. For example, we generally understand what is meant by the term "biomedical systems" used in reference to the digestive or the nervous systems, even if we can't name the component parts and can't describe exactly how these systems function. Similarly, we comprehend that a regional transportation system includes many modes of travel and transport from personal autos to mass transit buses and subways, from railways and airways to shipping and trucking. We also understand that systems like a water system can serve various functions—for example, human water supply, agricultural uses, transportation, scenic and tourist attraction, and so on. Systems thinking sensitizes us to the intersections between elements and thus helps us to develop empirical maps. Currently, systems thinking is developing with regard to the arts and culture because of a growing awareness of the intersections and linkages among nonprofit arts, entertainment, the unincorporated arts.

At present, we can identify five system functions that seem central to the operation of the arts. Broadly conceived, they are: creation, production and presentation, distribution and marketing, maintenance, and evaluation.

The scope and demand of adopting systems thinking into a new cultural policy paradigm would depend, in part, on how we define the boundaries of an arts sector or industry. If, indeed, the new policy paradigm expands to include broader artistic and cultural horizons, then the scope and complexity of a systems approach will be considerably more extensive than at present, producing many new and important challenges.

The creative system involves identifying talented individuals and teams; developing talent through education, apprenticeships, and on-the-job training; providing incentives and opportunities for creativity such as artist residencies and sequential educational programs; linking creative output to production and distribution; and working to preserve the creative legacy of this generation for the future. Activities that contribute to these tasks take place within all the arts across the arts sector as well as within educational and other institutions, though unevenly and with different degrees of success.

Numerous public policies, concerning matters ranging from copyright protections and tax incentives to fellowship grants and commissions, affect the maintenance and enhancement of our creative artistic infrastructure. Together, all this activity, in a variety of different arts practices, using a range of instruments and programs, constitutes the creative infrastructure of the arts in America. From a systems perspective, it is easier to identify where the nation's creative infrastructure is working, where it needs assistance, and what kind of assistance is necessary. The development of such system maps is a crucial task needed to guide and inform policy making for the new paradigm.

A further discussion of two other system functions—evaluation and maintenance—illuminates the notion and usefulness of adopting a systems approach.

Currently evaluation seems to engage at least three components or subsystems: professional review, political oversight, and public opinion. All three of these components have been operating for years at the NEA and other public arts agencies.

Under the old public leveraging paradigm, it was often assumed that the three evaluation components were, in large part, complementary. A decade of controversy regarding federal arts support has revealed that each evaluation component has distinctive standards; that knowledge about one (public opinion) is only rudimentary; and that another (political oversight) is neither static nor merely a supportive formality. Nor do all three function in lockstep.

The case of the NEA illustrates the operation and interaction of all three evaluative components. The practice of professional peer review was highly developed in terms of both the decision-making procedures and accepted networks that existed within each program of the NEA. It was augmented by private juried selection procedures and assisted by service and professional associations in each art discipline. Now, however, peer review at the NEA has been crosspollinated with political evaluative elements; laypersons have recently been included in peer review panels and members of Congress on the National Council of the Arts. Indeed, as the NEA continued to evolve, some peer review functions may gravitate to the service and professional organizations.

As the old public leveraging paradigm stabilized, political oversight seemed to become predictable and ritualized. Annual appropriation and reauthorization hearings were, for the most part, friendly "show-and-tell" events in which members of the arts community and local supporters endorsed current policy, praised the work of the NEA, and argued for more resources in order to do more good work. In this context, the arts community and the NEA abjured the very idea that political concerns or conditions were legitimate considerations for arts policy administrators. However, political controversies resulting from dramatic shifts in the partisan and ideological composition of Congress, have resulted in troubled or delayed reauthorizations and declining appropriations. They have vividly demonstrated that political evaluation is an inescapable fact in the life of a public agency. These conflicts over the NEA have clearly demonstrated that peer evaluation and political evaluation may employ different standards and reach different conclusions.

Finally, public opinion, the third evaluation component, manifests itself in audience participation, representative democracy, and survey opinion. It interacts with both the peer review and the political evaluation components. During much of the old paradigm era, relatively little was known about public opinion and the arts, although marketing and information about audience behavior, preferences, and composition in general became increasingly more sophisticated. Major gaps still exist in what we know about public opinion regarding the arts, arts policy, and the attitudes and preferences of that part of the general public who are not arts participants. Judging from limited public opinion studies, it appears that over the last decade public knowledge of and support for arts policy has tended to be ambiguous, ambivalent, and quite malleable. Opinion is essentially divided among those who are intensely supportive, those who are intensely critical, and a large group for whom the issue is not particularly salient.

Other insights emerge from a consideration of the maintenance function, which is the means by which a society sustains, encourages, and protects its artistic endeavors and heritage. The maintenance system might be thought of as comprised of four components or subsystems: advocacy, preservation, financial support, and public policy, all of which are interrelated.

The advocacy component for the nonprofit arts evolved out of the effort to organize, develop, and support these arts forms, to foster intradiscipline communication, to further professional development, and to mobilize political support for the NEA and its programs. The commercial arts have lobbyists to protect and advance their interests. Given the increasing global reach of the entertainment industry, they have also become active players in the formulation of international trade agreements.

The preservation subsystem includes a variety of institutions such as museums, archives, historic preservation societies, significant individuals such as folk art masters, collectors, entrepreneurs, and conservators. It encompasses concern with artifacts, artworks, cultural traditions, historic sites and buildings, books, films, audio and video recordings, and documents.

The financial support system for the nonprofit arts involves federal, state, regional, and local public agencies, private foundations, corporate contributions, individual patrons, direct and indirect tax incentives, and revenue considerations for nonprofit arts organizations, all of which are interconnected in an interdependent, cross-leveraging web. The financial well-being of the commercial arts depends upon a complex weave of tax, legal, and trade regulations that affect market and production conditions as well as various local tax, zoning, and investment incentives.

Finally, the policy component has brought together organized arts interests from both nonprofit and commercial sectors, congressional proponents, public arts program administrators, and lobbyists, as well as intermittently concerned presidential personnel and assorted political allies from other policy areas. Legislation that impacts on arts business is closely watched and influenced by the media and entertainment industries. Until recently, nonprofit players had been quite adept at securing annual funding for the NEA. However, the nonprofit policy subsystem was not well suited for dealing with sustained opposition to federal funding or with policy issues other than obtaining and distributing public patronage.

These four components, which were developed under the old paradigm, were seldom seen as interrelated parts of an integrated maintenance system. Examining them as parts of a system, however, we can see and address the importance of each component, tap the unrealized potential of each one, address and rectify their flaws, and focus on additional capacity building for the arts sector.

Some maintenance resources are currently missing or inadequate. A more effective maintenance system would require policy intellectuals with diverse political viewpoints and cultural academics and educators. It would be more active in identifying new policy issues, formulating policy alternatives, and devising methods for policy evaluation. To accomplish more expansive goals, the arts community must mature into a more sophisticated cultural policy community; a task that, while still in its infancy, is currently well under way.

A New Approach to the Arts and Cultural Policy Process

Developing a more complex, diversified, and comprehensive approach to the policy making process is the third apparent ingredient of an emerging cultural policy paradigm. Because of shifting paradigms, current policy concerns seem to emphasize what may be called the beginnings and ends of the policymaking process. That is, much debate and discussion focuses on the evaluation of old policies and programs and the identification of new issues and mechanism for dealing with them. In the language of public policy, these are the agenda-setting, issue-defining, and option-developing stages that occur at the beginning of the policymaking process and the evaluation and feedback elements that occur at its end.

While concern with these stages is a natural part of making policy, this focus marks a shift from what was the expected, standard practice during the heyday of the old arts funding paradigm. While a particular policy paradigm holds sway, attention is focused on the middle of the policymaking process—that is, on budgeting and program implementation. For the most part, policy attention is expended on securing more resources to support or augment variations on existing programs. Although new issues may arise and assert themselves while a paradigm is in place, they are treated within the context of an accepted set of issues and definitions, a continuing agenda, a stable set of policy actors, and implicit standards for evaluating how well the system is working.

After more than two decades of refining, adapting, and polishing the capacity of the old arts funding paradigm, the arts community was largely unprepared to deal with many new and insistent challenges.

The old paradigm assumed that potential audiences for the nonprofit arts were infinitely expandable. Today, this presumption is questioned in the face of intense competition for the time and money of cultural consumers across the arts, entertainment, and leisure spectrum. Even as cultural opportunities expand, consumer taste preferences seem to be reconfiguring. Some participants are narrowing their choices. Others are participating in a wide range of arts activities. Still others are domesticating their consumption habits, opting for at-home media participation rather than going to live performances and entertainment events. These taste shifts, coupled with years of inadequate in-school arts education, do not provide a common cultural literacy. Absent a familiarity with the high arts and hands-on learning for teaching, the nature of arts participation in the next generation remains unclear.

Another obvious challenge arose within the political environment. Although international affairs remain a concern, economic (rather than military and ideological) issues came to predominate following the end of the cold war. Electoral shifts produced dramatic political changes. The 1994 election of the 104th Congress gave Republicans control of the House of Representatives for the first time in forty years. Nationally, domestic politics became more ideological, more aggressively partisan, and more polarized. Opposition to the expansive, welfare-state basis of the PLA model was mainstreamed, eliminating or endangering many federal subsidies and entitlements. Republican control introduced new legislative oversight standards and expectations for many long-standing federal programs and agencies and prompted a move away from centralized federal leadership and toward decentralization of funding and program administration.

The country went through a two-decade-long erosion of trust in the institutions of government, especially those at the federal level. The consequences of such distrust can be seen in the demand for policy reform in welfare and education; for reinventing government (in part a concern with waste, fraud, and abuse); and an increased awareness of the unintended consequences of old policies such as welfare dependency, tax disincentives, environmental costs, and urban decay. In short, the assumption of programmatic positivism implicit to the formative era and the establishment of the federal arts funding policy paradigm shifted dramatically.

Calls for greater government accountability of arts funding proliferated, stoked by a polarized partisanship, a displacement of liberal dominance, and highly mobilized social conservatives. A very vocal and morally orthodox minority objected to what it saw as offensive, indecent, and even pornographic art. Governmental conservatives argued that there was no constitutional basis for a federal role in the arts. Fiscal conservatives decried what they considered to be the populism and political correctness of federal cultural programs.

Until quite recently the NEA was myopic about the necessity of coping with changing political forces and criticism. They found themselves on the defensive, rather than anticipating and dealing with the multitude of new issues arising out of changing political, social, and technological conditions. They were primarily reactive rather than proactive. In contrast, many state and local arts agencies were both more politically adept and publicly persuasive. As a consequence, state and local arts agencies have, on the whole, rebounded from the controversies and recession of the early 1990s with increased financial and public support.

New approaches to policy process at all levels of government began to be tested. The recent shift from the middle to the ends of the policymaking process is the effort to see policy and policymaking process as complex and variegated, predicated on a longer perspective, and based on a systems approach. For example, rather than a reliance on variations of the matching grant as the policy tool of choice for nonprofit funding, there is an effort afoot to develop a repertoire of implementation devices that could assist arts and cultural activities, such as program related investments, loans and underwriting funds, international trade and immigration agreements, copyright and spectrum "auctions," and public trust funds.

Whereas arts funding policy was seen to be the province of the NEA, now, with a smaller budget and staff, the agency is shifting and widening its activities from leveraging and catalyzing other funding contributors to brokering policy, project ideas, and information, as well as helping to forge alliances between the arts and other communities of interest. Leveraging support has become more innovative at all levels of government. Communities are experimenting with a variety of funding devices, from earmarking taxes and fees for the arts to searching internationally for models and examples of other revenue sources, and exploring the possibility of different kinds of federal assistance

The stable set of political and institutional arrangements that characterized the old arts funding system is swiftly becoming more open, variable, and fluid. New interest groups are asserting their right to participate. The system must now accommodate opponents, as well as advocates, growing and diverse interests and ideologies, artists, and analysts, and so forth. It engages the attention of numerous congressional committees as many executive agencies administer programs germane to the arts community. It remains to be seen in what varying and innovative ways these agencies will operate and interrelate in effecting arts and cultural programs.

Conclusion

A new arts and cultural policy is being born. People and interests previously outside it are being seen as an inextricable part of it. At present, there is no current consensus as to what is included under the rubric "art." We banter about undefined concepts such as an arts sector, arts industry, infrastructure, or ecology. We have only a vague sense of what is meant by the term "unincorporated" arts. Our systems approach is decidedly embryonic. Paradigm maps are concepts that we struggle to operationalize with clarity and utility. We still grope for ways to identify the public purposes of public art programs. But this is as it should be in the midst of a paradigm shift and a field-building effort.

Is this a justifiable reconceptualization, a useful perspective, a better vantage point on the ways things really work? So it appears, at least to those immersed in the public life of the arts in America. It remains to be seen what benefits and arrangements will result from the new paradigm and to what extent we can influence its composition for the betterment of the nation and its citizens.

Rethinking the role and relationship of the arts and the American polity is not an activity of a handful of self-interested arts professionals. It is predicated on the affirmative realization that the arts are essential because of their ability to bring transcendence, utility, joy, escape, meaning, and imagination to human beings. Tracking and reconfiguring their social arrangements is not only justifiable, but also can be potentially rewarding.

2 | Toward an American Arts Industry

This chapter summarizes twenty years of cultural economic research by myself and others in order to develop a clearer definition of the American arts industry. I map my findings into a mainstream economic framework—the Industrial Organization Model, or IO. More primary and secondary research is required to complete the framework; I call upon my colleagues in the arts and economics to aid in realizing this ambitious and important undertaking.

The Industrial Organization Model

IO is the brainchild of the late Joe Bain. His seminal work, *Industrial Organization*, was published in 1959 (Bain 1968). Using IO, Bain began what has become an ongoing process within the economics profession of linking macroeconomics (the study of the economy as a whole) to microeconomics (consumer, producer, and market theory) to better understand the way the real world works.

The IO schema consists of four parts (see fig. 2.1.). First, basic conditions face an industry on the supply (production) and demand (consumption) side of the economic equation. Second, an industry has a structure or organizational character. Third, enterprises in an industry tend to follow typical patterns of conduct or behavior in adapting and adjusting to a specific but ever changing and evolving marketplace. Fourth, an industry achieves varying levels of performance with respect to contemporary socio-economic-political goals.

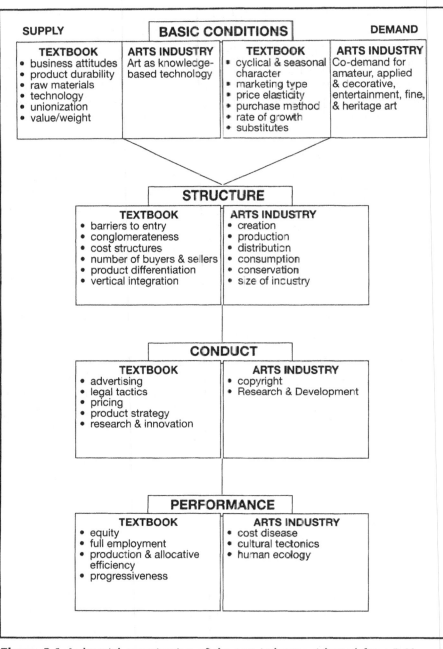

Figure 2.1. Industrial organization of the arts industry. *Adapted from F. M. Scherer,* Industrial Market Structure and Economic Performance, *Chicago: Rand McNally, 1971.*

Elemental Economic Terms

Four elemental economic terms will be used here. First, buyers and sellers exchange goods and services in markets, whether geographic or commodity based. Second, an enterprise is any entity engaging in productive activity, with or without the hope of making a profit. This thus includes profit, nonprofit, and public enterprises as well as self-employed individuals. All enterprises have scarce resources and are accountable to shareholders and/or the public and the courts. An enterprise is defined in terms of total assets and operations controlled by a single management empowered by a common ownership. Third, an industry is a group of sellers of close substitutes to a common group of buyers, for example, the automobile industry. Fourth, a sector is a group of related industries; for instance, the automobile, airline, and railway industries form part of the transportation sector. Often the terms "sector" and "industry" are used interchangeably.

The Arts Industry

In this chapter, the arts industry, or more properly the arts sector, includes all profit, nonprofit, and public enterprises (see fig. 2.2). This includes incorporated and unincorporated businesses that, and self-employed individuals who:

- use one or more of the arts including the heritage, literary, media, performing, or visual arts—live or recorded—as a primary factor of production; for example, in advertising, fashion, industrial, and product design as well as Internet, magazine, and newspaper publishing
- rely on one or more of the arts as a tied-good in consumption; for example, home entertainment hardware and software
- produce one or more of the arts as their final output; that is, they create, produce, distribute, and/or conserve artistic goods and services

By this definition, the arts industry can be seen as the center of a circle of circles made up of the so-called cultural industries or the widely defined arts and cultural industry (see fig. 2.2). The economic term "tied-good" requires explanation. An example is the old punch-card computer, which could not operate without such cards, which, technically, were an output of the pulp, paper, and publishing industries, sequentially. The computer and cards were tied-goods in the production of computational results. Similarly, there can only be a market for audiovisual software, for example, CDs and videotapes, if there is a market for home entertainment hardware, for example, cameras, CD players, TV sets, and so on. They are tied-goods in consumption, fitting hand in glove. In this regard, it is likely, but not proved, that home entertainment centers (HEC)

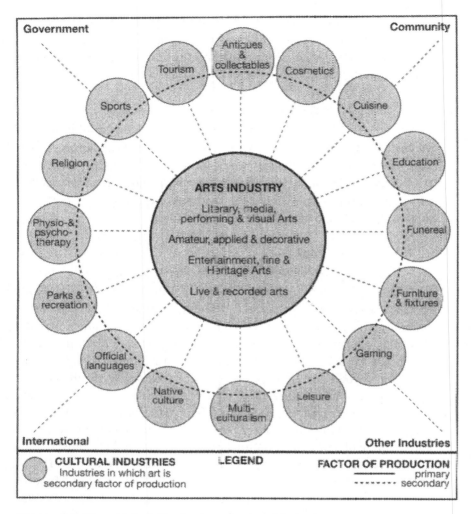

Figure 2.2. The widely defined arts and cultural industry

are the third most expensive consumer durable purchased by the average consumer after houses and cars Similarly, private collections of audiovisual software including phonographs, photographs, and videotapes constitute an enormous stock of American cultural wealth.

There are four biases inherent here. First, it is based on a compilation of findings stretching over decades; accordingly, much of the evidence needs to be updated. Second, the demonstration is incomplete. The full IO framework cannot be completed at this time. In some cases, the evidence required may be available, but I am unaware of its existence. In other cases, no primary research has been conducted. Third, the demonstration assumes a wide definition of art, including utilitarian art, entertainment art, and what is called art for art's sake. Finally, the demonstration is constructed by one economist. There is no consensus within the profession as a whole about the appropriate definition of economics and the arts.

Basic Conditions

The IO model requires information about basic conditions facing an industry on the supply (production) and demand (consumption) side of the economic equation (see fig. 2.1). Only two facets are examined. On the supply side, the economic meaning of knowledge, specifically art as a knowledge-based technology, is defined. On the demand side, co-demand for the arts is considered.

Supply

Economics recognizes three primary factors of production—capital, labor, and technology. Through time, understanding of these factors has changed and expanded (see table 2.1). Today it is generally accepted that improvements and changes in capital and labor, including education, have accounted for between 25 and 33 percent of growth in national income over the last century (Shapiro, 1970). The vast majority of growth is thus attributable to technological change.

In the Neoclassical period of economic thought (roughly the 1870s to the 1930s), economists first identified disembodied technological change reflected in general improvements in communications (telegraph and telephone) and transportation (steam, electric- and gas-powered engines). During the Keynsian period (roughly the 1930s to the late 1980s), the contribution of physical science research to the war effort—first the Allies and Axis powers (radar to ballistic missiles, and jet aircraft to the A-bomb) and then the Cold War warriors—expanded economists' vision to see embodied technological change—that is, change reflecting specific bits of new knowledge embodied in specific products such as the transistor in the transistor radio. Until the present, however, there has been one constant: We really do not know why some things are invented and others are not; and why some things that are invented are brought to market, and others are not. This was called by my college economics instructor, Harvey Lithwick, "the measure of our economic ignorance."

I have argued elsewhere that our economic ignorance (66–75 percent) is attributable, in part, to a narrow definition of technology (Chartrand 1989, 1990; 1992b). The word derives from the classical Greek *techne* meaning "art" and *logos* meaning "reason," that is, "reasoned art." In turn, the English word "art" means "skill" or "craft," forms of experiential knowledge gained by doing or applying as opposed to systematizing knowledge, which the ancient Greeks defined as science. Feedback between the application and systematization of knowledge results in learning or education, in the sense of *educe*, "to bring out an understanding of something outside oneself." In this sense, technological change in a knowledge-based economy results from application of new knowledge. This constitutes epistemologic, or knowledge-based, technological change.

Today's economic landscape is dominated by three primary yet interactive domains of human knowledge: the natural sciences and engineering (NSE), the social sciences and humanities (SSH), and the arts (Chartrand 1992a). Knowledge-based technological change results from increases in these domains when new information is applied in the real world.

Each domain rises up like a mountain above the lowlands and valleys of the traditional industrial economy. Each has its own historical and institutional foundation; each reaches up to its own lofty, specialized glacial summit of individual and institutional excellence. For the NSE and SSH, the traditional institutional peak has been the university. For the arts, it has been the arts academy, production company, conservatory, or school. Accretions to a domain takes place through research, the results of which, when applied, causes feedback resulting in learning how to do something better next time.

Institutionalization of knowledge domains varies between countries. In the English-speaking world, for example, Canada has the Canada Council for the Arts, the Social Sciences and Humanities Research Council, and the Natural Sciences and Engineering Research Council. In the United Kingdom, there are separate councils for the arts, engineering, humanities, natural sciences, and social sciences. In the United States, there is the National Endowment for the Arts, the National Endowment for the Humanities, and the National Science Foundation, which subsumes the social sciences.

In summary, knowledge-based technological change involves one or more of the following:

- new goods, services, and improved production processes, primarily emerging from NSE
- more effective, efficient, and humane ways of combining financial, human, information, and physical resources emerging primarily from SSH embodied in improved management methods and practices
- new aesthetics primarily emerging from the arts and embodied in better designed, more attractive, creatively advertised, and intelligently marketed goods and services

Table 2.1 Knowledge-Based Technological Change

NATIONAL INCOME = Y	INDUSTRIAL SECTOR	THEORISTS	EXPRESSION	ARTS & SCIENCES
$Y = f(K)$ where: f = a function of K = capital as gold, silver, and land conquered from other nations Spain in the seventeenth century	Primary farming fishing forestry mining	Preclassical English pamphleteers Quesnay Tourgot	Mercantilists, monetarists Gold standard & physiocrats, primacy of argiculture & monetary policy.	Symbolic
$Y = f(K, L)$ where: K = include capital as specialized industrial machinery L = Labor as division of labor England in early nineteenth century	Secondary manufacturing	Classical Smith Ricardo Malthus J. Mill Marx	Marketeers, manufactured goods source of national wealth; Marxists: only labor is productive of economic surplus.	Unproductive
$Y = f(K, L, T)$ where: T = technological change as disembodied or systemic change, e.g. steam power and electricity operating in competitive markets for K & L USA in late nineteenth to mid 20th centuries	Tertiary or Service communication financial services transportation	Neoclassical J. S. Mill A. Lord Marshall	Neo-Conservatives government should set business free.	Productive
$Y = f(K, L, T) g$ where: T = technological change as embodied in specific products sold in markets dominated by large corporations and trade unions where: g = government coordinates public and private sectors to: fine tune aggregate demand; adjust for externalities of private activity such as pollution; and support product and process innovation Japan in mid- to late 20th century	Public Sector Government	Keynesian Keynes	Liberals & Social Democrats, Government is primary engine of societal progress.	Merit Good
$Y = f(K, L, T, O, A) g$ where: T, O, A = forms of knowledge-based technological change where: T = physical change from the Natural Sciences & Engineering (NSE) O = organizational change from the Social Sciences & Humanities (SSH) A = aesthetic change from the Arts, ? in the twenty-first century	Quaternary Industries copyright industrial design patents trademarks know-how	Postmodern Bell Chartrand Innis Liebenstein McLuhan Porat Toffler Valaskakis	State of the Art (T) Search for Excellence (O) Elegance & Persuasion (A)	Source

These are the primary sources of value-added in a knowledge-based economy (Chartrand 1989). (See Table 2.2.)

Much research has been conducted about the socioeconomic characteristics of consumers of specific artistic goods and services, for example, modern dance, museums, and TV. Little, however, has been conducted about generic consumer demand for the arts as a knowledge domain.

Co-Demand for the Arts

Over the years I have evolved a fivefold framework to classify market demand for the arts (see table 2.2). In this framework, there are five motivations for consuming the arts. Each generates its own distinct industry with its own plant and equipment, talent pool, specialized repertoire of works and its own market made up of individual as well as public, private and nonprofit consumers (as investor, patron, or donor). All five are interrelated through crossovers between audiences (demand side, also called co-demand) and capital, labor, and technology (supply side).

Three terms require definition. First, "recreation" refers to the nineteenth-century British concept of time free to re-create a worker's ability to work. This contrasts with the aristocratic concept of "leisure" as time free to develop consumption skills, especially appreciation (Chartrand 1987). Finally, "philanthropic" refers to the altruistic giving of wealth, wisdom, or work to a nonprofit or public cause (Boulding 1973).

Amateur Art

Amateur art is motivated by self-actualization, -education, and -realization, including that of one's own cultural heritage. It is less concerned with pleasing an audience and more with developing self-expression and -understanding. Amateur art is practiced during and after primary, secondary, and tertiary school. It is in the amateur arts that talent is first disciplined in an artistic craft and an informed and appreciative audience is initially cultivated.

Amateur art is part of the public sector in the schools; part of the nonprofit sector in amateur or community institutions such as amateur theater and orchestras; and part of the profit sector through private teachers and instructors. It provides four kinds of experiences:

- arts education, that is, education in how to create art
- education through art, that is, art as a distinct way of understanding the world and of problem-solving

Table 2.2 Co-Demand for the Arts

	AMATEUR	APPLIED & DECORATIVE	ENTERTAINMENT	FINE	HERITAGE
Primary demand	self-actualization, -education, & -realization	elegance & persuasion	entertainment	enlightenment	enrichment, social cohesion, & tradition
Secondary demand	audience development, education, fulfillment, leisure, recreation, skill, development, status, & therapy	marriage of aesthetic & utilitarian values for style & persuasion	amusement, diversion, enjoyment, & recreation	art-for-art's-sake for freedom of expression, leisure, recreation, standards of excellence, status, insight into the human condition	marriage of scarcity & aesthetic value for preservation & conservation of residual creation for and/or by subsequent generations, leisure, recreation, standards of excellence, status, understanding the human condition
Tertiary demand	philanthropic, nonprofit, profit, & public	profit	profit	philanthropic, nonprofit, & public	philanthropic, nonprofit, profit, & public

- education of citizen consumers with respect to recognizing quality in advertising—commercial and political—and industrial and product design
- therapy—physical and psychological

Applied and Decorative Art

Applied and decorative art includes advertising, architecture and urban design, crafts, jewelry, and fashion, as well as industrial, product, and interior design. To a degree, it involves the use of style for enjoyment and persuasion. Production is motivated by the challenge of marrying aesthetic to utilitarian value. At its best it contributes elegance to the human environment defined as simple but effective, or the best-looking thing that works. From buildings to urban planning; from product design to effective advertising; from corporate imaging to designer fashion—applied and decorative art quite likely has the most pervasive and significant economic impact of any segment of the arts industry, accounting for 45 percent of the total arts labor force (Chartrand 1996).

Entertainment Art

Entertainment art generates enjoyment, amusement, and recreation. In the entertainment arts, America currently leads the world. Thus entertainment programming (film, recordings, and TV) is reported to be the second largest net export of the United States after defense products (*The Economist* 11 March 1989: 65–66).

Entertainment art is dominated by for-profit global media conglomerates with linked interests in television, film, music, video, and print media. The five largest firms in the world had combined revenues of $45 billion in 1988 and accounted for 18 percent of a $250 billion worldwide entertainment market (National Telecommunications and Information Administration 1990). Only one of the five, however, was American owned—Time/Warner. There has been significant merger and acquisition activity in the ten years since 1988. Concentration and foreign ownership have probably increased. There is, however, to my knowledge, no more recent comprehensive study of global integration and convergence of the broadcast, cable, film, publishing, and recording industries.

Fine Art

Fine art is motivated by what is called art for art's sake. It is the primary research and development segment of the arts industry. It generates enlightenment; that is, it sheds light on the nature of the human condition, for people as individuals and as members of societies.

It is primarily in the fine arts that new talent and technique are developed; new scripts and scores created; and, new images and styles set. Results of fine arts R&D, like the results of scientific research, are sometimes adopted by for-profit enterprises in and out of the arts industry. And, as in pure science, fine art is not financially self-supporting. It operates primarily in the nonprofit sector relying on public and private patronage. As in the natural sciences, a thousand new plays (experiments) must be tried if one is to become a box office smash. The right to fail is an essential artistic and scientific freedom that requires patience and risk-taking on the part of patrons, investors, and audiences.

Heritage Art

Heritage art subsumes the amateur, applied and decorative, entertainment, and fine arts as residuals of contemporary and past creation preserved for and/or by subsequent generations. It feeds back on contemporary art, setting standards and inspiring creators. It generates enrichment through the marriage of scarcity and aesthetic value including a sense of social cohesion and continuity. Heritage art thus links us back to our past reminding us of who we are and from where and when we come. It can also, however, impose the deadening hand of the past on contemporary creators who must compete not just with domestic and foreign peers, but also with works tried and tested through time.

Between 1969 and 1989, heritage art yielded the highest return of all financial investment opportunities (*The Economist*, 1 July 1989). Furthermore, theft of antiquities is the most lucrative international crime. Ounce for ounce, an antiquity can be more valuable than drugs. It can yield a higher return, at lower risk of being caught, and generally produces less jail time if one is convicted (Chartrand 1992b).

Structure

The second facet of the IO model is structure, or the organizational character of an industry. I examine only two facets here: the five-stage product cycle of the arts, and the statistical size of the arts industry.

The Art Product Cycle

The natural sciences are made up of three elementary disciplines: biology, chemistry and physics. The arts are made up of four: literary, media, and performing and visual art (see table 2.3). Each uses a distinct medium of expression:

- the written word
- the recorded sound and/or image
- the live stage
- the visual image

Creation. In all four disciplines, artists tend to be independent and emotive. They do not fit well into the "technostructure" (Galbraith 1968) except where the organization itself is artistic such as a symphony, dance or theater company, or architectural firm (Galbraith 1973). In advertising, broadcasting, films, and sound recording where enterprise is large and complex, dissonance between artists and management is usually solved by employing actors, composers, copyrighters, dancers, directors, producers, and scriptwriters through smaller subsidiary firms. The parent company then confines itself to providing advertising, broadcasting, marketing, exhibition, and/or production facilities.

In the literary and visual arts, the creative process tends to be solitary. The image of the solitary writer or painter is an approximate truth. When completed, a hand-written manuscript or a painting is a finished work standing on its own. It can be immediately consumed—that is, read

Table 2.3 Product Cycle of the Arts

	LITERARY	MEDIA	PERFORMING	VISUAL
Creation	writer &/or small creative team	broadcast, film or record producer, &/or small creative team	choreographer, composer, lyricist, or playwright, and/or small creative team	architect, designer, painter, photographer, or sculptor, &/or small creative team
Production	publisher & printer	broadcast film, or recording studio	performing arts company	studio
Distribution	book and other stores, mail order, & World Wide Web	audio-video stores, broadcast, cable, home entertainment center, movie houses, satellites, & World Wide Web	stage	dealer, gallery, museum
Consumption	reader	listener & viewer	audience	collector, client, viewer, visitor
Conservation	archives & libraries incl. personal & institutional collections	audiovisual & broadcast museums, including personal & institutional collections	performing arts repertoire and museums including personal & institutional collections	conservation institutes, galleries & museums, including personal & institutional collections

or viewed. The processes of creation and production of an artwork are one and the same.

The media and performing arts are interpretive, and the creative process is collective and linked to production. A play, film script, or musical score is usually created first, but it comes to life only through the efforts of interpretive artists like actors, dancers, or musicians and teams of artisans and technicians as well as directors, conductors, and producers. This differentiates creative from interpretive art.

In all disciplines, some artists work as one-person firms or in small partnerships, engaging larger firms to market their product. There is a specialized subindustry, artists' management, made up of dealers and agents who negotiate rates, terms, conditions, and scheduling for self-employed artists.

Production. Production in the solitary arts is similar. In literary art, a creator (author) writes a work, then a publisher mass-produces it. Essentially, however, the manuscript is a completed work ready for reading. In this regard, the printing press was the first engine of mass production and "His Majesty's Stationary" was the first proprietor of copyright in a work of literary art (Chartrand 1992a). Like a gatekeeper, publishers screen for marketability, then invest in editing, printing, manufacture, publicity, and/or distribution.

In visual art, creation tends to take place in an artist's studio. Exceptions include performance and environmental art, which may be created on site. Creation also results in production of a finished work (except framing) ready for distribution, or exhibition. Unlike literary art, in which an editor often is involved in the author's polishing a work, a visual artwork is seldom touched up by others.

Production in the interpretive arts is also similar. In media art, production requires a script and/or score, then a studio, to produce an animation, broadcast, film, or sound or video recording. Studios are generally owned by corporate producers who may rent out to independent producers. The producer acts as gatekeeper, screening for marketability and then investing in editing, production, publicity, and/or distribution. Unlike in the other disciplines, however, in media art copyright initially usually vests with the producer or corporation, which makes the complex arrangements to produce a media artwork.

Interpretive artists bring a work of media art to life. Such artists may be part of existing companies of players like bands, orchestras, or theatrical troupes, or hired individually on a one-time basis, like studio musicians. A sophisticated technical staff is required to operate equipment as well creating and maintaining costumes, sets, and props. They contribute production values to a media artwork.

Performing art also requires a script and/or score and then a venue, to present a live play, dance, or musical work. Venues are owned by profit or nonprofit producers or impresarios who may rent facilities out to independent companies or present their own in-house performing company. The impresario also acts as gatekeeper, screening for marketability, then invests in editing, managing the production, publicity, and/or distribution. As in media art, a sophisticated technical staff is needed to operate equipment, and create and maintain costumes, sets, and props, contributing production values to a performance artwork.

It is important to note that media art now provides interpretive artists with something that only literary and visual artists enjoyed in the past—performance after death. There may never again be a Richard Burton, but his image, his voice, and his performances will now endure like the Shakespeare plays in which he performed. Nonetheless, there exists a traditional suspicion of recorded art by those who engage in live art. At the birth of the arts-for-art's-sake movement, during the last quarter of the nineteenth century, new recording media emerged, including the steel engraving plate, the photograph, sound recording, and the motion picture. These created many new revenue streams (Hughes 1984). In the twentieth century, these new mass media were followed by radio, television, and video recording.

This suspicion is reflected in debate over the so-called substitutability of recorded and live art. Specifically, does the audience play a role in creating artistic excellence? Baumol argues that a gestalt exists between performer and audience feeding back and creating an aesthetic experience fundamentally different from a recording (Baumol and Oates 1972, 1974, and 1976). Tullock, on the other hand, argues that "canned" product may not be as aesthetically pleasing, but it does permit mass distribution beyond a small arts-going elite raising the general level of artistic appreciation in society (Tullock 1974, 1976).

The uncertain nature of employment in the interpretive arts, together with a hierarchy of talent, has resulted in a distinctive pattern of industrial labor relations. Thus, unlike other industries, arts unions and professional associations tend to set minimum rather than maximum rates for members.

Distribution. Traditionally, literary art is distributed by publishers who sell art wholesale and/or retail through chains, franchises, and independent book and stationery stores. In the last century, mail-order became another means to distribute directly to the "reading" public. Today, the World Wide Web has become yet another means to distribute literary art directly to readers by publishers and/or authors.

In media art, producers distribute wholesale and/or retail through chains, franchises, and/or independent audio-video stores (sales and rentals) and movie houses. They also distribute retail through broadcast, cable and satellite, and the World Wide Web. Media arts distribution requires a set of consumer capital goods collectively called the home entertainment center (HEC). The HEC, including the home PC, is possibly the third most expensive consumer durable purchased by the average American—after the house and car. The capital intensity of media art consumption has fueled vertical integration between hardware manufacturers and media art software firms. Acquisition of Hollywood and recording studios by Japanese consumer electronics giants like Sony reflects the legacy of Betamax's defeat by VHS. To ensure expensive long-term investment in the production of consumer hardware, such firms believe they must control the format of consumer media software products.

In performing art, distribution requires a stage. This may be as simple as a small riser in a club or bar or a soapbox in a park. It may, however, be an enormously complex performing arts facility with computer-operated lighting, extensive stage and special effects machinery, sound systems, and backstage facilities for costumes, sets and props, and dressing rooms for performers. Performing arts facilities are linked together in touring circuits, which permit distribution of works across states and countries, and around the world.

In visual art, distribution is accomplished through exhibition by dealers, galleries, and museums. In many cases a group or stable of artists is managed by a single dealer. Such dealers identify and occupy specific market niches for specific forms and schools of visual expression.

Consumption. Consumption of art is different from consumption of other goods and services. An artwork does not normally depreciate or become reduced in quantity by consumption. Essentially, consumption is affective rather than physical in nature. This is reflected in differing types of consumers. In literary art, the consumer is a reader; in media art, a listener and/or viewer; in performing art, an audience; in visual art, a collector, viewer, or visitor.

The affective nature of arts consumption has led some researchers to question the dominance of the traditional information processing model of consumer behavior, which views consumption as a consumer with a problem seeking information about the best solution. This neglects hedonistic phenomena, including play, leisure, sensory pleasure, daydreaming, fantasy, aesthetic enjoyment, and emotional response (Holbrook and Hirschman 1982; Holbrook 1987). The richest source of fantasy and contemporary psychic need is the arts. Many advertising copywriters and executives have found commercial success based on an arts experience. Is it coincidence that New York City is both the theatrical and the advertising capital of the world?

Conservation. Art is different from science. In art, the new does not necessarily displace the old. Conservation and preservation of past works is of greater importance in the arts industry than in any other. Specialized skills, expertise, plant, and equipment are required to conserve and maintain past works and constitute a distinct heritage arts industry, including archives, libraries, and museums.

In literary art, conservation is achieved through archives and libraries; in media art through specialized audiovisual and broadcast archives and museums; in performing art by maintaining works in repertoire and establishing specialized archives and museums for sets, props, costumes, plays, and playbills; and in visual art through conservation institutes such as galleries and museums.

A key aspect of art conservation is the personal art collection, including audiovisual recordings, books, fine furniture and fixtures, paintings, photographs (for example, those produced in the most popular and widespread amateur art—home photography), and statuary. Private collections of artistic and cultural goods constitute a significant stock of American cultural wealth, which becomes apparent when the role of auction houses and flea markets is taken into account.

Size

To measure the size of the arts industry, two data sets are used: the Baseline Input/Output Matrix for the 1982 U.S. economy, and the 1989 Standard Industrial Classification (SIC), both published by the Department of Commerce in Washington, D.C. Both were presented in my 1992 study, *The American Arts Industry*, for the Research Division of the NEA (Chartrand 1992a).

This was the first time the Input/Output Matrix was used to describe the arts industry. The 1982 matrix was published in 1991 (Bureau of Economic Analysis 1991). It is the best measure of the relationship between art and the American economy. A baseline 1992 matrix will not be available until the year 2000.

SIC data were derived from a special study, *Copyright Industries in the U.S. Economy*, commissioned by the International Intellectual Property Alliance (Siwek and Furchtgoff-Roth 1990). Rather than reinventing the wheel, I accepted the data presented in this study, with minor modifications, as the best available estimate of the SIC size of the American arts industry.

Arts Factor. One problem in estimating the size of the American arts industry is that art is used throughout the economy. How do we separate arts-based economic activity from the rest? One way is to apply an arts factor. Siwek and Furchtgoff-Roth used the copyright component of each industry's economic activity as estimated by the U.S. Copyright Office (Siwek and Furchtgoff-Roth 1990).

Copyright, however, provides only a partial measure of the size of the arts industry. A more complete factor would account for artistic activity embodied in registered industrial designs and trademarks. Assets reported in the balance sheet of Coca Cola, for example, includes the company's "goodwill," part of which relates to the distinctive shape of the bottle (industrial design) and the corporate logo (trademark). Both are intellectual property, like copyright, and like copyright they are rooted in artistic rather than scientific knowledge, as are patents. Unfortunately, no estimate of the economic contribution of industrial designs or trademarks is available. Accordingly, the arts factor used in this demonstration is based only on the copyright component of arts economic activity. Two estimates are presented: gross and net. Gross reports total economic activity, while net reports only arts-related activity, estimated using the copyright factor.

To some, the resulting net estimates will be high, because not all copyright economic activity is necessarily arts-related, for example, copyright in computer programs. To others, the estimate will appear low because it does not include the contribution of registered industrial designs and trademarks.

An additional caveat is in order. The inclusion of utilitarian industries like those that manufacture textiles, clothing, furniture, and leather goods, along with more obvious arts industries like publishing and films, is supported by Alfred Lord Marshall's observation that "development of the artistic faculties of the people is in itself an aim of the very highest importance, and is becoming a chief factor of industrial efficiency. . . . Increasingly wealth is enabling people to buy things of all kinds to suit the fancy, with but a secondary regard to their powers of wearing; so that in all kinds of clothing and furniture it is every day more true that it is the pattern which sells the things" (Marshall 1969, 177–178).

Standard Industrial Classification. Using the Standard Industrial Classification (SIC), the American arts industry accounted for at least 6 percent and at most 8.5 percent of the U.S. Gross National Product in 1989—that is, the sum of all goods and services consumed in the United States but not necessarily produced here. It ranked at most sixth and at least seventh among the ten primary sectors of the American economy recognized by the Department of Commerce including, in descending order of income size: (1) manufacturing, (2) services, (3) finance, (4) government, (5) transportation and utilities, (6) retail trade, (7) wholesale trade, (8) construction, (9) agriculture, forestry, and fishing, and (10) mining.

Input/Output. The input/output matrix reports the use (inputs) and production (outputs) of goods and services by each industry and between industries in the economy. In 1982, the arts industry generated nearly $304 billion in gross production, or 9.6 percent of the GNP. Net arts production was $162 billion, or 5.1 percent of the GNP.

Arts industry production ranked at most fifth, after the medical, educational, and service industries, and at least tenth after petroleum products among the seventy-seven private-sector industries identified in the input/output matrix. By the same measure, the arts industry contributed at least 13 percent and at most 45 percent to the American deficit in trade with the rest of the world. This last fact may seem strange given the popular belief that entertainment programming, including films, audio recordings, and TV programs are the second largest export of the United States, after defense products. The cause lies in the import of designer goods like Armani suits, which come mainly from Europe (Scitovsky 1976) and tied-goods like home entertainment equipment, including TV sets, audio and videotape recorders, amplifiers, and so on, which are imported mainly from Japan and other Asian countries. The result is that the export of entertainment programming is more than offset by the import of these arts-related goods.

Conduct

The third facet of the IO model is conduct, or the pattern of behavior, followed by enterprises in adapting and adjusting to an ever changing and evolving market. I explore only two issues: copyright, which provides the legal foundation for industrial organization of the arts is examined, and the unconventional nature of research and development (R&D) in the arts industry.

Copyright

Many types of law—statutory, regulatory, and criminal—affect the conduct of arts enterprises, including broadcasting and cable licensing, censorship, and copyright. Law can be used to prohibit certain types of economic activity—for example, antitrust statutes, resale price maintenance, predatory pricing, insider dealing, and so on. On the other hand, law can create markets where none existed before—for example, copyright. In fact, the evolution of market capitalism is characterized by the changing legal definition of property and of what can be legally bought and sold. Over the last two and a half centuries, the legal definition of property has matured from physical things toward intangibles and rights (Commons 1957).

Concept and Origins. Copyright and other forms of intellectual property rights—registered industrial designs, patents, and trademarks—are justified as a protection of and an incentive to human creativity, the production of which otherwise could be used freely by others. In return, creators are expected to make their works available in a market so that their works can be bought and sold. But while the state wishes to encourage creativity, it does not want to foster harmful market power. Accordingly, limitations are imposed that deal with both time and space. Rights are granted for a fixed period of time, and protect only material forms; that is, ideas themselves are not protected, but rather their production in material form. There are therefore inherent tensions in copyright. For example,

> Intellectual property is, after all, the only absolute possession in the world. . . . The man who brings out of nothingness some child of his thought has rights therein which cannot belong to any other sort of property . . . [but] We should start by reminding ourselves that copyright is a monopoly. Like other monopolies. it is open to many objections; it burdens both competitors and the public. Unlike most other monopolies, the law permits and even encourages it because of its peculiar great advantages. Still, remembering that it is a monopoly, we must be sure that the burdens do not outweigh the benefits. So it becomes desirable for us to examine who is benefited and how much and at whose expense. . . . (Chafee 1984)

This tension reflects the origins of copyright in the Tudor and Stuart periods of English history in the midst of the Protestant Reformation and the Catholic Counter-Reformation. To keep heretical works from being reproduced, the Crown granted to selected printers the copyright, that is, the right to copy approved works. It should be kept in mind that the printing press, as the first engine of mass production, generated more anxiety at the time of its innovation than radio, TV, satellite communication, and the World Wide Web in our time.

Copyright thus began as a Crown grant of industrial privilege to printers and a means of censorship. Only with the Statute of Queen Anne in 1710 did authors gain any rights, and even these were explicitly balanced by rights granted to "proprietors" (MacDonald 1971). To this day, all rights of the creator can be extinguished by contract with a copyright proprietor. The legal instrument used to extinguish creators' rights, after a one-time payment, is the "blanket licence," which strips away the artist's rights to any subsequent exploitation of a work.

In most cases, therefore, creators do not sell work directly to the public. Rather, they sell or license its copyright to corporate market intermediaries—dealers, employers, publishers or producers. These intermediaries act as gatekeepers, screening new works for marketability and then investing in production, advertising, sale, and/or distribution.

A corporate copyright proprietor, having purchased all or part of a creator's rights, then exploits the many revenue streams flowing from such copyrights. Consider a book written in India that, through sale or licence of its copyright, becomes a play in London's West End theater district. The play becomes a movie in Hollywood from which posters, a soundtrack, T-shirts, and toys are spun off and manufactured in Taiwan.

The movie is then broadcast on Italian television and the soundtrack on rock radio in Ghana. The styles and fashions of the film inspire a Munich designer, who previews a fashion collection in Paris. Furniture makers in Ohio license the design and manufacture look-alike furniture. A book is then written in New York City about the making of the movie, and a film sequel is shot in Saskatoon. All associated income streams have their source in the copyright vested in the initial work—in this case, a book. The bargaining power of the average creator to set prices or retain residual rights to such a work is limited.

International Differences. There are five distinct legal traditions of creator's rights illustrating the fact that copyright is as much a cultural artifact as a law (Chartrand 1996). First, there is the British tradition in which copyright is subject to a restrictive concept of "fair dealing," which exempts only a very small number of very specific uses from infringement. "Crown copyright" also exists in all documents published by the government.

Second, there is the American tradition, which has two strands. First, copyright is subject to a liberal concept of "fair use," which exempts most not-for-profit uses from infringement, including private copying. Unlike in the British tradition, there is no equivalent to the Crown copyright—that is, works of the government and its agencies are in the public domain. The second strand is a tradition of granting preference to domestic manufacturers. Thus, prior to 1909, no English-language work could be sold in the United States unless it was printed there (Hanson 1973). From 1909 until the mid 1980s, the Manufacturers' Clause of the U.S. Copyright Act specified that any book written by an American could only be sold in the United States if it was printed there. This effectively stopped Henry Miller's works, published in Paris, from being sold in America. This tradition continues with certain rights being granted outside of the U.S. Copyright Act and applicable only to Americans.

Third, there is the civil code tradition in Europe and Japan. Under this tradition, a creator's rights are inherent in and inalienable from the individual creator. Some rights can never be transferred by contract. The code does not accept that a corporation has the same rights as an individual. The ability of copyright proprietors to exploit copyright is limited relative to both the British or American traditions (Vaver 1987).

Fourth, there is a distinct Islamic copyright tradition based on Islamic law, the Shar'ia. The following summary is based on private correspondence between the author and Mustafa Salman Habib, Ph.D., Barrister at Law (Lincoln's Inn) in London, England (Habib 1998). The roots of Islamic copyright lay in the Koran and the traditional portion of Islamic law based on the Prophet Mohammed's words or acts but not written by him, known as the Sunna. This traditional portion of Islamic law is accepted as authoritative by the Sunni branch of Islam but rejected by the Shi'ite branch. One relevant saying in the Sunna is: "The works of a person that do not cease even after his death are three: a continuing charity, a beneficial know-how, or a worthwhile son." Such know-how is recognized as generating a continuous benefit that outlives the author. Sunni jurists are also unanimous in their high regard for authors, researchers, and scientists, who are collectively called "A'Lem" and to whom several references are made in the Koran and the Sunna.

Early Islamic jurists recognized copyright and offered protection from pirates. Unlike written legal codes of today, traditional Islamic copyright treated copyright infringement as a breach of ethics, that is, a moral rather than a criminal act. Punishment took the form of defamation of the infringer and casting shame on his tribe. An exception was blasphemy or incitement against Islam. The infamous case of Salman Rushdie is an example of what an author can expect if he is convicted of writing such a work. Only in recent years have formal copyright statutes been drafted, for example, in Saudi Arabia eight years ago.

Fifth, there are aboriginal heritage rights (AHR). These are based on a collectivist or communal concept of creation. To tribal peoples, a song, story, or icon does not belong to an individual but to the collective. Rights are often exercised by only one individual in each generation, often by matrilineal descent.

Outside Rights. There are creators' rights that exist outside of the Copyright Act. Generally they derive from the civil code tradition and cannot be transferred by contract from a creator to a proprietor. Furthermore, national treatment often need not be extended to nonresidents, allowing a nation, state or province to target and reward the creativity of its own citizens. Some U.S. examples illustrate this.

The Chip Protection Act provides copyrightlike protection for the design of integrated circuit chips, but only for U.S. manufacturers. Similarly, a proposed new Industrial Design Act recommended rights only for U.S. residents (Andrews 1990).

Aboriginal heritage rights (AHRs) are outside rights. For example, Public Law 101–601: The Native American Graves Protection and Repatriation Act of 1990, converts native art and artifacts into "inalienable communal property." This right may eventually be extended to include folktales and sacred tales (Farrer 1994).

The Visual Artists Right Act of 1990 provides special rights to creators of "recognized stature," including the right to prevent destruction of their work (Sullivan 1996, 43). This right is similar to "moral rights" granted to creators under the civil code and by the Canadian Copyright Act.

At the state level, the right of following sales (*droit de suivre*) has been granted to visual artists resident in California. The work of a young artist is sold at a low price, but as his or her career progresses, earlier works increase in value. While collectors benefit from the resale of early works, the artist gets nothing. The right of following sale insures that a percentage of all subsequent sales goes back to the artist.

Two foreign examples demonstrate that outside rights are available not only in the United States. Canadian public lending rights (PLRs) are granted for books written by Canadian authors and held in Canadian libraries. PLRs assume the public benefits from libraries, but authors suffer lost sales. Therefore, market failure exists justifying a public policy response. PLRs compensate authors from a special federal fund. Payment is capped so no one author receives too much. Payment is restricted to Canadians and goes directly to the creator.

The Republic of Ireland (Eire) exempts copyright income earned by resident creators from income tax. The exemption applies only to individuals, not to corporations. The result has been an influx of creative talent who pay sales and other taxes, offsetting the tax expenditure to the public treasury. In addition, such talent enriches the cultural and economic life of the country.

Research and Development

Research and Development (R&D) in art is different from R&D in the sciences. Natural sciences and engineering and social sciences and humanities research is centered in the university; arts research is not. This is reflected in federal subsidies to universities. Roald Hoffmann, professor of chemistry at Cornell University, determined that the ratio of federal funding to science and art was "about 500:1" in 1992 (Hoffman 1997). Arts research also does not benefit from contracts between industry and universities, targeted research by private foundations, or industry research institutes inside universities.

Art R&D primarily takes place in the nonprofit fine arts, where most new talent and technique are developed, new scripts and scores created, and new images and styles set. Results of arts R&D, like the results of pure scientific research, are sometimes adopted by for-profit enterprises, in and out of the arts industry. Results can inspire societywide changes in design, fashion, and style, as with art nouveau and art deco in the early part of the century.

There is anecdotal evidence of increasing private business support

of arts high schools in California and planned animation training institutes in Canada. Unfortunately, the only comparative industrial evidence
is quite outdated. In 1984, *Business Week* published a comparative analysis of sixteen major American industries, of which only the entertainment industry spent nothing on R&D (*Business Week* 1984). An update
of this comparative analysis is long overdue.

The university also plays a lesser role in professional development
(Busch 1985; K. Robinson 1982), and there is a well-documented gap
between graduation from university in the arts and attainment of professional status. Art is learned by doing; it is experiential. Traditional
craft methods, apprenticeship, and master classes survived the Industrial Revolution and remain the most effective methods of professional
training in the arts.

Artistic knowledge is also unlike scientific knowledge. Scientific
knowledge tends to depreciate through time; Greek deductive science
was displaced by modern experimental science. In art, however, knowledge can appreciate through time. King Tut, Shakespeare, and Bach still
speak, still sell. In media art, Hollywood film libraries have become multi-
million-dollar assets. The preservation of classical repertoire in the performing arts provides continuing inspiration to contemporary creators
and establishes standards of excellence against which new work is judged.
This religio (linking back) is embodied in heritage art that conserves and
preserves past and present creation for subsequent generations.

Performance

The final facet of the IO model is performance or the
socioeconomic results achieved by an industry. The three examined here
are the cost disease, cultural tectonics, and the contribution of the arts
to human ecology, both physical and psychic.

The Cost Disease

As has been confirmed in studies conducted around
the world, the arts (both live and recorded) suffer an inherent cost disease. In the live arts it takes the same time to rehearse and perform a
Mozart concerto today as was the case in his own time. In other industries, new NSE or SSH technology can substitute, complement, or better motivate workers, increasing the productivity of labor and allowing
wages (per remaining worker) to rise without increasing the price of other
goods and services (Baumol and Bowen 1966).

In the live arts, substitution of NSE or SSHs technology for artistic
labor is usually not possible and often not desirable. Consider an example from music: In the case of NSE technology, a seventeenth-century

Stradivarius outperforms any contemporary violin; Carnegie Hall is a
better venue for Mozart—with respect to sight line and sound—than the
Kennedy Center. In the case of SSH, conservatory training takes the same
time today as it did in Mozart's time, allowing for the randomness of
genius.

In effect, the live arts are a nonproductive industry in which there
is an income gap between what can be reasonably charged at the box
office and the rising costs of production. One factor filling this gap has
been artistic labor, which traditionally has been less well compensated
than other professions requiring similar years of tertiary education and
training. Low wages have been somewhat offset by what economists call
psychic income—that is, love of the job.

Nonartistic personnel, however, such as administrators, backstage
artisans, office workers, technicians, and other support personnel must
be paid relatively competitive wages. Eventually, no matter how great
their love of the job, ticket prices inevitably increase unless the gap can
be filled. In the past, princes and popes filled the gap, as the so-called
patrons of the arts; today, they have been replaced by government and
the philanthropic sector.

From an economic perspective, patrons patronize for self-serving
purposes (Boulding 1973). They have two primary motives: preservation of a particular vision of the collective cultural past or of themselves,
and/or selective promotion of contemporary creativity. Only limited consideration is given to live-arts R&D. A recent exception is the Disney
Corporation, which has reversed the traditional pattern of stage-to-screen
with *Beauty and the Beast*. The live arts community has responded positively (Chartrand 1998)

Studies of media art, including broadcasting, film, and audio recording, reveal the same cost disease (Baumol and Baumol 1984). In television, for example, about 10 percent of the budget is for transmission,
which benefits most from NSE technological change. However, more than
60 percent is for programs that, like the live arts, benefit least from this
type of technological change. While new NSE technology may enormously increase productivity at the outset, causing a decrease in cost
per audience member, once these productivity gains are made, the cost
of media art suffers in the same way. A similar situation exists in the
computer industry, where rapidly falling hardware costs are accompanied by more slowly decreasing costs of programming. Inevitably, labor-
intensive programming becomes the dominant cost factor. The media arts
and computers are thus called initially productive industries.

A corollary to the cost disease is technoaesthetic progress. During
downturns and depressions, the scale of art production grows, due to

the decline of real wages. In upturns and boom times, rising real wages result in smaller-scale productions, for example, one-person shows. Thus there is an inverse relation between economic prosperity and scale, if not quality, of arts production (Leroy 1980).

Cultural Tectonics

Using the geological analogy of tectonic plates, it has been argued that the Cold War between Marx and markets has been replaced by a clash of cultures based on language and religion (Huntington 1993, 22–49). One example is the Balkans, where Catholic Croats, Orthodox Serbs, and Moslems are at each other's throats yet are of the same race and speak the same language. With respect to the arts, language and religion are ongoing fault lines within and between the arts and society—for example, clashes between freedom of expression and religion, between multiculturalism and mainstream culture. Three such tectonic plates involve ideology, law, and geography.

Ideology. Ideology is the basis of political economic systems. It continues to be a disruptive force, as in the clash between those who believe in public funding of the arts and those who place their faith in the free market and philanthropy. At the international level, there is a related clash between the United States and countries that protect their arts industry. Many nations argue that artistic and cultural goods and services are carriers of values, not just utilitarian functions like a coffee pot, an automobile, or a bank account. Accordingly, they encourage production of artwork consistent with their national values and beliefs. This argument fuels ongoing international debate about "cultural sovereignty" and the "morals clause" of the GATT agreement. In international trade, all countries reserve the right to prohibit import of goods and services that threaten public morals. For example, Islamic countries prohibit public dissemination of images of the naked human body, and the United States prohibits the importing of child pornography.

Legal. Beyond ideology there are legal tectonics. The civil code concept of creators' rights differs from common law copyright. The battle between the French and Americans in the World Trade Organization reflects not just nationalist animus but a clash of legal philosophies. The United States wants Europe to extend the moral rights of individuals to corporations; Europe resists. There is also controversy between developed and industrialized countries over who is a creator. In the preamble to the treaty concerning trade-related intellectual property (TRIPS), community intellectual property rights are excluded. TRIPS includes only individual or corporate intellectual property, and only if it can have industrial application. By definition, this excludes all kinds of knowledge, ideas, and innovations produced in the intellectual commons, for instance, in villages among farmers, in forests among tribal peoples, and in universities (Shiva 1993).

Another legal tectonic concerns aboriginal heritage rights. The question of appropriation has become a painful problem in the artistic community. Some in the community accept ownership by aboriginal peoples of their own cultural heritage; others believe if artists restrict themselves to their own culture, humanity will be deprived of a significant cultural enrichment (Chartrand Winter 1996).

Geography. The final cultural tectonic involves geography, specifically, geographic mobility of people, by immigration and mass movement of populations from one continent or country to another. Peoples of different continents, races, languages, and religions are coming into closer and closer daily contact—inside multicultural societies like Australia, Canada, and the United States, with those remaining in the mother country, and with tourists. The result is a cross-pollination of art and art forms and a growth of multicultural expression in the literary, media, performing, and visual arts.

Human Ecology

As a species, humanity occupies, shapes, and is shaped by its physical and psychic environments. The arts industry contributes to both.

Physical. The physical human environment is molded by architects, designers, and urban planners. They are the visual ecologists of society. If architects and designers are concerned about the present, preservationists are concerned about the past and planners are concerned about the future. Architects and designers apply art to the skylines of our cities, the clothes we wear, the malls at which we shop, the picture on our cereal box, our homes and furnishings, the cars we drive, the places at which we work and the churches and temples in which we pray. From Frank Lloyd Wright through the German Expressionists and the Bauhaus movement to the International Style, architects and designers have believed that good design could change the world. They wanted to contribute to the *kosmos*, our sense of the right ordering of the multiple parts of the world (J. Hillman 1981). Together, architects and designers make up more than 45 percent of the total arts labor force (Chartrand 1996b).

Psychic. Beyond the physical environment there is the psychic commons filled with the values, images, and attitudes that shape both our own self-image and how we treat one another. Ongoing controversy about sex and violence in the media is an example of art shaping the psychic environment. On one hand are those who argue that sex and violence in the media provide a catharsis, allowing psychic release and reducing antisocial behavior. On the other are those who argue that the media fosters and encourages antisocial behavior, creating a "psychic epidemic."

From a welfare economist's perspective, there are two types of social behavior. The first are onerous activities not performed for inherent satisfaction but for what they yield—that is, work. Thus the disutility of work is theoretically to be compensated by a pay check. Second are the activities that are the opposite of work. They give satisfaction to those performing them. There are two types of such activities. The first are antisocial activities that give pleasure by inflicting pain or suffering on others. Social costs usually outweigh benefits, because benefits are transitory while suffering is often long lasting or permanent. Third, there are social activities that impose no physical burden or harm on anyone yet can give satisfaction or pleasure to all. They include the most benign and valuable of human activities such as love, learning, and the arts (Scitovsky 1989).

Conclusions

I intended, as an economist, to demonstrate the concept of an American arts industry. I did this by applying a textbook industrial organization framework drawn from mainstream economics and partially filling it with evidence collected over more than two decades of cultural economics research conducted by myself and others. As a citizen, I have a broader intention.

The concept of an American arts industry has significant implications. First, it could help cool traditional tensions between professional and amateur art, contemporary and heritage art, high and popular art, and profit and nonprofit art—what I call artistic apartheid. It shows each to be part of a larger, greater, and potentially integrated whole.

Second, it could be the first step toward a unified public, private, and philanthropic arts strategy like those of more politically coherent sectors such as business, environment, government, health care, science, and technology. It should enhance public discourse by permitting the arts to communicate with these sectors using the common language of contemporary society—economics.

Third, it could help explain transformation from an industrial to a knowledge-based economy; national wealth will come increasingly out of heads, not out of the ground or from the strength of our arms. A knowledge-based economy does not, however, mean the end of farming, fishing, mining, or manufacturing. Like Maslow's need hierarchy, economic development is a process of adding to, not subtracting from, the means available to satisfy human wants. In economics, this means that national income at the margin will increase fastest in knowledge industries. "At the margin," in economics, means that an increase in resources available to knowledge industries will generate the greatest increase in national income relative to other industries.

The content and the mechanism of this new economy are the arts, and natural sciences and engineering. The natural sciences and engineering provide the medium, the arts provide the message, and the social sciences and humanities provide the social context. Computers, fiber optics, and satellites require actors, dancers, directors, impresarios, musicians, painters, playwrights, producers, sculptors, and teams of highly skilled artisans and technicians to fulfill their destiny as much as any empty theater stage in ancient Greece. The difference today is that we have more stages than plays, more medium than message.

Finally, in this century the natural sciences and engineering have given us a futuristic vision of the earth from space—one world, one biosphere, and one human race. In the next century the arts must mold and sculpt a humanistic mask for this new vision, a mask to transform a world of warriors into a celestial sphere filled with artists and creators in all domains of human knowledge.

MARGARET J. WYSZOMIRSKI

3

Raison d'Etat, Raisons des Arts
Thinking about Public Purposes

The arts of government . . . rightfully order all lesser arts for the greater good and the higher glory.
—W. Carey McWilliams discussing the Puritan view of the arts in "The Arts and the American Political Tradition" (1985)

Democratic government and the arts are . . . in league with one another, for they both center on the individual and the fullest development of his capacities and talents . . . To free men, the arts are not incidental to life but central to it.
—John D. Rockefeller III testifying before the U.S. Senate subcommittee on Education, Arts, and Humanities on 31 October 1963 on behalf of Joint Resolution 104 to establish a National Council on the Arts and National Arts Foundation (quoted in Biddle 1988, 24)

The arts and public interest in the United States are intertwined in what has been called "an awkward embrace" (Burns 1975). History is replete with debates and shifting tides of opinion about which public interests are furthered by the arts, how the interests of the arts and of the public coincide or diverge, and how the organizations of the arts and of government interact. There is no simple or best answer to these questions; nor is there an enduring answer to them, since responses will vary over time. Thus, this chapter does not attempt to resolve such debates. Instead it sketches out some of the key issues, public interests, and policy values present in current debates and recent programs.

The Question of Public Purpose

Public purposes are not immutable; they evolve and are reinterpreted as conditions and social concerns shift. However, all public purposes must meet one fundamental requirement: the assembly and sustainment of a manageable consensus that recognizes the value of each purpose and therefore legitimates the allocation of public effort and resources.

It might be said that certain basic purposes have a standing consensus that is codified in the Constitution or in the Declaration of Independence. The declaration asserts as "self-evident" the "inalienable rights" of life, liberty, and the pursuit of happiness. The Bill of Rights extends protection to life, liberty, and property and provides details on the civil rights and liberties that the government is obligated to recognize and guarantee. The Bill of Rights includes an explicit protection for freedom of expression, which is generally regarded as the constitutional anchor for freedom of artistic expression as well as for the academic freedom of humanists and other scholars.

In general, the Constitution may be regarded as an outline of the responsibilities, powers, processes, and limitations of the federal government and its constituent branches. As such, it is a signal reference point in the public policymaking process. The Preamble to the Constitution identifies a number of general public purposes that have enjoyed an enduring consensus: "to form a more perfect Union; to establish Justice; to ensure domestic tranquility; to provide for the general welfare; to provide for the common defense; to secure the blessings of liberty for ourselves and our Posterity."

Each of these purposes was more extensively developed in other sections of the Constitution, through subsequent statutory law and judicial decisions, and through two centuries of practice and experience. Within these broad guidelines and over the course of our history, many specific concerns have come to be accepted as public matters, while the treatment of others have come to be regarded as private concerns. Our current interest in devolution and privatization reflects the continuing redefinition of private and public concerns. In the American context of limited government, capitalism, and individualism, it might even be said that it is an implicit public purpose to facilitate the achievement of many private purposes, as long as these do no harm to others.

The formation of a more perfect union is the enduring challenge of democracy and civil society—a quest that engages government and citizens, public and private spheres. While this and other basic public purposes find expression in the fundamental and authoritative documents of our system of governance, such purposes are not solely the responsibility of government. Rather they are also public in a larger sense, in that they represent what we, as a people, decide is important to us as a society, an economy, and a democratic polity.

Although none of the broad Constitutional purposes explicitly mentions the arts, an artistic or cultural manifestation of each can be perceived. Among the liberties that bless the Republic are cultural activities, including freedom of expression, which is guaranteed in the First Amendment. In the course of providing for the general welfare, the specific property rights of authors and inventors were protected through copyrights and patents that Congress was empowered to grant under article I, section 8. Certainly the arts can make an important contribution to the pursuit of happiness (Wollheim 1985). As Joseph Conrad observed, the arts and artists "speak to our capacity for delight and wonder, to the sense of mystery surrounding our lives; to our sense of pity, and beauty and pain" (PCAH 1992, 25). Similarly, cultural literacy plays a role in "domestic tranquility," since it is through "shared symbols, and the shared information that the symbols represent, [that] we learn to communicate effectively with one another in our national community" (Hirsch 1988, xvii). As an extension, global cultural literacy provides us with the basic information needed to thrive in an increasingly interdependent and interconnected world.

Each of the general public purposes asserted by the Constitution has been subject to numerous reinterpretations over the years, accommodating changing circumstances and shifting expectations about the legitimate scope of governmental action. The federal government has the authority to make all laws that are "necessary and proper" for carrying out the powers and responsibilities enumerated and implied by the Constitution. This idea is embodied in the "elastic clause"—a clear indication that public purposes, objectives, and means were likely to change over time. Such adaptation is also prompted by changing private needs and interests. Once shared and acknowledged by others, private interests can become matters of public purpose. If public purposes are to be politically legitimate, they must be arrived at through processes of open deliberation and consensus-building. As part of this process, it is incumbent upon the private interests and their representatives to be ever mindful of the coincident public aspects. Without attention to and articulation of how public interest coincides with self-interest, the longevity and effectiveness of supportive political coalitions will erode.

Political scientist Edward Banfield raised a set of related issues with regard to government spending on the arts. He asked: "Is the activity one that is properly within the sphere of government, especially that of the national government? Does it have a purpose that was arrived at by deliberation and with an understanding of the situation? Are the means employed for the attainment of the purpose effective? . . . Are the means employed more likely to achieve the purpose, or to achieve it at less cost, than some other means? (1984, 5)

Banfield's answer to all these questions was "no." Others have reached quite different answers, ranging from "yes" and "perhaps" to "sometimes" or "in this instance." It is appropriate and necessary for public debate to grapple with the issue of determining public purposes and the strategies and means for addressing such purposes.

A persistent challenge of American democracy has been to allow for the simultaneous pursuit of individual self-interest and of public interest or common good. Remarking upon this hallmark characteristic of American political thought, Alexis de Tocqueville called it "the doctrine of enlightened self-interest properly understood." As he saw it, enlightened self-interest holds that it is "to the individual advantage of each to work in the good of all" and to strive to find "those points where private advantage does meet and coincide with the general interest." Tocqueville described this doctrine as "universally accepted" by Americans and used in "explaining almost every act of their lives" (Tocqueville 1969, 525–528). More recently, this tendency was recapitulated by Harvard social scientist Gary Orren: "People do not act simply on the basis of their perceived self-interest. . . . They are also motivated by values, purposes, ideas, goals, and commitments that transcend self-interest or group interest" (Orren 1988, 13).

Clearly, neither all personal interests nor every common interest are the subjects of government action. Americans also have a long tradition of addressing shared interests through voluntary activities and associations. This innovation has given rise to what we now see as a third sector of society, composed of informal community organizations and formally incorporated nonprofit organizations (NPOs) of a stunning variety—including many arts and cultural organizations. Whether directly by government or indirectly through private organizations (not-for-profit and for-profit), when private interests become a public concern, there is often an implicit quid pro quo involved wherein public services or public procedures are expected from the private interests. For example, it has long been assumed that "all charitable purposes . . . are designed to accomplish objects which are beneficial to the community" (Austin Scott quoted in Swords 1985, 128). In return for these public services, NPOs are granted certain public benefits such as exemption from taxes and are expected to operate in a public manner (for example, with public reporting requirements and without regard for individual profit). Similarly, private, commercial interests that are licensed to use a public good (such as the airwaves) are also expected to provide public services in exchange (such as news and weather reports, public service announcements, and children's educational programming).

Clearly, any answer to questions about what constitutes public purpose, how such purposes should be addressed, and what kinds of organizations should address them must be capacious, contingent, and evolving. One way of understanding which concerns are viewed as appropriate for authoritative public action and the allocation of public resources lies in Tocqueville's notion of "coincidence"—those concerns in which private interests and public interests coincide with and complement one another. Alluding to such a coincidence with regard to public funding for the arts through the NEA, political scientist Kevin Mulcahy has written that "just as every government program must in some way address an identifiable public need, so too must the NEA address a legitimate public need . . . [such as] the aesthetic needs of the American public as well as of American artists and promote the cultural welfare of the general citizenry as well as the artistic resources of the nation" (Mulcahy 1995, 206).

Enlightened self-interest takes shape in public policies, government operations, and political processes, as well as in voluntary and community action and in nonprofit organizations. This chapter focuses primarily on the governmental and policy aspects of public purpose and also discusses implications for the nonprofit and commercial sectors.

Public Purpose and Public Policy

Public policy is a course of governmental actions—and their consequences—intended to address a public purpose. In common usage, phrases like "public interest," "common good," "public purpose," "public problem," "public need," and "policy goal" are used fairly interchangeably. While we might quibble about fine distinctions, I think we can agree that these terms are interrelated. In this chapter, I use the phrase "public purpose."

Each policy entails its own particular interpretation of enlightened self-interest, identifying what public purpose is involved and how it may be linked to particular private interests. This linkage is often forged through core values that are so broadly accepted in the polity that they cannot be seriously contested (Baumgartner and Jones 1993; Cobb and Elder 1983). Values such as equality, pluralism, efficiency, liberty, and accountability are historically persistent and inherent in American civic culture. For example, the provision for a common defense is obviously in the public's interest in securing liberty and maintaining sovereignty. Equally obviously, the provision for a common defense is of particular and tangible benefit to industries that manufacture weapons and military materials. Maintaining what is perceived to be an acceptable balance between what is necessary for a common defense (a public purpose) and what is profitable for defense industries (a private purpose) is a continuous and shifting challenge for defense policy.

In the cases of cultural policies such as government funding for the arts, facilitating international and domestic trade in cultural products and services, protecting artistic freedom or intellectual property, preserving cultural heritage, or licensing broadcasting and recording industries, the private concerns may often seem more evident than the public purposes. Discerning a public dimension of commercially produced art is particularly nettlesome. The legacy of our Puritan forefathers, combined with the Protestant work ethic, makes us hesitant to recognize a governmental concern in leisure, entertainment, or recreation—which generally are presumed to be private and perhaps trivial. Creativity and innovation confront an expectation that they will be useful and propel progress. In economic terms, the commercial arts are private sector activities and their audiences—whether mass or niche—are seen as consumers. Both in terms of ownership and in terms of individual tastes and consumption, the private interest is self-evident, but where is the public interest to be found? Refocusing on public benefit allows us to see that the commercial arts can be engines of international trade (van Hemel, Mommaas, and Smithiujsen 1996), resources for public diplomacy, and instruments for exercising international cultural leadership and projecting the American spirit abroad.

Historically, another general public purpose has been the protection of society from frivolous and/or dangerous activities and products through regulatory policies. Recent public debates have focused on finding ways to regulate the distribution of commercial arts products in order to protect the public from harm in the form of excessive violence on television and in the movies or of pornographic or obscene art through FCC decency regulations, the V-chip, or broadcast, movie, and recording rating systems (Galligan and Brown 1992).

Each age finds its own way of defining what is public and what is private, as well as of linking and relating across these interests. As societal conditions change, public purposes may also change, and certainly the ways in which we seek to achieve such purposes will vary. While essential political values endure, the way we put them into practice is subject to change, as is the manner in which we prioritize and balance among these values. At the end of the twentieth century, as Americans refocus on values and rethink their expectations of government and of themselves, we are engaged in a wide-ranging process of redefining the character of our common purposes. Consequently, the arts—like defense, foreign affairs, welfare, education, telecommunications, or intergovernmental relations—find themselves in the midst of a changing conception of enlightened self-interest. In the case of the arts, such flux has made formulating public policy and assembling a sustainable public consensus a formidable task.

Moving from Public Purpose to Policy Impact

The mere identification of public purpose does not automatically translate into policy, nor does a declaration of purpose determine effective action. Instead, it is but one step in a complex decision-making process that draws upon various kinds of knowledge, information, experience, and belief. Graphically, one might think of this as a decision tree (see fig. 3.1). A brief explanation of this analytical device is in order before a discussion of the specific topic of public purposes and the arts.

Public purposes might be considered the trunk of this tree, since they represent broad, sturdy goals that are considered to be appropriate subjects for government action. However, these purposes are not the sole foundation for public action. Values constitute a root system that anchors public purposes and nourishes policies that address these purposes.

Part of the root system is composed of values particularly important to the members of a policy community—those individuals and organizations that are most directly affected and have the most distinct interests at stake (Wyszomirski 1996). For the arts and cultural community, such values include artistic freedom, creativity, and individualism. Some would argue that aesthetics—whether referred to as excellence, beauty, or truth—is also a core value of the cultural community (Kimball 1997). Basic values of the general public and the polity at large constitute another part of the root system. For Americans, these values would include liberty, pluralism, fairness, and equality, as well as general support for the practices of free market capitalism, representative and limited government, and popular sovereignty. Ideally, to strongly support and sustain a public purpose, both parts of the root system must be intertwined and healthy; that is, values held by the cultural community must commingle with values of the general public, and both sets of values must be related to a public purpose.

Clearly, there is a link between artistic freedom and liberty, but they are not exactly the same thing. For example, artistic freedom (or academic freedom) as it is thought of by artists (and scholars) may seem somewhat removed from the average citizen's sense of liberty. Some people focus on liberty as "freedom to do" (as in the artist's sense of freedom of self-expression); others focus on the aspect of "freedom from"

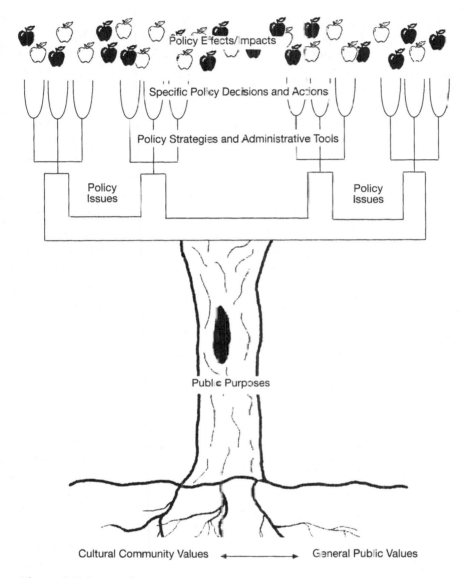

Figure 3.1. From values to impacts

intrusion or imposition (as in some citizens' desire for freedom from exposure to art that they consider pornographic, blasphemous, or offensive).

Relatedly, the artistic community places a high value on innovation and experimentation, which often translates into an emphasis on change. However, public opinion research on the sciences tells us that the public is ambivalent about the value of innovation and experimentation and that it has become increasingly less positive about progress and change, often finding change to be unsettling if not outright threatening. These differing views of innovation and change can weaken the anchoring roots of certain public purposes. Clearly, the meaning of each value is subject to interpretation. For example, citizens may differ as to how limited they believe government should be. Some hold a strict and narrow interpretation, while others have an expansive and flexible sensibility. Yet, while citizens may differ on the particular meaning of limited government, they nonetheless agree that the concept itself is valued. It must also be recognized that there are inherent trade-offs and combinations among values and that individuals may hold different opinions as to where the appropriate and legitimate balance among values is to be struck. With regard to the arts and culture (Kreidler 1996), our knowledge about such attitudes and values is relatively inadequate and fragmented. We have only a general understanding of which values are most important for artists and how they interpret these values; we know far less about how these values and attitudes compare with those of the general public. Most other subjects of public policy have a better, more extensive, and more subtle understanding of what "enlightened self-interest" means. A better understanding of the values of both the cultural community and of the general public is an important part of finding where public and private interests coincide and can sustain cultural policies.

To return to the tree analogy: Above the trunk of broad public purpose, one finds the major branches that represent various policy issues. Public purposes can be advanced or hampered by many factors or conditions, thus giving rise to different policy issues or problems. These policy issues may be addressed singly or in combination, sequentially or simultaneously.

While issues attract governmental attention (and often carry connotations of causality), actions need to be operationalized through specific program strategies or administrative tools (Salamon 1989). With regard to the arts, some of the most common policy tools are matching grants, public art commissions, copyrights, communication regulations, and tax incentives. Just as a purpose may involve a number of issues, an issue can be approached with a variety of program strategies and using many types of policy tools. During most of its history, the NEA had eighteen program divisions, each of which used a set of policy tools including grants, fellowships, contracts, and partnerships (whether in the form of public-private collaborations or interagency agreements).

It might be argued that mature, well-articulated, and deeply legitimated policy arenas are capable of dealing with a collection of issues using a repertoire of policy tools and program strategies. This versatility can facilitate adaptability to changing value perceptions and circumstantial factors. For example, in discussions of economic policy, we talk about using fiscal and monetary strategies. In social welfare policy, a host of strategies have been employed, ranging from punitive, to preventive, to alleviative, or curative (Rushefsky 1995, 131–139). Alternatively, some analysts speak of general policy strategies that are distributive, regulatory, or redistributive (Lowi 1964; Ripley and Franklin 1991). Federal arts policy has inhabited a rather tenuous policy arena largely reliant on a distributive strategy and focused primarily on the issues of expanding access and coping with the market failure of nonprofit arts organizations. The broader construct of cultural policy has been a fragmented and amorphous policy arena, using regulatory, distributive, and redistributive strategies and many types of administrative tools to address a variety of seemingly unrelated issues.

Growing out of program strategies and policy tools are the "leaves" of specific decisions and actions—specific grants, licenses, commissions—that are awarded to particular artists, art organizations, and/or industries or the application of rules and regulations to particular cases and instances. In recent years, much attention has been focused on this level, as particular grants, institutions, or individuals have become controversial and the subject of intense public scrutiny and debate. Yet as this analogy suggests, such leaves are relatively ephemeral manifestations of the public purpose. Such policy leaves change with the seasons, are numerous, and exhibit differing characteristics a new crop can be grown each year. The leaves are unlikely to be healthy if the program strategies are ill conceived or outdated or if administrative tools are flawed. As conditions and issues change, entire branches of policy may need to adapt and change course or may wither or require pruning. If the policy trunk—composed of values and purpose—is essentially strong, then it can probably endure political storms, issue redefinitions, administrative mistakes, and programmatic change.

Finally, to carry the metaphor to its full application, the fruits of these values, purposes, and programs are the impacts and outcomes that actually affect people, organizations, and conditions (Barsdate/NASAA 1996; Wyszomirski 1997b). For example, it took nearly three decades of careful cultivation in arts policy to produce three major fruits: a national crop of nonprofit professional arts organizations; growth in the number of artists and the size of audiences; and a vibrant state, local, corporate, and foundation financial support network for the arts. Other fruits have included new and additional artworks that add to our cultural resources and legacy. There are also infrastructure fruits in the form of arts service organizations, program models, and information resources. Along the way, the arts policy tree flowered annually with grants that often seemed of particular benefit to specific beneficiaries and interests (grantees and the arts disciplines) while the public benefits were less apparent (and more long term). Historically, specific policy branches have been pruned, such as the WPA arts programs of the New Deal era.

This tree metaphor distinguishes and relates a series of policy elements that are frequently confused and provides a visual and organic model for thinking about the arts and public purposes. Purposes are anchored in values and grow in the environment of their political, social, and economic circumstances. Public purposes branch out toward various issues and sprout many program strategies and administrative tools. Policies may develop in many patterns and directions. Public purposes, like trees, seldom follow only one line of development and may develop in different ways at different times. Public purposes are neither linear, unadaptable, nor inevitable; they evolve, adapt, and can be shaped.

Public Purposes and the Arts

With regard to the arts, the articulation of public purposes has often been implicit or indirect. Generally public policies and decisions have been undertaken while those who formulate them allude to, rather than declare, the underlying public purpose. Indeed, the reluctance to focus on public purpose and policy concerning the arts has been so pronounced that it has prompted Joseph Epstein, a former member of the National Council for the Arts, to ask whether "the arts . . . have a peculiar resistance to being discussed in the frame of reference known as policy" (Epstein 1996, 29).

The expression of public purposes has taken many specific forms and the choice of particular objectives and means has varied through time. The law that established the NEA and NEH begins with a section called "Congressional Declaration of Purpose." The report of the Independent Commission on the NEA observed that the NEA "as a public agency, has a responsibility to serve the public interest and to promote the general welfare" (1990, 58). The history of government actions with regard to the arts, as well as the range of explanations and intentions behind those actions reveals at least five basic public purposes. These five public purposes include: (1) furthering the quest for security, (2) fostering community, (3) contributing to prosperity, (4) improving the quality and conditions of life, and (5) cultivating democracy.

For the purposes of discussion, figures 3.2 through 3.6 identify likely core values in either the cultural community, the general public, or both. I have sketched in a set of major policy issues and program strategies for each. This is not an exhaustive catalogue of all issues or programs, either current or historical, although it does draw upon an extensive awareness of past and present practices. Nor do I intend it to present a definitive analysis of the values value interpretations, and value conflicts that characterize public debate about cultural policies. Rather this analysis is offered as a lens through which to bring a range of phenomena and experience into clearer focus.

Security

Whether economic, international, or societal, security has historically been an important and legitimate public purpose underlying government action concerning the arts. Although security has taken many forms, the term "security" is seldom used explicitly with regard to the arts. Perhaps because of this, security has been one of the least explicit public purposes of the arts. At least three policy issues can be discerned that have involved the arts in the quest of our common security: helping to ensure national security, protecting the survival of our cultural patrimony, and helping to maintain social and moral order. Each of these issues has given rise to a variety of programs or strategies (see fig. 3.2).

The role of the arts in ensuring our national security has taken many forms. Cultural historian Neil Harris points out that during both world wars, the federal government turned to artists—from both the entertainment industry and the so-called high arts—to help arouse patriotism and mobilize public support for the war effort. Artists participated in rallies at home and helped entertain the troops abroad; they went on tour selling war bonds and designed recruiting posters (Harris 1996). During World War II and the long years of the Cold War, the federal government supported programs that sent artists abroad as cultural ambassadors engaged in public diplomacy. Cultural diplomacy programs were used to cultivate stronger ties among allies and friendly nations and as a long-term strategy to improve understanding between unfriendly or unallied nations (Coombs 1964; Frankel 1966; Mulcahy 1982). As recently as 1992, a report from the President's Committee on the Arts and Humanities argued that "cultural exchanges are a rich source of global communication furthering a unique level of understanding among distant nations and societies" (PCAH 1992, 14).

During the cold war era, national security took on elements of scientific and cultural competition as well as military and ideological conflict. Take the case of Van Cliburn's success in winning the 1958 Tchaikovsky piano competition in Moscow playing the work of Russian composer Sergei Rachmaninoff. Upon his return to the United States, he was greeted as a national hero, his success all the more satisfying to his compatriots because it came only a year after American scientific confidence

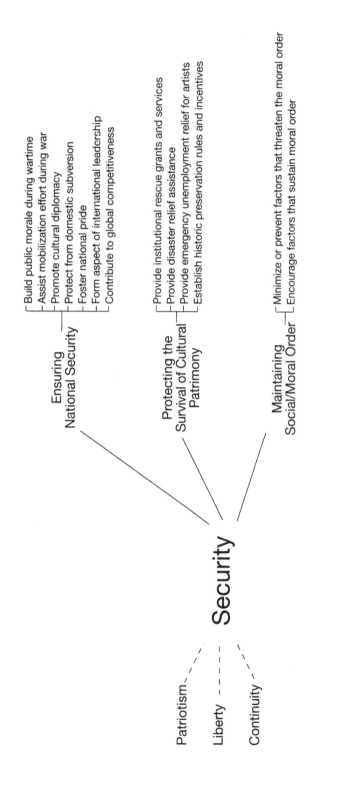

Build public morale during wartime
Assist mobilization effort during war
Promote cultural diplomacy
Protect from domestic subversion
Foster national pride
Form aspect of international leadership
Contribute to global competitiveness

Ensuring
National Security

Provide institutional rescue grants and services
Provide disaster relief assistance
Provide emergency unemployment relief for artists
Establish historic preservation rules and incentives

Protecting the
Survival of Cultural
Patrimony

Minimize or prevent factors that threaten the moral order
Encourage factors that sustain moral order

Maintaining
Social/Moral Order

Security

Patriotism
Liberty
Continuity

Core Values   Public Purpose   Policy Issues   Program Strategies
                                                        and Administrative Tools

Figure 3.2. Security

had been shaken by the successful Soviet launch of the first *Sputnik* satellite into space. Clearly, this artistic accomplishment was regarded as a source of patriotic pride and marked a symbolic American triumph in the ongoing cold war. Conversely, during the 1940s and early 1950s, the House Un-American Activities Committee and Senator Joseph McCarthy were engaged in what they saw as an attempt to protect the country from internal subversives, including some artists (Larson 1983). Thus, the role of artists and the arts in the quest for national security can cut both ways; the arts can be seen either as assets or as threats.

The Librarian of Congress, James Billington, points out that "stronger cultural and education programs enable us to sustain and support longer term forces working towards democratization" throughout the world and that building democracies is "in the interest of world peace" (Billington 1991). National security and international stature were alluded to by the legislative founders of the National Endowment for the Arts in 1966. The Preamble of the NFAH Act states that "world leadership . . . cannot rest solely upon superior power, wealth and technology, but must be solidly founded upon worldwide respect and admiration for the Nation's high qualities as a leader in the realm of ideas and of the spirit" (NFAH ACT: Sec. 951, sec 2, 9).

In the post–cold war era, national security concerns have taken on a distinctly economic character, such that national security has been redefined in ways that highlight economic matters such as competitiveness and trade. The arts contribute to national economic security both directly and indirectly. America is "the world leader in the creation and distribution of intellectual property, particularly copyright products" (Siwek and Furchtgott-Roth 1990). These creative products include newspapers and periodicals, book publishing, radio and television broadcasting, records and tapes, motion pictures, theatrical productions, advertising, and computer programming and software, art, photography, and architectural services. Today, these cultural products and services constitute one of America's largest and fastest-growing export industries. So, just as military capacity has long been a cornerstone of our national security policy, now American cultural capacity is becoming an important national asset in the competition for global economic security. Indirectly, the arts help other businesses compete more effectively in the global arena. Corporate leaders recognize that knowledge of history and culture enhances their ability to react to the complexities of global business (Lehman and Merrill 1986). Some corporations have even adapted the cultural ambassador approach to the economic realm, recognizing that sponsoring artists and arts organizations to tour abroad can open doors and help forge good business relationships (PCAH 1992, 16).

Security is not only a matter of "the common defense" but is also manifest in the survival imperative (Stone 1988, 69). In many other countries, this takes the form of a concern for the protection of a nation's cultural patrimony. While this issue is not typically discussed this way in the United States, it has, nonetheless, been implicit to a number of policy strategies and programs during the past fifty years. Both the unemployment crisis that faced American workers (including artists) during the Great Depression and the financial crisis that confronted some of our most renowned nonprofit arts organizations in the early 1960s threatened the nation's cultural patrimony. During the New Deal, federal WPA programs provided emergency economic assistance to artists who were in need of a job and sought a living wage. In 1961, a musicians' strike and inadequate financing threatened to close down the Metropolitan Opera, one of America's preeminent cultural institutions. President Kennedy directed the secretary of labor to mediate the dispute, and the settlement helped establish the rationale for direct federal support for the arts (Cummings 1995). In 1966, one of the first grants of the newly established National Endowment for the Arts went to rescue the American Ballet Theatre from the brink of financial disaster. More recently, emergency grants made by the NEA to local arts organizations battered by natural disasters (for example, hurricanes or earthquakes) or community traumas (for example, the Los Angeles riots or the Oklahoma City bombing) also address the survival imperative.

Emergency assistance is clearly of great value to the individual workers and organizations that receive aid, but the coincident public purpose is not merely the sum of these individual interests. Rather, the public purposes inherent in such government programs lies in the effort to protect the nation's cultural resources for posterity. The New Deal art programs are credited with having saved a generation of American artists and thereby setting the stage for the resurgence of American arts in the postwar years. Similarly, in the 1960s, fear of losing major cultural institutions helped galvanize public action leading to the creation of the NEA (Cummings 1995). In the 1960s, public awareness of the precarious state of many historic buildings and sites increased, resulting in public and private conservation efforts. At least in part, institutional support from the NEA for the past thirty years has sought to protect and expand what in other countries is thought of as the nation's cultural patrimony.

Security can also pertain to preserving social or moral order. As former chairman of the NEH William Bennett observed, "the issues surrounding the culture and our values are the most important ones" and that "Government, through law, discourse, and example, can legitimize and delegitimize certain acts . . . [and values]" (Bennett 1992, 36–37). The role of the arts in preserving, reflecting, and shaping the moral order has long been recognized. One might even say it is ingrained in the political traditions of the United States.

The Puritans, whom many regard as having been against art, had rather a highly moral understanding of the role of art in society. As political philosopher W. Carey McWilliams pointed out, the Puritans believed that human beings were meant to "live Bright and Civil, with fine Accomplishments"; however, with regard to the arts, one had to guard against overemphasizing self-interest. Thus from the Puritan perspective, the arts were worthy of cultivation and public support to the extent that they pointed the soul toward excellence or fostered civic virtue and the harmony of the community (McWilliams 1985, 17–18). During the age of Jackson and the advent of mass democracy in the 1830s, the Aristotelian view was revived: The quality of democracy was defined by the excellence of its people. As a consequence, the arts were not only regarded as a manifestation of the American image and ideal but were important in the education of citizens in the art of democracy (McWilliams 1985, 27). The Progressive Party observed in 1948 that the arts were "a potentially powerful force in the moral and spiritual life of a people" (Cornwell 1985). In the current era of mass media and popular entertainment, television, radio, magazines, newspapers, film, and popular music, theater, and literature are seen not only as a reflection of social and political reality but as a force to "define reality, shape the times, give meaning to history" (Hunter 1991, 225).

Thus, Americans retain a fundamental agreement about the capacity of the arts to influence the social order through the inculcation of moral and civic virtues. Currently, however, disagreement churns over whether the moral effect of the arts is positive or negative. Some see the instructive potential of the arts as leading to individual and social betterment, while others blame the popular culture for encouraging teenage sex and violence (Kolbert 1995). Some see some aspects of the arts (or some of the arts) as a force supportive of social order and cohesion; others see them as a socially disturbing or a coarsening force.

Both moral views can be seen in any number of political statements. For example, the Prohibition Party platform of 1932 voiced concern about the "degrading influence of immoral pictures and insidious propaganda connected therewith" and called for federal controls and preventive efforts (Cornwell 1985). After observing in 1988 that the arts and humanities should emphasize "those ideas and cultural accomplishments that address the ethical foundations of our culture," the Republican Party platform in 1992 asserted that "Government has a responsibility . . . to ensure that it promotes the common moral values that bind us together as a nation . . . no artist has an inherent right to claim taxpayer support for his or her private vision of art if that vision mocks the moral and spiritual basis on which our society is founded. . . ."

Alternatively, the 1984 Democratic platform, noting that "the arts and humanities are at the core of our national experience," went on to sound a recurring theme that "the arts flourish where there is freedom and where individual initiative and imagination are encouraged" (1960 and 1984). This atmosphere is "firmly rooted in the First Amendment's freedom of expression guarantee" (1992). A 1994 publication by People for the American Way warned that recent art controversies are "a critical warning sign of the fraying public consensus behind free expression . . ." and that the debate over the arts presents "an opportunity to bring more of the American public into a broader discussion that encompasses the principles that formed this nation—free expression, mutual respect and tolerance" (PAW 1994, 7, 14). Inherent in these latter statements is a sense of the moral order of American society—what some have called secular humanism or our civil religion. From this perspective the Constitution and the Bill of Rights are living documents that exert a fundamental moral authority in the service of the ideals of freedom and justice (Hunter 1991, 113–114).

While conceptions about the moral order may differ, this does not detract from a basic agreement about the importance of moral order to security and that the arts play a part in that purpose. Differing perspectives do, however, make it difficult to forge a working consensus about this aspect of the public's security concerns. As Hunter points out, such "disagreements poignantly signify a loss of the UMUN, the 'center,' the moral consensus in American public philosophy . . ." and asks whether "a liberal democracy [can] remain . . . without an elementary and somewhat universal agreement in the public realm about the criteria for distinguishing the social good from the socially destructive. . . ." (Hunter 1991, 314).

Fostering Community

This is a second public purpose to which the arts have contributed (see fig. 3.3). Fostering community may invoke any of a number of core values, some of which present the potential for fundamental tensions. Within the context of community, we value both individualism and pluralism, equality and representativeness, freedom of expression and mutual responsibility. At different times and in different programs, various of these values may be emphasized, or a balance among them may be cast differently. Sometimes these strategies have been so implicit that we hardly recognize them for what they are. As political

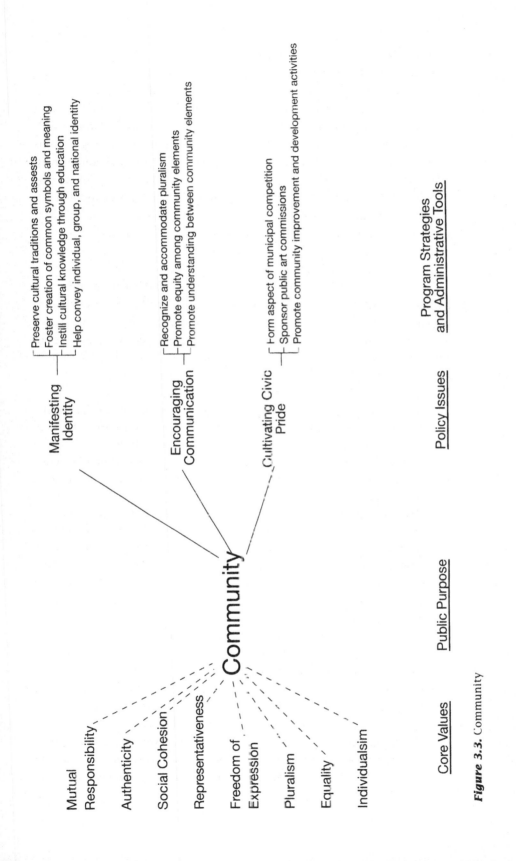

Preserve cultural traditions and assests
Foster creation of common symbols and meaning
Instill cultural knowledge through education
Help convey individual, group, and national identity

Manifesting
Identity

Recognize and accommodate pluralism
Promote equity among community elements
Promote understanding between community elements

Encouraging
Communication

Form aspect of municipal competition
Sponsor public art commissions
Promote community improvement and development activities

Cultivating Civic
Pride

Program Strategies
and Administrative Tools

Policy Issues

Community

Public Purpose

Mutual
Responsibility

Authenticity

Social Cohesion

Representativeness

Freedom of
Expression

Pluralism

Equality

Individualsim

Core Values

Figure 3.3. Community

theorist Benjamin Barber observed, "the arts have . . . the capacity simultaneously to offer expression to the particular identities of communities and groups (including those that feel excluded from the dominant community's space) *and* to capture commonalities and universalities that tie communities and groups together into a national whole" (Barber 1996).

At least three policy issues can be identified as underlying various programs and approaches that are intended to help foster community. These include: manifesting identity, encouraging communication among diverse groups, and cultivating civic pride. Figure 3.3 also identifies a number of program strategies and policy tools (such as public art commissions) that have been used to implement these strategies.

Contributing to Prosperity

This is a third public purpose that has been addressed by the arts and by public policies concerned with the arts and culture (see figure 3.4). Once again, a number of possible core values are involved, some of which are different from the core values underlying other public purposes. For example, concerns for property and efficiency imply decidedly economic values. Prosperity can also concern creativity, excellence (or quality), and fairness.

At least four prosperity-related issues can be discerned that find a coincidence between the interests of the arts and the public. These issues and the strategies used to address them have included:

Promoting shared economic utility through the development of positive externalities such as economic impact, redevelopment, tourism, or competitiveness.

Coping with market failure problems through direct subsidies and indirect tax expenditures, by helping to underwrite labor or to develop markets, by creating a common good in the form of field or market information, or in assisting particular industries or companies adapt to systemic or societal changes such as new technologies. This issue is primarily concerned with nonprofit organizations (NPOs) and, for the past three decades, has focused on increasing the proportion of their contributed income rather than boosting earned income as a proportion of organizational revenues (L. Stevens 1996).

Promoting public access and choice has been a strategy used with regard to both not-for-profit and commercial arts, through programs that have expanded the distribution of cultural products. Through program strategies like building and supporting public television or licensing commercial broadcast corporations, the federal government has sought to provide more people with greater access to more cultural opportunities and choices. Other policies have been concerned with ensuring quality

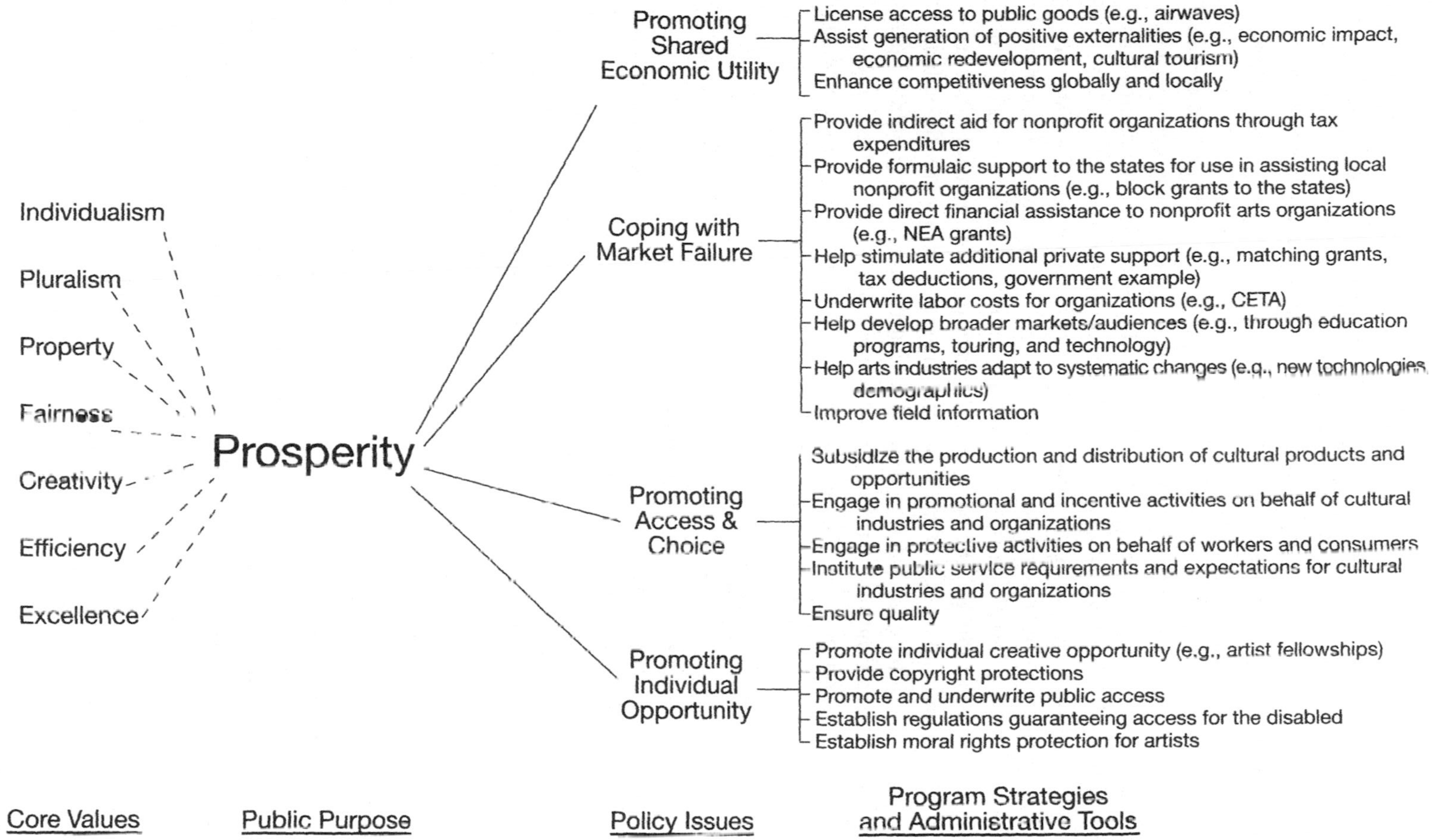

Core Values   Public Purpose   Policy Issues   Program Strategies and Administrative Tools

Prosperity

Core Values
- Individualism
- Pluralism
- Property
- Fairness
- Creativity
- Efficiency
- Excellence

Public Purpose
- Prosperity

Policy Issues
- Promoting Shared Economic Utility
- Coping with Market Failure
- Promoting Access & Choice
- Promoting Individual Opportunity

Program Strategies and Administrative Tools

Promoting Shared Economic Utility
- License access to public goods (e.g., airwaves)
- Assist generation of positive externalities (e.g., economic impact, economic redevelopment, cultural tourism)
- Enhance competitiveness globally and locally

Coping with Market Failure
- Provide indirect aid for nonprofit organizations through tax expenditures
- Provide formulaic support to the states for use in assisting local nonprofit organizations (e.g., block grants to the states)
- Provide direct financial assistance to nonprofit arts organizations (e.g., NEA grants)
- Help stimulate additional private support (e.g., matching grants, tax deductions, government example)
- Underwrite labor costs for organizations (e.g., CETA)
- Help develop broader markets/audiences (e.g., through education programs, touring, and technology)
- Help arts industries adapt to systematic changes (e.g., new technologies, demographics)
- Improve field information

Promoting Access & Choice
- Subsidize the production and distribution of cultural products and opportunities
- Engage in promotional and incentive activities on behalf of cultural industries and organizations
- Engage in protective activities on behalf of workers and consumers
- Institute public service requirements and expectations for cultural industries and organizations
- Ensure quality

Promoting Individual Opportunity
- Promote individual creative opportunity (e.g., artist fellowships)
- Provide copyright protections
- Promote and underwrite public access
- Establish regulations guaranteeing access for the disabled
- Establish moral rights protection for artists

Figure 3.4. Prosperity

through peer panel review of grant applicants or through public service requirements for children's or public affairs programming on commercial broadcast channels. Both quality and choice can be seen in policies that enhance the provision of public information through rating systems so that citizens can make informed choices about their selection of movies, recordings, and television shows.

Promoting individual opportunity for both creators and consumers is a policy strategy that includes some of our oldest programs (for example, copyright protections) and some of the most recent regulations (access for the disabled as well as moral rights protections for artists).

All these strategies combine self-interest—whether of artists, arts organizations, entertainment corporations, consumers, or audience members, with public interest—whether that public is composed of a community, an industry, the economy, the nation, or the general citizenry. These four policy issues are well recognized and frequently the subject of public attention. Yet it is surprising that the underlying public purpose of contributing to prosperity is seldom explicitly recognized; rather, the resultant policy strategies and programs are generally portrayed as based on economic arguments (Cwi 1982; Netzer 1978). This obscures the link to the public purpose of furthering prosperity. Furthermore, defining the issue primarily as a matter of the financial needs and interests of artists and arts organizations draws attention away from the public benefits derived from the outcome of creative activities. Thus, while economic evidence is essential to demonstrating the role of the arts in fostering prosperity and economic principles are an important factor in devising effective policy strategies, prosperity—rather than economics—is the policy purpose.

These observations prompt questions and may provide a clue concerning recent debates. One might ask whether a prolonged period of a strong economy, combined with surging free market ideals and more conservative political principles, has undermined concern for market failure, redistributive strategies, and public subsidy programs. Certainly this has been the case in other policy areas such as welfare reform. With regard to the arts and culture, there has been an increase in the popularity of programs that invest in and promote mutually beneficial activities such as cultural tourism and cultural trade. Perhaps this provides a clue about designing programs or communicating policy ideas that might prove useful for dealing with arts policy controversies. Certainly a recognition that the arts can contribute to the commonwealth and that the public has an interest in furthering that capacity is appealing in an era highly skeptical of special interests and the effects of globalization.

Improving the Quality and Condition of Life

This can be thought of as derivative of the government's role in the provision for the general welfare of a free and pluralistic society. As is illustrated in figure 3.5, there are three common ways that the arts can address this purpose: enhancing educational achievement and educational utility, helping to mitigate and/or prevent social pathologies, and recognizing the importance of quality of life factors. Undoubtedly other strategies have also been used to address this public purpose. Certainly, cultural organizations, though in both the nonprofit and the commercial sector their pursuit of innovation, excellence, and art for art's sake have made important contributions to the quality of life.

Cultivating Democracy

Finally, this is virtually an intrinsic public purpose of all public policies in the United States. However, until fairly recently, the processes and strategies involved in cultivating democracy seemed almost invisible. In the past two decades, some of the elements and practices that contribute to a vital democracy have been increasingly evident. In this regard, at least two issues can be discerned: building social capital and moral resources and maintaining the political system through procedural "correctness" (see fig. 3.6).

With regard to the first of these, we have come to realize that not-for-profit organizations can help promote the effectiveness of public institutions as well as the economy; can foster the habits of democracy and of the heart (Bellah et al. 1985); and can be an alternative to government for collective action. As mediating structures, nonprofit organizations seem to have an essential role in cultivating democracy. James Morone (1990) explains, "The democratic wish is suspended between the democratic promise of limited government for individual liberty—which is rooted in the dread of government and trust in economic markets—and the democratic prospect of social and economic equality—which is rooted in a yearning for community. . . . "

Lester Salamon observes that, as mediating structures, nonprofit organizations are potentially both a prerequisite and an instrumentality of democracy. As a prerequisite, they preserve the liberty of citizens to act apart from government by permitting their members representation and participation in the sociopolitical arrangement of the neighborhood, community, nation, or state. They may also be instrumentalities of democracy when they forge bonds of trust and cooperation beyond the boundaries of their group membership to persons and groups outside

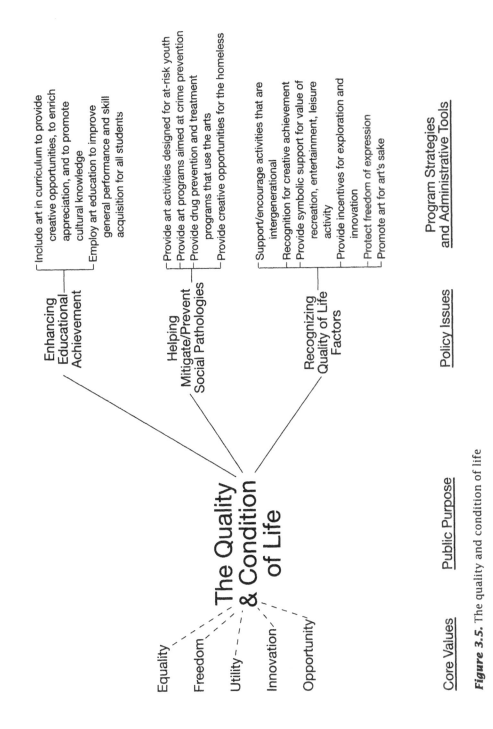

Enhancing Educational Achievement
- Include art in curriculum to provide creative opportunities, to enrich appreciation, and to promote cultural knowledge
- Employ art education to improve general performance and skill acquisition for all students

Helping Mitigate/Prevent Social Pathologies
- Provide art activities designed for at-risk youth
- Provide art programs aimed at crime prevention
- Provide drug prevention and treatment programs that use the arts
- Provide creative opportunities for the homeless

Recognizing Quality of Life Factors
- Support/encourage activities that are intergenerational
- Recognition for creative achievement
- Provide symbolic support for value of recreation, entertainment, leisure activity
- Provide incentives for exploration and innovation
- Protect freedom of expression
- Promote art for art's sake

The Quality & Condition of Life

Equality
Freedom
Utility
Innovation
Opportunity

Core Values   Public Purpose   Policy Issues   Program Strategies and Administrative Tools

Figure 3.5. The quality and condition of life

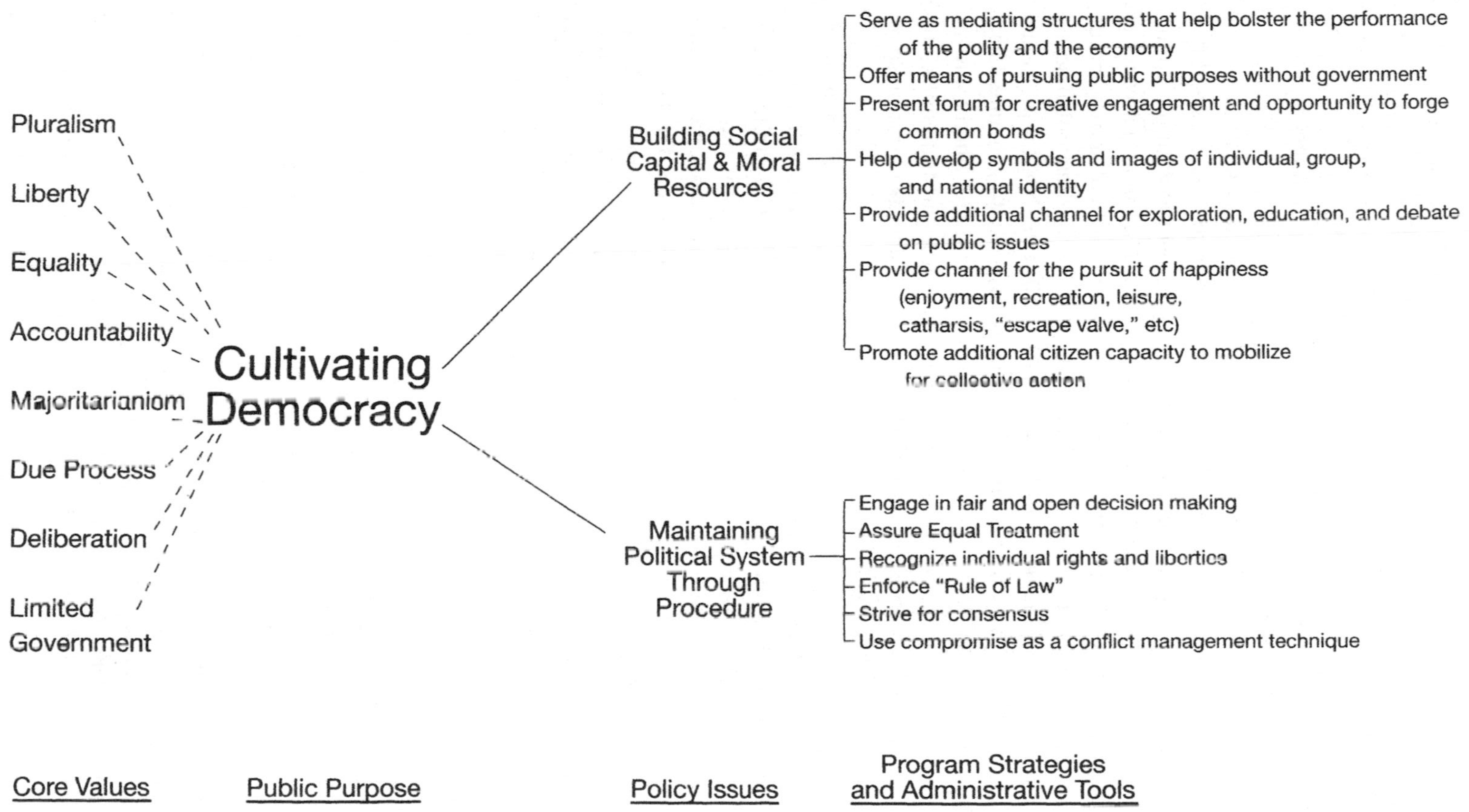

Cultivating Democracy

Core Values

- Pluralism
- Liberty
- Equality
- Accountability
- Majoritarianism
- Due Process
- Deliberation
- Limited Government

Public Purpose

Building Social Capital & Moral Resources
- Serve as mediating structures that help bolster the performance of the polity and the economy
- Offer means of pursuing public purposes without government
- Present forum for creative engagement and opportunity to forge common bonds
- Help develop symbols and images of individual, group, and national identity
- Provide additional channel for exploration, education, and debate on public issues
- Provide channel for the pursuit of happiness (enjoyment, recreation, leisure, catharsis, "escape valve," etc)
- Promote additional citizen capacity to mobilize for collective action

Maintaining Political System Through Procedure
- Engage in fair and open decision making
- Assure Equal Treatment
- Recognize individual rights and liberties
- Enforce "Rule of Law"
- Strive for consensus
- Use compromise as a conflict management technique

Policy Issues

Program Strategies and Administrative Tools

Figure 3.6. Cultivating democracy

it. Finally, not-for-profits may also be relevant to democracy when they provide or advocate for efforts to meet human needs and reduce socio-economic inequalities (Salamon 1993). To varying degrees, art and cultural organizations can provide forums for such participation and cooperation as well as serve as commentators (and sometimes as provocateurs) on social conditions.

Robert Putnam has argued that nonprofit organizations have a key role in fostering democracy through their creation of a public good that he calls "social capital." Social capital provides people with the opportunity and occasion for interactions that create horizontal networks of engagement that help participants solve dilemmas of collective action. In these recurring interactions, people learn trust, and establish social norms and working relations (Putnam 1993, 175–176). Not-for-profit arts organizations are a part of this civil society capacity to generate social capital. As Ben Barber asserts, "a free society gains its liberty and its democratic vitality from civil society and the arts and humanities invest civil society with its creativity, its diverseness and its liberating spontaneity" (Barber 1996).

The role of the commercial arts in building social capital seems more ambiguous. Putnam points to television as the most likely "culprit" in "civic disengagement" and a consequent decline of social capital in contemporary America (Putnam 1995, 677–680). Conversely, movies, television, and popular music provide a set of common experiences and a source of shared cultural literacy for millions of Americans. Furthermore, American popular culture has become a global phenomenon that helps transmit democratic values and taste preferences, while at the same time it threatens to diminish the cultural capital ledgers of other nations, as has been asserted by such countries as Canada and France. Thus the arts—both in nonprofit and commercial forms—appear on both the positive and the negative sides of the social capital ledger.

Second, the cultivation of democracy can also be thought of as a process of system maintenance. Within the polity, democratic norms and expectations condition how government operates, how (and what) public policies are engaged, and how public programs are run. Similar norms and expectations carry over to the operations of many nonprofit organizations, either because they are viewed as public institutions (such as museums) or because they act as "third-party agents" in the accomplishment of public purposes. Even some commercial enterprises assume a systemic aspect, particularly when they become agents or contractors of government. They may also assume a public role as responsible corporate citizens. In all cases, operating procedures are expected to be "correct" in that they embody democratic values such as fairness, due process, equity, and accountability. Thus, democracy in procedure reflects and legitimates democracy in principle on a day-to-day basis.

The Arts and Public Priorities

Five public purposes have been identified as engaging and concerning the arts. Each has been characterized as giving rise to a set of policy strategies and programmatic approaches. In practice, however, public policy strategies and programs are not mutually exclusive from one purpose to another; rather, they overlap and intersect. Indeed, strategies and programs that serve multiple purposes may be particularly likely to attract and maintain public legitimacy and support.

Furthermore, additional public purposes may be served by the arts. Here, the characterization of public purposes has intentionally been broad. The assumption is that purposes broadly defined are more likely to sustain a manageable public consensus while allowing strategies and programs to change through time in response to new or evolving issues. The characterization of these five purposes has been intentionally resonant with the ideas and language of our founding and fundamental public documents. The assumption is that although our specific concern is with the arts, public purposes are basic because they are based in the abiding needs and character of the polity.

Finally, it must be noted that at least two important questions have not yet been addressed. One set of questions concerns how policy priorities are established among various purposes. How are priorities set among different, perhaps competing, public—and private—purposes? How and why do these priorities shift over time? And what are the consequences for individuals, organizations, industries, and governments when these priorities change?

Another set of questions focuses on the importance of the arts regarding each public purpose. For example, the arts clearly can, and have, played a role in securing national security, but not as great a role as military defense or scientific research. The arts make a significant and growing contribution to national and community prosperity, and we have become increasingly aware of that role. For the most part, it would seem that the arts are regarded as a minor contributor to many of the purposes identified. Is this a matter of being underappreciated and underestimated, or of incomplete or inadequate evidence of effect, or is this an accurate reflection of basic capabilities? Are there changes in the wings that might accord the arts a higher priority? In other words, how do we assess the importance of the role that the arts presently do and potentially can play in addressing essential public purposes? These important questions go far beyond the scope of this chapter.

Implications, Observations, and Questions

The arts not only serve many public purposes, but they do this as a consequence of many kinds of policy strategies, using a variety of programs and tools. In this chapter alone, fifteen different policy issues that prompted seventy kinds of programmatic strategies have been identified. This not only should heighten our appreciation of the repertoire and diversity of policy devices that have been employed with regard to the arts, but should reinforce the point that there is no one best or only way in which the arts and public purpose pursue a coincidence of interests. There has been a history of inventing new strategies as demanded by changing times and circumstances.

Security, as seen from a new perspective on recent cultural controversies, is a potent and multifaceted public purpose that involves the arts. The quest for security—national and individual, economic and moral—is of heightened importance in this era of profound changes. These changes include increased global competition, domestic economic restructuring, fast-paced technological innovation, significant demographic shifts, and the end of the Cold War. Indeed, given the current and sustained prosperity, public attention may be shifting from the economic issues that underlay many cultural policies during the last thirty years. If the relative priority given to security in its current forms, and to prosperity, is shifting, this might suggest that it is increasingly important to seek public consensus for policies that advance our mutual security.

In the 1970s and 1980s the nation became increasingly aware of the finiteness of resources and the limits of our societal capabilities. The language of budget constraints and ecological sustainability factored into all sorts of public and private debates, including those concerning the arts. There seems to be a pervasive sense that long-standing assumptions about education and markets, training and growth, leadership and citizenship, change and progress must be reexamined, redefined, and reinvented. In such circumstances, prosperity and good government are less likely to be assumed. As a consequence, the values of efficiency and accountability may be acquiring new emphases and, along with them, a stronger focus on assessment, evaluation, and demonstrable impact. Indications of this can be seen in calls for performance/outcomes-based budgeting at the state and federal levels as well as repeated criticisms of government waste, fraud, abuse, and inefficiency. For example, when the House Republican Conference (HRP) called for the elimination of the National Endowment for the Arts, one of the key arguments pointed to the agency's inefficiency as detailed by the agency's own Inspector

General (HRP 1997). It can also be seen in growing concerns about the costs and risks of cultural production both in the nonprofit and the commercial realms, whether this concerns investing in a new Broadway play or commissioning a new orchestral work, the cost of making and marketing Hollywood films, or the risks of launching the career of a new author, singer, or musician.

Education is a useful program strategy for addressing a number of policy issues. Clearly education plays a role in preserving both national security and social order; it is crucial to fostering community and expressing identity, in achieving economic prosperity, and in cultivating democracy. Indeed, the multipurpose importance of education may cast new light on public thinking about the role of arts education. This, in turn, suggests a factor to consider in designing other program strategies. A program that has multi-issue utility may find it easier to attract a supportive political coalition than one that is more narrowly construed.

Clearly, both the nonprofit and the commercial arts can be involved in addressing all five of the public purposes identified. However, how and to what extent this will be the case will vary from one sector to another, from one art form to another, and from one policy strategy to another. Perhaps a better understanding of the patterns and options of this variation will prompt new ideas for crossovers between the for-profit and the not-for-profit realms; for adaptations of products, processes, and policies between the sectors; and for the potential phase-out or reinvention of existing policy approaches. Indeed, new policy possibilities are inherent in the shift of attention from the direct target of policy to its public purpose. Similarly, program and tool options are evident in a comparison of a number of cultural policy issues and strategies.

For example, if we recognize that neither institutional survival nor market failure is an imperative concerning all arts organizations, then we might choose to redirect policies on the basis of the public purposes addressed by specific kinds of organizations. Today, many prestigious arts organizations are well financed, well managed, and not particularly susceptible to market failure problems. In contrast, many small and midsized arts organizations are financially precarious and acutely susceptible to potential market failure.

It can be argued that recent controversies over the NEA have highlighted a curious and problematic fact: Public debate has often focused on the outer leaves of the tree. Specific program decisions and procedures have attracted much of the contention. We can now see more clearly that this focus literally leaves advocates (pro and con) out on a limb—arguing about details without much sense of the larger purpose, issue, or strategy involved. Conversely, other aspects of recent debates have tended to focus at the level of values with relatively little attention to what purposes might not be served and what fruits might be lost if a tree is cut down to save the roots. Implicitly, the tree metaphor helps us see the fallacy of common assumptions. The relation of the arts and public purpose is neither self-evident nor an oxymoron; rather it is purposive, organic, and varied. The commercial arts and the not-for profit arts are not antipathetic; rather they are as two sides of a single coin—the currency of culture.

Asking what might be absent from this analysis—the road not taken—seems to reveal a paradox. If there is something that can be called an American national character, then a key element of it would be America's creative spirit (MacNeil 1997; PCAH 1997, 2). Whether in the form of innovation, can-do-ism, entrepreneurship, or artistic imagination, creativity has historically been part of the American identity. Yet there has been relatively little consensus on fostering what might be called the preconditions for creativity and valuing creativity as a matter of public purpose. The creative spirit has long been recognized as a matter of personal accomplishment and private purpose. How a public interest in creativity might be more fully perceived would seem to be a current and future challenge.

The habits of democracy must be actively cultivated and can be fostered as matters of public policy. Perhaps we are on the verge of realizing that the capacity for imagination, creativity, and recreation are in the public interest and also serve a variety of public purposes. And perhaps thinking about the public purposes of the arts will promote a better understanding of the organic linkages of values, purposes, policy, and programs in other policy arenas.

Note

Special thanks go to three graduate students who were invaluable to the preparation of the manuscript and charts in this chapter: Sue Anne Lafferty, John Paul Lucci, and Melanie Buffington.

PART

II

The Public and the Arts

JUDITH HUGGINS BALFE
MONNIE PETERS

4

Public Involvement in the Arts

Bobby McFerrin . . . complained: "People always ask me about the difference between classical music and jazz, or pop. I never know how to answer. When you think of all the rooms in your house, you'd never consider spending all your time in the bathroom, would you? That's how I feel about music. I grew up with all kinds of music, and I certainly don't think any one kind is better than another."

—Steve Mencher, *Symphony Magazine*
(January/February 1997, 19)

In the United States, non-profit and commercial creative enterprises all interact and influence each other constantly. . . . This flowing exchange among the amateur, non-profit and commercial segments of culture deserves special attention because it expands our understanding of how culture operates and the many avenues for participation.

—PCAH, *Creative America: A Report
to the President* (1997, 3)

What the American arts do best, what they've long done best, is fusion—mixing a variety of cultural influences within individual works. The history of theater, music, dance and art in America is the story of artists borrowing freely from classical idioms and spiking them with elements taken from other cultures and forms. The American musical drew on black music. Made-in-the-U.S.A. blues grew out of both African and European musical traditions. American tap had its roots in Irish and Scottish step dancing and English clog dancing as well as in African tribal dance.

—Jan Breslauer, *Washington Post*
16 March 1997, G1)

Discussions about involvement in the arts have traditionally started with some premise about what are "the arts" and what is meant by involvement in the arts. In most discussions a dichotomy has been created between what was "high" or "fine" art and what was "popular", mass, or commercial art. Today, these categories are blurring, and the distinction hardly holds. This is as true of the supply side of artistic production as of the demand side. No longer can we only describe and differentiate an audience for the fine arts versus consumers of the popular arts. Rather, all those involved must be understood as participants in the production of the arts' meanings, and therefore in their public purposes. This calls for a reexamination of the traditional assumptions about how involvement in the arts serves the public purposes.

In this chapter we explore the origins and persistence of categories of art, then provide evidence of Americans' current involvement in the arts that demonstrates the limitations of our present knowledge of the issues and use of common terms. We then suggest some new ways of thinking about and measuring involvement, as well as considering the social consequences of both involvement and noninvolvement in general and how it may relate to policy considerations.

The Failure of Our Thinking About Involvement in the Arts

What are we to include in our broad understanding of the arts? This is an obvious yet important starting point. Appendix A provides a tentative listing of the arts, a departure point for discussion of this most vexing question. As *homo sapiens*, we make qualitative distinctions via perceptions learned through socialization, which can be applied to almost anything, including aesthetic analysis. On what then do we base our selection of those entities that we have come to define as "the arts" versus the "nonarts"? What has been the effect of our inclusion of some forms and the exclusion of others in terms of social cohesion, economic, and political concerns, all of which are germane to any assessment of the public purpose of the arts?

Traditional conceptualizations of the arts were built upon related dichotomies, going back to the classical Greek distinction between the beautiful and the useful, and are imbedded in Western culture as a religious distinction between the sacred and the profane. In America (and elsewhere) during the last century, various art forms have been institutionalized as either fine art or entertainment; as non-profit or commercial; and as elite or popular or having mass appeal. Technology—particularly film and television—has had an independent effect on assigning the arts to one side or the other of this presumed great divide. Most cultural models have reflected differences in numbers and status, rather than in inherent quality, and have been based on the traditional value-laden distinctions. And there is little question as to which side is considered sacred, based upon the quasireligious values of art for art's sake rather than on the profane or profit motive.

Indeed, the history of these traditional categories is of such duration that they have been built in to our structures and institutions of direct as well as indirect public support for the arts and culture. Yet today, despite often overt conflicts between the respective supporters of the high arts and the popular arts the dividing line continues to grow hazier. In the postmodernist late 1990s, crossovers, hybrids, mixed-media, and "outsider" arts are becoming curated at "insider" institutions (Zolberg and Cherbo 1997); Gregorian chants are at the top of the pop music lists; and Grandma Prisbrey's "Bottle Village" of recycled glass in Simi Valley, California, has been designated for historic preservation (Brown 1997). *Smithsonian Magazine* heralds old diners along with old masters, art glass, country music, and everything else you could mention, as does Garrison Keillor, the radio humorist of *A Prairie Home Companion*. With the dissolution of previous boundaries by discipline, medium, and level of professionalization, the old categories don't line up so neatly anymore.

How do traditional categorizations contribute to the difficulty in assessing public involvement in the arts? Dichotomized categories exclude much that should be included. These inadequate conceptualizations also plague the data gathering by which we heretofore have measured public involvement in the arts. Current data do little to inform us about what people have actually been doing—how they themselves participate—and define what they consider to be the arts. It is time to rethink the categories and be in a better position to then assess how people are actually involved in the arts as they define and use them.

Most studies have failed to exhaust the most obvious examples of arts and entertainment participated in by adults. For example, in the 1993 Port Authority of New York and New Jersey study of the impact of the arts on the economy of the region, the production of movies and video (including commercials) was included, but there was no assessment of movie box office or video rentals (or employment at either venue), nor of the publishing industry and bookstores (only "nonprofit literature"— presumably that found in libraries and published only by university presses—was included). There was no effort to calculate wages paid to freelance musicians doing gigs at clubs, weddings, and bar mitzvahs; nothing was said about studio and rehearsal hall rentals, nor about the impact of providers of arts education, from volunteer museum docents to Juilliard professors. Yet these are all aspects of the full spectrum of the public involvement in the arts: the anonymous casual art consumers, the live audience seeking entertainment, the identifiable collectors, members, and patrons, the amateur hobbyists and the semipros and professionals.

What is involvement, and how involved in the arts is the American public? Regarding an art museum, for example, I can be involved through the purchase or rental of books and other media (such as videos, CD-ROMs or the Internet) on its collections; I can order merchandise from its catalogue; I can attend in person, become a member, or raise that status to become a "Friend", volunteer, or patron, or serve on its board. I can take classes from the museum's educational offerings, or become a volunteer or docent. Consider a commercial movie such as *Star Wars*; I can be minimally involved by buying a ticket; increase my involvement by buying tickets for repeat showings; buy a video of the film; buy some of the commercial spin-offs from toys to T-shirts; join a club of *Star Wars* partisans for ritual re-viewing of the video; subscribe to a "StarWarz" chat group on the Internet, and so on. Given enough disposable time and disposable income, I can simultaneously engage in a variety of activities in a number of artistic disciplines.

We know this from our own experiences, but there are no data that report the extent and depth of involvement *across* art forms. Field or genre-based studies that examine the range of activity in a specific institution or discipline seldom look at what people are doing in other arts areas and thus cannot assess *aggregate involvement* in a more inclusive set of arts activities and institutions. For example, in its survey of all types of museums (aquariums to art museums) in which the American Association of Museums asked for a count of objects and lots (groups of objects) by the type of object (historical, art, botanical, anthropological, and so on), less than 15 percent of the art objects and less than 40 percent of the art lots were held by art museums. The majority were held by history museums (see appendix B). Do those attending the latter consider that they are participating in "the arts"? Thus, if we look only at art museums for information on the arts, we will miss more than half the picture.

Amateur arts activities, such as informal book groups, church choirs, or photography, are seldom considered because they are not easily amenable to data collection. Yet these activities must be included in any analysis of Americans' arts involvement. Because much of the informal involvement in the arts is missed, arts industry dollar figures and ticket sales provide insufficient information—other than by inference—about the full range of public activity in the arts and culture.

A Short History of Categorizing the Arts

The now-traditional distinctions between high and popular arts were a part of America's European heritage. They were re-created in nineteenth-century America as a means of validating status distinctions as the migrant population grew, as Lawrence Levine demonstrates in his book *Highbrow/Lowbrow: The Emergence of Cultural Hierarchy in America* (1986). Paul DiMaggio's analysis (1982) of the development of high-culture arts institutions in Boston, describes this process. About 1870, in the aftermath of the Civil War, and with a large influx of immigrants coexisting with the new merchant class, two distinct social purposes were served by these new elite arts organizations: The cultural superiority of the new monied class was asserted and maintained, and a structure was provided for the emulation of their taste by, and the ultimate assimilation of, the so-called uncultured immigrant class.

Among the immigrants fleeing the European wars of the 1870s were many accomplished artists who became the supply of skilled and talented personnel for the institutions founded by the merchant class. Many of these artists (and their immediate audiences) were steeped in the "religion" of European high culture, which contributed to the American desire to emulate European arts institutions and repertoires in new museums, symphony orchestras, and opera companies. Thus, even though P. T. Barnum had brought Jenny Lind to American audiences of his traveling circus and Edwin Booth played King Lear in mining camps in mid-century, by the century's end, the line between high and low culture was tightly drawn.

In 1917, the new federal income tax structure granted not-for-profit status to these arts institutions, widely understood as serving civic, charitable, or educational purposes. In the provision for charitable deductions by donors, they were aligned with religious, medical, and educational institutions as comparably deserving of philanthropic support. With this new affirmation of their public benefit as merit goods and to be appreciated for their own sake, nonprofit arts organizations were seen as equal to the charitable work of the Little Sisters of the Poor. Accordingly, the nonprofit arts were enshrined in their legal and social distinction from the commercial sector.

In the first half of the twentieth century, technological advances in what would become the mass media (film, radio, and television) enhanced that distinction, both in terms of their respective reputations and in terms of the size and status of the audiences being served. As was the case with the nonprofit arts, the commercial ones were advanced by upwardly mobile immigrants and their children Many of East European and Russian Jewish ancestry, not born to the old elite that supported the museums, operas, and orchestras, provided the energy, talent, and risk-taking that established the new film and radio industries. Never having entree to European high culture, they looked to the future rather than to the

Table 4.1. Size of the Entertainment/Communications Industries

COMMUNICATIONS INDUSTRY	GROSS INCOME ($ MILLIONS) FROM CONSUMER EXPENDITURES, 1994 OR 1995	
Television, video, film	$90,992	($90,992,000,000)
Television broadcasting	$30,635	
Subscription video services	28,984	
Filmed entertainment	31,373	
Radio, recorded music	23,642	
Radio broadcasting	11,320	
Recorded music	12,322	
Publishing	98,657	
Newspaper publishing	50,387	
Book publishing	24,877	
Magazine publishing	23,393	
Other communications	38,182	
Business information services	30,560	
Interactive digital media	7,622	
Total communications industry spending	251,473	
Noncommunications arts spending (1994)	40,250	
Performing arts	16,850	
Visual arts and design services	18,400	
Heritage arts (estimated)	5,000	
Total arts/entertainment consumer spending (approx)	$ 291,700	
Gross domestic product (United States economy)	$ 7,247,700	
Consumer spending on entertainment/ communications as a % of GDP	4.0%	

SOURCE: *The Veronis, Suhler & Associates Communications Industry Forecast* 1996, 35; *Statistical Abstract of the United States*, 1996, 257, 263.

past, to the creation of wealth rather than the preservation of traditional culture. The new entertainment industries institutionalized popular culture for a wide audience. With ever rising sophistication, these industries provided an attractive and successful alternative to the fine arts.

The entertainment industry is now extraordinarily large and economically successful both domestically and internationally (see table 4.1). Recordings, movies, and videos are the second largest U.S. export after defense. In response, some advocates of the fine arts have asserted their sacred quality even more and insisted upon the profane quality of mere entertainment.

Our increased understanding of the arts industries is the result of accumulated academic analyses along with the traditional commentary. Public funding of the arts has increasingly required measures of accountability like those applied by corporate investors interested in the bottom line. At the same time better technological and methodological means have been developed to do analyses (see appendix C). We have also realized that the for-profit and not-for-profit sectors are linked by tax laws in which the general public provides both direct and indirect support. One can take a tax write-off for a business loss caused by investing in a failed Broadway show or a movie just as one can take a deduction for a donation to the Metropolitan Opera, and the same individual may do both.

Breakdown, Interpretation, and Fusion of Categories

Given this anecdotal information on the breakdown of traditional arts categories, how then might we assess the interpenetration of art forms and the fusion of the high and the popular arts? There have been various recent attempts. For example, to get a sense of the geographic spread of both nonprofit and commercial cultural institutions, sociologist Judith Blau studied cultural production by SMSA (standard metropolitan statistical area). Activities were measured in terms of numbers of institutions per 100,000 capita, such as commercial movie theaters and dance halls as well as nonprofit opera companies and museums (1989). (She did not include institutions of cultural dissemination such as schools, libraries, and video rental stores.) She found that many forms and institutions of high culture were more geographically widespread and more available on a per-capita basis than were many forms of popular culture, which showed more regional variation. Blau concluded that given the previous twenty-five years of public art support, in terms of the geographic accessibility for live audience participation, the high arts had won parity.

Thus, the concern of the mass culture theorists that the "bad" (that is, commercial popular culture) would drive out the "good" (that is, traditional elite culture) appears to be unfounded. High culture has become more popular, in the sense of being more widely distributed, than what we call popular culture (1989, 26–27).

To be sure, Blau's findings do not demonstrate that most individuals are involved in both levels of culture, but given the simultaneous presence in most SMSAs of both high and popular culture—especially in areas with economic homogeneity and a preponderance of the middle classes who can afford both—it makes that conclusion more probable.

Herbert Gans's analysis of American 'taste cultures" (1985) shows that involvement with high culture is more typical of the professional upper middle classes than of the wealthy elites. Status rivalries and efforts at upward mobility are spurs to high arts participation today, just as they were in the late nineteenth century (Balfe 1993). Such aspirants do not necessarily leave the popular arts behind, but blend the two. Today, status competition can be indulged in through the popular arts and their related paraphernalia as much as through the fine arts.

Consider film scores: On one hand, the expiration of copyrights for some works of the traditional elite culture allows this music to be appropriated for movies so that new works need not be commissioned. On the other hand, outside academe, composition of movie and television scores provides the bulk of employment for contemporary classical composers. As the classical tradition is being mined for popular cultural forms, media stars such as Sting want to show their talent in high culture venues thereby to gain increased legitimization. High culture venues wanting to attract new audiences do so through the crossover performances of popular culture stars such as Bobby McFerrin and Wynton Marsalis, both of whom are involved with both jazz groups and symphony orchestras. This fusion is not new, but it seems more pervasive today, and, as our opening quote from Jan Breslauer's article suggests, it is a critical component in the strength of the arts in America.

Furthermore, technology has now created common distribution systems for both the high and the popular arts, especially through the broadcast media, recordings, videos, and film. Other technological advances, such as the Internet, are contributing to the undermining of previous status hierarchies among the arts and their institutional bases by increasing their accessibility.

This fusion and interpenetration have contributed as well to a greater valuing of so-called multiculturalism. If one purpose of the arts is to provide novelty and stimulation, having the whole world at one's disposal helps. If another purpose of the arts is to provide solace and stability, having one's own culture affirmed and widely available helps as well. In fact, one can have it both ways: Whirling dervishes may celebrate with fellow believers even as their performances are reviewed by dance critics of the *New York Times*. To be sure, such enrichment of the cultural palate comes at the cost of the old certainties and hierarchies, including established standards of criticism through which some works were elevated to the canon and others excluded.

Public Involvement in the Arts

Obviously, large numbers of the public are involved in arts on both sides of the old divide. How many? To what degree? And how? We're not sure, because the traditional analytical categories no longer fit the current situation. We do know that American adults, when asked about participation in specific arts during the past year, reply overwhelmingly that they have participated in some activity. The 1992 NEA-sponsored Survey of Public Participation in the Arts (SPPA) conducted

Table 4.2. Public Participation

TYPE OF ART PARTICIPATION/INVOLVEMENT	PERCENTAGE OF ADULT AMERICANS	EST. NUMBER[a] (MILLIONS)
Watch/listen via media (a benchmark art[b])	65.1%	121.0
Attend/go to see (a benchmark art[b])	42.5%	79.0
Take an art class/lesson	8.6%	15.9
Create/perform (benchmark arts plus additional arts activities[c])	57.9%	107.6
Any participation in the arts (any of the above)	80.8%	150.2

TYPE OF ART/CULTURAL PARTICIPATION/INVOLVEMENT	PERCENTAGE OF ADULT AMERICANS	EST. NUMBER (MILLIONS)
Go to the movies	59.0%	109.64
Read literature	54.2%	100.72
Go to art/craft fairs	40.7%	75.64
Go to historic parks	34.5%	64.11
Any participation in the arts and culture	94.9%	176.36

[a] In 1992 the adult population in the United States was 185.84 million. As the categories from the SPPA are expanded to include other cultural activities, the percentage of the population that is involved increases to almost 95% of the adult population (176.36 million adults).
[b] Benchmark arts included: classical music, opera, musical theater, theater, jazz, ballet, modern dance, and art museums.
[c] Additional activities besides playing or singing one of the (performing) benchmark arts include: weaving, crocheting, quilting, needlepoint, sewing, pottery ceramics, jewelry, leather, metal work, making movies, photographs, videotapes, creative writing, owning or purchasing artworks, composing music, singing in a chorale/choir/glee club.
SOURCE: The first half of this table comes from M. Peters and J. M. Cherbo, tab. 6, p. 11 *Americans' Personal Participation in the Arts: 1992*, a Monograph describing the data from the *Survey of Public Participation in the Arts*. (Research Division, NEA, 1994). The second half of this table is a new calculation.

by the Census Bureau asked adult Americans whether they had participated in various arts, cultural, and arts leisure activities during the previous year. Over 80 percent said they had participated in some form of arts activity; the figure rose to almost 95 percent when cultural activities (such as visiting a historic site) were added (see tab. 4.2; Cherbo and Peters 1995). We also know a lot of other disjointed facts about involvement.

An attempt to make sense out of the current data on arts involvement is an exercise in frustration. The data cover a wide variety of art forms, are gleaned from numerous sources and cover different years. The measures of involvement include numbers or percentages (seldom both) of adult Americans who participate in arts activities (informal, hobby, amateur, or professional involvement), both live and media attendance and sales figures, the number of organizations and their gross or net incomes, and other disparate figures. This "mix 'n' match" creates difficulty for interpretation, comparison and aggregation into one big number or even several big numbers. Thus, although we can theorize, we can count only small areas of the full range of involvement in the arts industry.

New Measures of Public Involvement in the Arts

A few analysts, for example, Rolf Meyersohn on arts participation in the Bronx (1988), have adapted the Surveys of Public Participation in the Arts (NEA 1982 and 1992) to better understand how people define the arts and their own involvement in them. Meyersohn's study was conducted in 1986. His research design followed the SPPA 1982 structure and was based on a sample survey of over six hundred residents; he took care to control for problems created by carrying out research in an area in which living arrangements and lifestyles are not always neatly arranged. Face-to-face interviews supplemented telephone interviews. Residents were asked the same live arts participation questions as were used in the national SPPA study and were also asked about participation in other cultural and leisure activities located in the Bronx. Meyersohn concluded, "Linking populations to cultural activities works most effectively when the connections are made not for some lofty purpose of educational uplift (according to exogenous criteria of excellence) but to provide pleasure and entertainment with a mixture of the familiar and unfamiliar, the friendly as well as the strange" (1990, 149).

Other researchers have faced those issues from other directions. To grapple with this issue, we present a listing of the ways one can be involved in the arts that is free from historical tradition. The first step in the process of measuring involvement in the arts is to enumerate the panoply of ways one can be involved in the arts. Individual involvement can entail both consumption and production. Although we often think of producers as those who have artistic vocations, many of their activities are carried on at the amateur, avocational level of involvement. In fact, the average American is not only a consumer but also a producer, albeit on an informal level. Consumer and producer involvement must be examined together, then juxtaposed against a listing of art forms to simply enumerate the range of different types of involvement (see appendix A).

In addition, if the nature of arts involvement is to be understood in its multifaceted complexity, then the additional components (or dimensions) of range, venue, and intensity must also be examined. First, however, the various underlying purposes of arts involvement must be considered.

Purposes of Involvement in the Arts

Because of their subjectivity, purposes present a difficult topic. Any attempt to assign them to categories underlines the subjectivity and values inherent in the definition and application of such a measure. The nature of motivation may change from moment to moment and from culture to culture; but it does contribute a great deal to what an individual may get out of an artistic involvement. The primary purpose(s) of the involvement may be:

background or enhancement of another experience (driving, cooking, sex)

entertainment (enjoyment, passing the time)

education (self-realization, acquiring knowledge)

aesthetic experience (inspiration, enlightenment)

economic or status rewards (power, wealth)

Much of the past analysis regarding why individuals participate has started at this purpose level and typically has been limited to educational and aesthetic experience. It thus overlooks the myriad of reasons for arts involvement, including those arts activities done at home for pure enjoyment.

Involvement of the Arts Consumer and Producer

The biases built in to the traditional dichotomous categories of the fine versus the popular arts are also implicit in the categories of consumer involvement and producer involvement. These categories or dimensions do not describe art types, genres, or disciplines, and are not attached to specific time periods, as with the previous list of possible purposes. However, the list does connote a greater or lesser degree of involvement, and suggests resultant evaluations of increasing seriousness.

The arts consumer can:

listen, watch, read, interact (with) the arts (at home or in some nonarts space, such as in a car, on a train, at the beach) via broadcast/cable (TV, radio, computer, cable) or a tangible object (videotape, CD-ROM, CD/tape/record, book, art object)

learn about the arts in a formal setting or independently (education)

go to see or experience the arts (as audience/visitor at an event, exhibition, fair/festival, performance, cultural or historic site, and so on)

purchase, collect or invest (also borrow, rent) the arts includ-
    ing objects, books, CD/tape/records, CD-ROMs, videos
volunteer (as member, usher, board member, patron)

The arts producer can:

collect and preserve (museums, libraries, archives, historic sites,
    or personal collections)
sell, rent (objects, media products, art-related services)
provide administration, technical assistance, support, capital for
    investment (consultation, space, patronage, legal and busi-
    ness services, advertising, manufacture and distribution of
    arts materials)
exhibit, perform, produce, broadcast
create (visual, media, literary, performing, building and design arts)
teach (artists as well as the public)

The NEA-sponsored 1992 SPPA included the first three of the consumption activities as its "benchmark" art forms (classical music, opera, jazz, musical theater, theater, ballet, dance, visual art and literature).
For the benchmark and other arts, over 80 percent of the adult American population said they had participated in one art form at least once
during the past year, if only via the media (Cherbo and Peters 1995, 56–
58). Adding other cultural and entertainment activities of reading and
listening to literature and attending movies, art fairs and historic monuments, sites, houses, the participation of adults rises to almost 95 percent (see tab. 4.2. Tab. 4.3 provides further measures that enumerate
involvement).

Now let us turn to three other components of arts involvement: range
(in how many different arts/genres an individual is involved); venue
(place of involvement: at home, locally or at greater distance); intensity
(time, effort, money involved).

Range. This refers to the number of different art forms or genres in which
an individual is involved. Using the SPPA surveys which included a number of questions about "liking" for a number of types of popular music,
Richard A. Peterson and colleagues (1992 and 1996) determined that the
traditional distinction between "snob and slob" no longer holds. Between
the 1982 and 1992 SPPA surveys, they found a considerable increase in
the number of "omnivores" (those whose taste crosses many musical
genres) and a decrease in the number of "univores" (who like only one
type of music). The former had increased among "high brows" (those
who like classical music and opera and also jazz, rock, reggae and blues)

even more than among "middle" or "low brows," with much of this increase found among younger cohorts (Peterson and Kern 1996). For nearly all forms of popular music, rates of "liking" were higher among those who also participated in at least one of the "high" arts than those who did not so participate. Peterson did not see this greater range of liking as evidence of any decline of taste and discrimination among the "highbrows," ascribing this pattern as being "better adapted to an increasingly global world managed by those who make their way, in part, by showing respect for the cultural expression of others" (Peterson and Kern 1996, 906).

That view is given further support by Bethany Bryson, who examined specific musical genre dislikes by those with more or less education as demonstrated by 1993 survey data. She concludes that "cultural breadth has become a high-status signal that excludes low-status cultural cues" (1996, 895). In her analysis, such multicultural tastes can still have an exclusionary dimension, one now based on education rather than on race or other aspects of social class. Thus the greater inclusiveness of the multiculturalists can serve to discriminate between haves and have-nots, just as the previous distinctions between high and popular. The grounds of greater inclusivity of musical taste, as well as its prevalence, suggest that we must analyze public involvement in terms of how many artistic genres of art people participate in (asking as well what they don't want to participate in), and include as options all the various popular forms.

Venue. Another measure of involvement is concerned with its location. How geographically accessible to me is the art in which I am participating? It is certainly easier to be involved in a locally based chamber-music society than it is to be similarly involved in a more distant though more prestigious arts organization. If I participate in the arts primarily at home through the various media at my disposal and at very little cost, that is a very different level of involvement than my paid-for, live participation at a distant place. And long-distance participation can be differentiated between what I may do as a tourist and what I may do at home. If I set foot in a museum only when I am abroad, I am not as involved in the arts as I would be if I attended one regularly near home.

In considering venue, we also need to take into account the level of institutionalization of the arts organization. How large and formally structured is the presenting group or organization? I may hear chamber music played locally in a church by well-qualified amateurs because my neighbor is in this group. For a professional performance, while on vacation, I may go to a summer stock show of *Cats*. I may even get nostalgic about my youthful roots and go to some local arena for a rock concert. Where does this put me on the scale of arts involvement? (See appendix D for a list of possible venues.) The geographic spread of venues may be large, but so too may be the range of organizational structure, the production values, the ticket prices, and so on. Do people who follow amateur-level activities differ from those who are involved only in polished, high-tech ones? Do those who are themselves amateur performers keep their involvement primarily with other amateurs, in community-based art-center activities, or is their involvement a wannabe step toward the professional level? Do people who favor the nonprofit high arts, at whatever level of institutionalization, avoid the local for-profit organizations that may provide some of the same fare? Local jazz clubs are usually informally organized, and mostly commercial. Do those who attend consider this profit-making a form of selling out? We don't know, because we haven't asked.

Intensity. While both range and venue contribute to involvement in the arts, the level of investment of time, money, and education must be considered independently as another measure of involvement. Arts education can include parent-induced piano lessons, marching bands promoted by high school teachers, self-determined adult education, and so forth.

Consider different levels of intensity. One level could be media consumption, another a collection of recordings or videos. A different but not necessarily higher level may be live audience participation. I may have to plan in advance, pay for tickets, hire a baby-sitter, pay for a space in a parking garage. How often do I do this? How many hours a month or year, at what real cost to me in terms of my income? On more invested levels, I can not only attend but become a member of an arts organization, supporting its activities while enjoying the ambiance and the heightened aesthetic experience and status it provides to increasing degrees as I become a sponsor or patron.

Yet another level is amateur or hobbyist activity, which can also vary in intensity. I may be a museum docent working at a museum twenty-five hours or more a week; I may get together with my friends in a rock band and play every weekend for fun; I may sing in a church choir. I may take snapshots or home videos and exhibit them locally. When are these categories of involvement considered more than merely amateur? When are activities like knitting or quilting considered to be an arts activity? For most who participate in such amateur activities, their aesthetic sense is being expressed, shared, and heightened, even if they may receive little public recognition except from their families and neighbors.

Does the highest measure of arts involvement, then, rest upon public acclaim and/or income as a by-product or mark of professional stature? Where would we put Grandma Prisbrey, who earned no income from her Bottle Village constructions, compared to the Three Tenors, who earn a great deal for their performances? Perhaps the highest level of involvement in the arts includes time devoted as well as income derived, thereby linking amateurs with professionals, nonprofit, and commercial arts; media consumers and live participants.

Finally, something must be said about the designers, media tech specialists, arts educators, managers and administrators, entertainment lawyers overseeing contracts and protecting copyrights, functionaries in the various professional artists' associations and unions, arts policy analysts (and those who teach them), all of whom make their living by helping to facilitate the arts. Other industries include technical support functions and personnel in calculating their gross statistics (such as percentage of GDP or number of employees); so too should the arts. Accordingly, such measures as range, venue, and intensity among consumers and producers across the whole spectrum of the arts must be noted and assessed. Only then can we grasp the scope and impact of the arts in American life and the public purposes served by the arts. Only then will we be in a position to formulate appropriate policy agendas.

Noninvolvement in the Arts

Measures that record the full range of arts involvement can indicate as well how many do not so participate. The question of noninvolvement has considerable political significance, especially in terms of (non)support for continued public funding of the arts and culture. (The so-called culture wars are based, in part, upon the differences between those who do and those who do not participate at all in the fine arts and what and how they think about public culture.)

Consider, for example, the implications of changes in the audience and nonaudience for the fine arts. As measured by SPPA in 1982 and 1992, there was a precipitous decline in rates of participation for most of the forms of the fine arts (museums are the primary exception) among the younger baby boomers (born in the early sixties), compared to the older cohort born right after World War II, who attend at the highest rates. The decline is most critical for classical music, and can best be understood in the following table, which includes only those members of the two compared cohorts who have had some college education (higher education being the best predictor of arts participation). The two cohorts were selected for this comparison because across all the art forms examined in SPPA 92, they generally ranked respectively highest and lowest in rates of participation.

Table 4.3. Classical Music Attendance and Nonattendance for 1941–1945 and 1961–1965 Cohorts with One or More Years of College

	1941–1945	1961–1965
Cohort size	6.93 Mil	10.32 Mil
Attendance rate	31.30%	17.60%
Audience size	2.17 Mil	1.82 Mil
Nonattenders	4.76 Mil	8.50 Mil

SOURCE: Peterson et al. 1996, 116.

Given its comparative size, the number of nonparticipants in the younger cohort was nearly double that of their fellows in the older cohort, and the increase nearly equals the combined audience total of both cohort segments. Multiply this example across other age groups and other art forms where the same phenomenon occurs, and one sees new dimensions of the problem. Such nonparticipation is reflected in turn in the sharp declines in sales of classical recordings as part of the total music market. It turns out as well that sales of popular music recordings have also declined, as has attendance at rock concerts. Thus the questions of participation—or its absence—arise for areas of popular as well as for high culture. We need to understand these declines and their possible interrelatedness.

What Are the Consequences?

We have argued that without an accurate assessment of how Americans are actually involved in the arts and culture on their own terms, across the previously dichotomized areas, we do not have the basis to establish sound public policy. At the same time, we know enough to make some interesting and reasonable speculations that could or even should impact on policy considerations.

We have very sound data at the micro level about the very beneficial impact of the arts on cognitive development in early childhood, and we know that SAT scores improve for those who study the arts (PCAH 1997, 10). Improvements in mental health occur among those whose diagnoses have brought them to the attention of arts therapists or who simply attend live performances under the sponsorship of Hospital Audiences Inc. (Spencer 1997). A recent study on the Swedish population found that frequent attendance at cultural activities was associated with lower mortality (Bygren, Knolaan, and Johansson 1966). However, extrapolating from these data to determine the impact of the arts at a societal level is risky. While cognitive development through the arts can be assessed, larger social consequences have yet to be determined, as aesthetic appreciation appears to have few moral or ethical resonances. Consider the long-term social and political impact of Herbert von Karajan or Leni Riefenstahl and many other artists who artistically colluded in the worst events of twentieth century.

Numerous, detailed studies of the economic impact of the arts in various communities demonstrate how many people are making how much money and contributing to the tax revenues because of their professional or audience participation in the arts industry. Such studies are usually commissioned to show government officials that some public support for the arts should continue and, indeed, be increased, because the arts more than pay their own way. While useful, such studies are limited in their ability to answer why the arts matter socially, and to whom, in part because they have not measured involvement as we advocate.

We are not alone in the dilemma caused by changing paradigms compounded by inadequate data. The European countries have always assumed that the arts should be supported as part of national culture and economic considerations. Today we are seeing these nations move toward an American version of cultural privatization, reducing the role of the state and attendant funding, becoming more of a "facilitator" on the American model rather than that of "patron" or "impresario" (Chartrand and McCaughey 1989; Cummings and Katz 1987; Mulcahy, chapter 6 in this volume; Zimmer and Toepler 1996).

In part the social and political effects of the arts are less clear today due to the deficiencies in instruments of measurement of public involvement. The lack of clarity is also built in to the nature of the inquiry. Consider the thousands of studies of the impact of sex and violence on television with their conflicting conclusions, which demonstrate primarily that it is exceedingly difficult to determine cause and effect. Do I watch the XXX cable channel because I have fantasies of violent sex, and this channel just enhances my taste, or do I learn these fantasies from the videos and then go on to act on them? Obviously, the American advertising industry is based on the latter premise, but the sociological evidence is mixed.

Even the SPPA data and other surveys tell only a small part of the story. In SPPA 1992, one third of those who had had music lessons in their youth (a small number) did not go to classical music events, while one third of those who did go to such events had had no music lessons. While the large majority of those who attend opera have some higher education, most of those with a college education don't attend at all, and some without it do attend. Correlation does not define causation; in areas of culture, it seems even more problematic.

Furthermore, what of art forms and works whose popularity and social meaning appear to transcend social class and the arts education related to it? Beethoven's Symphony No. 9 was played at the official destruction of the Berlin Wall; the Beatles accompanied the thoughts of an entire generation; some try to revive Woodstock; black rap music provides outlets for the normal rebelliousness of white suburban teenagers while making millionaires of the rappers. And then there is the Internet, with the Louvre and the National Gallery at anyone's disposal on CD-ROMs along with the most appalling pornography, racist invective, and sheer nonsense. How can one measure such broadly defined cultural participation, the evident inequality of its distribution, and its significance for society?

What Is to Be Done?

Obviously, we believe that public policy agenda should include research on arts involvement. While we know from SPPA a great deal about people's participation in the traditional fine arts, we can make inferences from the trade data about public involvement in the entire industry (as in tables 4.1 and 4.2). If we operate from the assumption that public involvement in the arts benefits society as a whole and not just those who are so involved, we must provide evidence of that benefit. As Margaret Wyszomirski has pointed out (1987), fine arts participation can be thought of as comparable to political participation. According to SPPA, in 1992, 42 percent of all adult Americans participated in at least one live benchmark art, while 37 percent of the American electorate went to the polls in the November elections. If the popular and amateur arts were to be included, as well as arts education, the recognized degree of live participation would escalate. One might then conclude that as a nation, we are more invested culturally than we are politically.

Whatever may be demonstrated by future analyses of public involvement in the more broadly defined arts, the policy questions must be dealt with. Given a history of limited direct and indirect public funding for the arts and culture, in combination with increased competition for private and foundation philanthropic support by those with economic and social needs, how are choices are to be made? Who will determine the priorities? Which cultural forms will receive public legitimacy and support, to what degree, and at whose expense? We can prepare to answer these questions only by better understanding the range and nature of activities in which people are actually involved.

Appendix A:
What Are "the Arts"

The following is a taxonomy that can be used as a departure point for discussing the vexing and confrontational question: What constitutes the arts? It is broad, based on our assessment of the need to fuse the old arts categories with actual practices of the today's (multicultural omnivore) consumers of the arts. This is an exercise in inclusiveness. Undoubtedly we will omit an important activity, which the reader can gleefully note and add to the list. We start with five broad categories and then list multiple activities and art forms. The activities listed are mostly dimensions of involvement, of both consumer and producer, but some are venues. On the level of the broad categories of the arts, the same generality and timelessness exist as for the consumer and producer involvement lists in the text. However, as the list becomes more detailed, the specificity of "the arts" becomes more related to culture, time periods, values, taste, purpose, status, and so on. It is at this level of detail that each of us may disagree about what is to be included, and the problem of "what are the arts" stops the discourse.

Broad Categories of Art
Visual
Design, building, decorative (also visual but part of things utilitarian/functional)
Literary
Media
Performing (what is presented in front of an audience at an event)

Table 4.4. Types of Art

VISUAL ARTS

painting, drawing, printmaking
sculpture
photographs
film, video, commercials
ceramics, jewelry, leather, metalwork, basketry, pottery, glass
weaving, crocheting, quilting, needlepoint, sewing
tattooing
ancillary activities that are part of the product
    Examples: Framing, casting sculpture, film editing art supplies (paints, crayons, and so on); design, building, decorative arts (applied to and used in the design of functional items).
architecture
interior design
graphic design
landscape architecture
furnishings (furniture, clocks, and so on)
crafts
fashion

LITERARY ARTS

nonfiction (biography, history, and so on) and fiction (novels, short stories)
poetry
drama, screen plays, documentaries
ancillary activities (editing, small presses, publishing)
book making, paper making (are these visual, literary or both?)

MEDIA ARTS

animated film
computer art
choreography
composition of music videos

MUSICAL ARTS

composing (and song writing)
ancillary activities: music publishing, instrument making

DANCE AND OTHER MOVEMENT ARTS

choreography (original and derivative)
gymnastics, skating

PERFORMING, EXHIBITING (A PRESENTATION TO THE PUBLIC)

playing a musical instrument or singing

classical (symphony orchestra, chamber, historical)
opera
musicals (show tunes, operetta)
jazz
choral/glee club

parade, march
ethnic/national
country/western
folk, bluegrass
big band

Table 4.4. Continued

hymns, gospel, religious	blues, R&B/soul
latin/salsa, reggae/rap	seasonal, historical
rock, new age, mood/easy listening	

dancing or movement

ballet	ice dancing
modern dance	music revues (Rockettes)
ballroom, tap dancing	gymnastics dancing
ethnic, folk	
precision movement (Stomp, Kodo)	

acting (musical and nonmusical)

plays	one person acts
musicals/opera	mime, clowning, puppetry
ethnic/folk	comedy revues
film/movies/TV	

literary presentation

poetry reading
story telling
lectures

multimedia or other performances

music videos	circus
musical comedy	happenings
sheet performers	
exhibition of art/cultural objects	

ancillary activities within all these performing, exhibiting activities

directing
technical: design of lighting, sets, costumes
movie/film/video production
production of musical instruments, sets, costumes, dance footwear

MEDIA[a]

film/movies/TV
animated film
computerized art
commercials
internet art

SELLING, RENTING ART OBJECTS, MEDIA PRODUCTS, ETC.

fairs, festivals
antique shows
arts and crafts shows/shops
galleries
book stores
video/CD stores

Table 4.4. *Continued*

COLLECTING, PRESERVING (HERITAGE FUNCTIONS)

objects (art, historic)
sites (historic, artistic, natural)
media products

done at/through these venues

libraries
archives
museums[b]

museum types[c]

art museums/centers	planetariums
history museums	science museums
historic houses/sites	children's museums
arboreta/botanical gardens	zoological parks
nature centers	aquariums
general museums	specialized museums
natural history/anthropology museums/sites	

TEACHING ABOUT ARTS AND CULTURE

topic

history of (sociology of, politics of, cultural economics of) music, visual
    arts, dance, etc.)
theory/appreciation (what is music, what is painting, etc.)
studio/performance (how to play a piano, make a ceramic pot)
arts management

educational level

preschool, K–12
college
grad and professional schools
artistic training (apprenticeships, residencies)
adult/general learning (classes, workshops, lectures)

ADMINISTRATIVE, TECHNICAL, GOVERNANCE, FUND-RAISING

Artists' spaces, collaboratives	Technical (lighting, stagehands, frame makers, etc.)
Board members	Arts service organizations
Executive Administration	
Fund-raising (development)	

[a] Media arts are usually performing or visual arts; some use performing arts (acting, music, dance) as a basis such as music videos.
[b] Common museum functions of exhibition and education are in other categories.
[c] These are all the types of museums (institutions that "collect, preserve and/or educate the public") as categorized by the Institute of Museum and Library Services and the American Association of Museums. Any type may have art, although many have a primary focus other than aesthetics.

Appendix B:
Art Held by Nonart
Museum Institutions

This illuminates the extent of the problem of traditionally defining art that arises when counting art objects in museums. The 1989 American Association of Museum survey asked museums of all types to give a count of objects (and lots, that is, groups of objects) held in their collections classified into five broad categories: anthropology/archeology, art, history, nature, and other. It was known before this survey that art museums held historical material, history museums held science material, nature museums held art objects and so on. For art objects (and lots) the results of this enumeration were surprising to most. Less than 15 percent of the art objects and less than 40 percent of the lots of art are held by art museums. So, if accounting for art objects is a goal, then one must include museums of all types in the art universe.

Percent of Art Objects and Art Lots Held by Type of Museum

	OBJECTS	LOTS
History museums	55.0%	45.4%
Art museums	12.5%	38.7%
Historic sites	11.4%	2.3%
Natural history museums	4.1%	9.0%
Specialized museums	6.6%	3.6%
General museums	5.8%	0.4%
Science museums	4.0%	0.1%
All other museums	0.6%	0.6%

SOURCE: *The Data Report from the 1989 National Museum Survey* (Washington, D.C.: American Association of Museums 1992, 225).

Appendix C:
Improvements in
Measuring the Arts

Over the last twenty-five years there have been enormous advances in computer technology. An explosion of data is now accessible to the average interested individual, simply because of the advent of PCs and the ease of data transmission. More organizations collect more data, and there are more sources of data that are readily accessible. In addition, there have been vast improvements in measuring and sampling in survey research, in standards and definitions, and in the inclusivity of organizations in surveys and data sources.

Accounting guidelines for not-for-profit organizations have undergone significant changes in the last twenty-five years. Prior to the 1970s the accounting profession did not pay much attention to the not-for-profit sector except for colleges and universities and hospitals. For the rest of the sector there were no specific guidelines about how to report and record many monetary transactions until the release of the audit guide by the AICPA for "Certain Nonprofit Organizations" in 1981. An important result of these changes has been general standardization throughout the nonprofit arts industry and the changes in format on the IRS Form 990, Return of Organizations exempt from Income Tax, which has made the return a possible source of information.

The Independent Sector has worked with government reporting sources to improve the categories of organizations in arts and cultural industries (the Standard Industrial Classification [SIC] codes). Within the arts world the National Assembly of State Art Agencies working with the National Endowment of the Arts mounted a large effort in the late

1970s and early 1980s to develop the classifications for the National Information Standard which has been the basis of the state reporting systems used by every state arts agency. Even the service organizations and trade associations have improved their methods, definitions, and standards for gathering and reporting information about their members.

In government surveys about the arts there has been a continually growing participation by arts organizations. In part this is a result of government reporting sources (that is, the IRS and the Social Security Administration) changing reporting rules and then making sure these organizations actually report. But also it is in part due to greater numbers of organizations that have grown large enough to cross the minimum threshold for reporting ($25,000 in gross receipts), and they have become sophisticated enough to have the resources to report accurately. Thus more of the nonprofit art world is being included in government statistics.

The Research Division at the National Endowment for the Arts has been making slow but steady progress in improving the statistics on the arts at a national basis. The Survey of Public Participation in the Arts completed its fourth cycle of data collection in 1997 and was thus able to show more interesting results with each new cycle. In the 1998 Statistical Abstract of the United States, there are several tables on this data set. The SPPA, however, has its limits, which we and others note frequently. One of the inherent problems is that it is a data set that is designed to be a time series. If the definitions or data items are changed, the ability to measure change over time is compromised.

There is continuous work by NEA Research Division on how the arts fit into larger national economic surveys, but progress is slow in part due to lack of financial resources and because the nonprofit arts sector is small and perceived as of lesser importance than other national concerns. There is some serious work being done to explore the feasibility and practicality of how to collect data nationally on arts organizations. A report for the NEA Research Division, *Data on Arts Organizations: A Review and Needs Assessment, with Design Implications* (Kaple et al., Center for Arts and Cultural Policy Studies, Princeton University, November 1996) provides a good discussion on the difficulties.

There are massive practical problems to collecting good data for both consumption and production (demand and supply) and for involvement in the arts. There is a lot of potential creativity not just in the production of the arts but also in the organizational structures that make the arts world. And we will need the time, the money, the talent, and the will to better document our artistic enterprise.

Appendix D

What venues for the presentation of art can you name?

When the SPPA questionnaire asks "In the last twelve months did you go to a _____," the respondent isn't asked where. So below are all of the places we have thought of. (On the SPPA questionnaire, only high schools were specifically excluded.)

Cultural centers

Museums

Theaters

Schools, colleges

Churches (lots of art that doesn't get counted is in the churches)

Military bases (even more art goes on here)

Community Centers

Clubs: Civic, country, etc.

Hotels

Nightclubs

Restaurants

Cafes, coffeehouses

Shopping Malls

Bookstores (Borders has a huge arts/cultural program in the Washington, D.C., area)

Musical instrument stores

Dance studios

Corporate headquarters, corporate spaces

Embassies

Other NGO spaces and government spaces
Outdoors:
    Parks
    Monuments
    Stadiums
    Street fairs
    Outdoor festivals in public spaces
(Semi-) private spaces
    Weddings
    Bar and bat mitzvah celebrations
Home (personal consumption)
Autos

JOHN P. ROBINSON
THERESE FILICKO

5 American Public Opinion About the Arts and Culture
*The Unceasing War with Philistia**

... in the unceasing war with Philistia ... [artists] have forgotten that they are measuring their own success by standards that artists and wise men of the past would never have dreamed of invoking. They are asking for circulations and audiences that were never considered by any *artist until the last few generations.*
—Walter Lippmann (1922, 106; emphasis added)

Thus did Walter Lippmann in his classic *Public Opinion* discuss how pictures and words are used to enlist public support for a cause or idea. In order for an event to mean something to the public, people "must be allowed to exercise the love of struggle, suspense, and victory." Lippmann argued that few masterpieces in museums captured suspense in the same way that popular movies did. While producers of popular entertainment felt bound to fit their works into stereotypes, artists often challenged or altered stereotypes—often with minimal popular acknowledgment.

Lippmann's view of the public's perception of the arts may be a bit pessimistic. Coming to terms with whatever acknowledgment, acceptance, or appreciation of artists and the arts exists in the public is a necessary element in any public policy discussion of the arts and culture. If we wish to know what role the arts play in our community life, we must ask the public what they know about the arts, how they feel about culture, and what role they see for the arts in their lives.

* Revised version of paper originally prepared by John P. Robinson and Nicholas Zill for American Assembly Conference on the Arts, May 1997.

American citizens have been polled about almost every imaginable aspect of their lives. In particular, much energy and time have been devoted to discovering their opinions and behaviors related to their consumption of goods, services, and media, as well as their policy preferences and political choices. One area that remains underexplored is their attitudes and behaviors regarding the arts and culture, and in particular their knowledge of the arts, their preferences and attitudes with respect to the role of the arts in local communities, and the range of cultural activities in which they engage. One reason is that there are difficult measurement and conceptual problems regarding the arts and culture in general.

Public opinion surveys about the arts and culture have been sporadic and fragmented, and there are very few high-quality long-term data sets to consult. Most opinion surveys touching on the arts have included only one or two questions about arts activities. Those that have examined cultural issues more broadly have had limited utility as they are generally the products of advocacy or public relations organizations (such as the *Americans and the Arts* studies, among others). Few questions on the arts have been repeated using quality samples across time to document trends in public opinion, and few questions address long-term policy concerns.

We begin this chapter by reviewing evidence from the various national surveys that have dealt with the arts and culture, and by evaluating what is known about the public in this respect. We draw a distinction between surveys dealing with attitudes about the arts and those dealing with arts behavior. We then turn to those few studies that have highlighted interesting issues, specifically the "culture questions" that have been asked in the General Social Survey (GSS). We explore findings from the GSS as part of a discussion of how "culture" is understood as synonymous with, as complementary to, and as distinct from "the arts." Having reviewed the available information on public opinion and the arts, we return to the relationship of these data to questions of public policy and identify important arts issues that have yet to be addressed.

The Public and the Arts—What Do We Know?

While a number of survey questions have been asked about the arts in America, few have been asked with any consistency or in ways that allow us to say much that is definitive about how Americans view the arts. There are perennial issues that arise regarding 1) the place of the arts in education and the need; 2) desire for a national arts program and/or agency.[1]; and 3) national funding for the arts.[2] Fundamental questions of definition and purpose have rarely, if ever, been posed. Questions about the nature of a national arts agency or program might be taken as implicitly asking about public purposes. For example, such questions might examine the role of the arts in America, whether there is an American culture, what are the defining elements of that culture, and to what extent are the preservation and promotion of such things public concerns. In contrast, while much has been written about the benefits of the arts to the proper functioning of a democracy (Barber 1996; Mulcahy and Wyszomirski 1995), almost nothing is known about the role of the arts in America, *as perceived by the public*. Until this is clarified, the reasons this should be a public policy concern rather than strictly a concern for the private market and/or for the nonprofit sector will not be clear.

The lack of survey data on what the mass public sees as the place of the arts and culture in American public life contrasts with the lively discussions among the participants at the American Assembly conference about what public purposes are served and ought to be served by the arts. In her discussion of public purposes and the arts, Wyszomirski (chapter 3 in this volume) takes the question further to explore the policy strategies and programs that have accompanied various purposes. The discussion draws on implications from the U.S. Constitution and its Preamble to explore the question of what interests can be assumed to be public—shared by all citizens and/or benefiting all citizens.

Only rare polling about the arts fits into any discussion of public purposes and/or policy goals as evident in the review of survey questions in Filicko (1996). There are questions that ask what it means to be an American (or what in other cultures can be contrasted with American culture), but it is difficult to assess notions of democracy, pluralism, and so on. More interesting are questions that deal with the role of the arts in both creating a sense of community and in educating good citizens, but the link between a broad notion of public purpose and a specific policy is difficult to find in survey responses. Related questions deal with the perception that the arts improve a community by attracting business and improving the economic well-being. Finally, some questions try to measure how well the arts improve the societal quality of life, but it is difficult to measure opinions on this question particularly in ways that allow respondents to answer in the negative—that is to say that the arts are not beneficial.

Survey questions on the arts are of two types: behavioral and attitudinal. Attitudinal questions may focus on abstract goals (for example, the value of the arts to the community) or on what the respondents would like someone else (e.g. a legislator, a bureaucrat) to do. Alternatively, a question might address the respondents' preferences to engage in arts vs. other behaviors when all other things (e.g. costs, distractions) are equal. In contrast, questions about behavior measure specific actions or particular experiences. More subjectively are questions about perceived influences on behaviors, such as barriers to participating in activities.

Elsewhere (Filicko 1996; Robinson 1989), authors have separately critiqued behavioral and attitudinal survey data on arts and culture. The work of DiMaggio and Pettit (1998) provides an additional review of surveys. One obvious matter that remains to be addressed is the link between behaviors and preferences in the arts.[3]

Public Participation in the Arts

Few attitude surveys match the solid behavioral data collected by the National Endowment for the Arts in its periodic national Surveys of Public Participation in the Arts (SPPA). These surveys have the advantages of replicating identical survey questions, interviewing large representative samples, being repeated across time (1982, 1985, 1992, 1997), and using highly-trained interviewers. The questionnaire was developed by the NEA after considerable input from arts professionals and undergoes continual pilot testing to ensure its relevance for arts policymakers. (Chapter 4 in this volume, by Balfe and Peters, reviews the data on arts behaviors in greater detail.)

Data from the 1997 SPPA "indicate that half of the U.S. adult (18 and older) population attended at least one of seven arts activities (jazz, classical music, opera, musical plays, non-musical plays, ballet, or art museums) during the past twelve months."[4] The data suggest that the average American adult attends three arts events per year, which probably translates to fewer than ten hours per capita per year. The 1997 SPPA also examined "personal performance or creation" in the arts, and found that two-thirds of the respondents participated in at least one of fourteen categories.[5]

The "Americans' Use of Time" project offers a means of comparing arts participation with other leisure time activities. [6] That project, which collects detailed single-day accounts of what Americans did "yesterday," shows closer to thirty hours a year spent attendance at arts events—but also nearly fifty hours a year spent in playing music, writing, and other personal arts production. This contrasts with more than a thousand hours a year devoted to TV viewing and two hundred hours to reading unrelated to the arts.

Data from both the time-diary studies and the SPPA mainly track behavior (for example, the proportions of the public attending ballet versus jazz performances), rather than not attitudes in the form of public preferences, values, and opinions about the arts. However, the SPPA surveys do contain a few attitude questions about music preferences, barriers to participation, and the types of arts events respondents would like to attend more often. All of these offer insights—direct and indirect—into public responses to the content of the arts programming available in their communities.

For example, it could be argued that music preferences are among the most informative indicators of public taste levels. For example, one could argue that the finding that increased proportions of the American public say that they like classical and jazz music compared to ten years ago is a key indicator of increased audience "sophistication" (Robinson and Zill 1994).

Attitudes about the Arts and Culture

In contrast to the data on arts activity, most of the other arts data collections often appear sketchy, hastily conceived or deficient in sampling. Filicko (1996) has provided a comprehensive review of 885 questions about the arts contained in the voluminous Roper survey archives at the University of Connecticut. The Roper Center contains public responses to hundreds of surveys that have been conducted by Gallup, Roper, the *New York Times*/CBS, NBC/AP, and other groups over the last sixty years. She searched the Roper archives for all relevant questions on the arts and arranged them under fourteen general categories. Behavioral questions ("Participation" and "Contributions/Volunteering") account for 16.5 percent of the questions, and "Attitudes about Participation" constitute an additional 10.7 percent of the total questions. The other two major categories of questions are "Schooling/Classes" and "Funding," each of which accounts for slightly over 15 percent of the questions. Questions about "The Role of Government, Political Leaders, and Institutions" account for under six percent of all questions archived.[7] While some subjects do show up frequently, very few questions have been asked in ways that allow comparisons across time, and many questions do not allow for drawing conclusions beyond the event or artist specified in a given question.

The review of the archived questions turns up few insights into how Americans perceive the importance or role of arts and culture in their lives and American life in general. Only two open-ended questions were found in the Roper archives that provide in-depth reasons or insights into how people feel and think about the arts. One concerned culture; the other, the arts. A review of the responses reveals that (1) for a plurality of those surveyed (37 percent), the term "culture" evoked images of the arts (other responses included "education, learning" [19 percent]; life style, way people live, behavior [16 percent]; refinement, finer things, anything uplifting [14 percent], and so on); and (2) that the term "arts" evoked images almost equally of the visual arts (for 81 percent of respondents) and the performing arts (for 72 percent of respondents; no other answer was given by more than 17 percent of those surveyed). These results are minimally meaningful in terms of what the arts or culture mean to people in their daily lives, or how they respond to the many political issues and debates that animate civic discourse about culture. The fact that the 37 percent mention the arts in relation to culture but only one percent mention culture in relation to the arts indicates how little overlap of the two terms there is in the public mind—or perhaps how confusing this overlap may be. In other words, "A consensus on the arts is likely to include things cultural, but our understanding of things cultural does not necessarily focus on the fine arts" (Filicko 1996, 237).[8]

Even direct questions about support of the arts fail to address aspects of support apart from simple funding or funding in relation to other government activities. Many questions are superficially phrased in ways that make it unlikely that survey respondents would disagree with them. For example, a Research & Forecasts (1990) finding that 83 percent of the public agrees that the NEA serves a useful purpose for American society contrasts with a Roper finding that only 14 percent support federal funding for the arts. Much the same skepticism arises in connection with the many other "soft" questions in the Research & Forecasts study, such as the 95 percent agreement that the arts "provide children with a means of self-expression" and the 87 percent who agree that "the arts bring people together."

The Americans and the Arts *Series*

Much of what we know about attitudes on the arts does come from this series of studies done by Louis Harris and his associates. The first study is from data collected in 1973 (published in 1975); the fifth and most recent is from 1992.[9] These are national surveys and include questions on attendance and participation in the arts, the place of arts in education, and support for a national arts program and funding for the same, among other things. Across the two decades, there were significant shifts in American social life, and questions were asked to gauge the impact of such phenomena as economic recessions, the advance of technology and telecommunications, and the decline of leisure time on Americans' attitudes about the arts and their participation in the arts.

While the Harris studies provide the most extensive series of surveys about arts attitudes, they are often seriously biased in both sample composition and question-wording which is likely to result in artificially high levels of demonstrated support for the arts.[10] For example, a potentially interesting Harris finding in both 1980 and 1992, that close to half of Americans would be willing to pay $25 or more income tax annually to support the arts, must be interpreted in light of these potential data biases. Likewise, ambiguities arise about interpreting seemingly contradictory trends such as a slight increase in support for federal government assistance for the arts (from 50 to 57 percent) over the 1980–1997 time period; compared to the public feeling that businesses should be responsible for this, which rose from 72 percent to 80 percent; and the sentiment that "individuals" should help the arts, which stayed at about 84 percent until it dropped in the 1990s to 74 percent.

On many questions, the data from the *Americans and the Arts* series show a great deal of stability over the past several decades. For example, support for arts classes in the public schools is consistently high, and majorities consistently believe that such courses should be part of the regular curriculum and funded as such. People show consistent patterns in their attendance at arts events, though these vary across standard demographic variables and across the different arts disciplines. Majorities consistently say they would like to have more opportunities to experience the arts in their communities, and they would like their children to be able to experience the arts. The arts are consistently seen as important to the quality of life in a community as well as in the communities' ability to attract business. Majorities frequently support raising taxes to pay for the arts.

Each of the reports from this series notes that the public's support for federal financing of the arts is not particularly strong, but this is assumed to be because the public misunderstands how the arts are financed. The implicit—at times explicit—argument is that the public would support federal financing for the arts if they only knew better. Questions are asked to determine what people believe to be the sources of funding for different arts disciplines that receive most of their funding. To the extent that more people believe institutions to be publicly funded (for example, libraries are assumed to be, but the performing arts are not), a greater proportion of the public is willing to support continued funding. To the extent that more people believe the arts to be profit-making, fewer people are likely to support public funding for the arts. Also, there is consistently more support for state and local funding of the arts than for federal funding.[11]

Some of the most interesting questions in the recent studies are on the advances in telecommunications and technology (especially VCRs, cable, and now the World Wide Web) that have made the arts more accessible in many ways but may serve as a deterrent to support for live performances. At this point, the studies merely note the the increased presence of these media; it is difficult to gauge their impact yet.

The questions that might prove to be most helpful in some ways are also the most troubling. Beginning with the 1976 report, the studies ask about attitudes on the arts—how beneficial the arts are seen to be to the community, how hardworking artists are believed to be, how much artists deserve benefits similar to other professions, and how well the National Endowment for the Arts performs its role These questions begin to get at the issue of the role that the arts should have in our public life. Again, there are serious problems with question wording. The questions on artists and the questions on the NEA begin with statements that define "professional artists" and the National Endowment for Arts, respectively, in glowing terms, and then go on to ask about support for them. The attitudinal questions often have an implicit tendency to establish a choice whereby the respondent can either support the "pro-arts" position or define him- or herself to be a simpleton or a boor.[12]

Trends in Public Opinion on Policy Issues

Few survey questions on three policy areas—the arts in education, the federal role in the arts, and sources of financial support for the arts—have been asked in identical ways across time. Still, some insights can be drawn from the available survey data.

The Arts in Education. This includes questions about support for art(s) classes in the public school curriculum (usually in primary grade school), about whether such courses should be funded as part of the regular curriculum or treated separately, and about the benefits of the arts to children. There is general support for the idea that arts education makes one more well-rounded, a better communicator, and more able to appreciate the arts. However, art classes are not considered a top priority in education nor an item that would be supported in a time of budget cuts, limited resources, or competing priorities. Moreover, while respondents say they believe that exposure to the arts benefits children in many ways, they do not place much significance on their own exposure to the arts during their school years.

While majorities support providing arts classes as part of the regular curriculum, there was a shift between 1987 and 1992 in public opinion toward having classes taught after school and not for credit. This could be taken to mean one of two things: either that in a budget, time, or resource crunch, arts classes are considered by many to be expendable; or even in crunch times the arts are considered necessary, and opportunities for students must be made available in some form.[13]

Support for a Federal Arts Program. When asked about the role of government in the arts, both the questions and responses have been inconsistent. A 1981 Roper poll found a majority of people did not think that the federal government should be involved in fostering the arts—with 26 percent saying this was best left outside of government, 24 percent favoring local government support and 19 percent favoring state government arts support. Only the remaining 14 percent felt the federal government should be providing support for the arts. However, less than a decade later, a 1990 Research & Forecasts study showed general support for the National Endowment for the Arts, (that is, for federal involvement in the arts), with 76 percent agreeing that the NEA "directs money to deserving artists and arts organizations," 69 percent disagreeing that the Endowment "is wasting the taxpayers' money," 83 percent agreeing that the NEA "serves a useful purpose for American society," and so on. Thus when asked whether the federal government should be involved in the arts, most people say no, but when presented with the federal government's actual involvement in the arts, most people support it.

One of the problems with assessing the role of government in the arts is in defining what "support" means. One might assume that support for a cause is always through funding, but support need not be financial; it can also come from the endorsement of privately run programs by federal agencies. Whether the typical survey respondents are thinking of support as involving their tax dollars or from hearing the president praise a group of artists, or from some other endorsement, is not clear.

Some attempts to assess the public's policy preferences involve comparisons between the United States and other countries. While the following question has the advantage of using a concrete example, its preamble provides information that encourages a "nationalistic" response.

> Other countries in the western world, such as Canada, France, the Netherlands, Scandinavian countries, and others all have programs to help individual artists develop. Their governments and private contributors set up special funds that sometimes buy the works of developing artists, sometimes give artists direct grants

of money, and sometimes set up professional training facilities for artists. In the U.S., almost no such facilities or programs exist. Do you think there should be such programs for individual artists in the country or not? (Survey Organization: Louis Harris and Associates; Research Sponsor: Philip Morris Companies)

1987	1982	
65	70	Should be such government/private programs
31	26	Should not be such programs
4	4	Not sure
100	100	

As can be seen about two-thirds of Harris respondents in both 1987 and 1992 chose the "should" response.

Federal Funding for the Arts. When one moves from abstract financial support (for example, funding for the arts), to specific amounts or trade-offs in support for other areas (education, defense, and so on), support may be much more difficult to obtain. In part, this is because the amounts of money and the trade-offs are not clear.

Americans and the Arts 1980 found that 51 percent of those polled would be willing to pay twenty-five more dollars per year in taxes if they knew the money would be going to the arts. Twelve years later, a similar 49 percent of 1992 respondents would be willing to pay that twenty-five more dollars in taxes (although that twenty-five dollars is worth relatively less).

Alternatively questions can ask who or what organizations should be helping the arts, and here again the findings are mixed. When they were asked in 1980 what specific organizations should give financial assistance to the arts, 50 percent felt that the federal government should help, 60 percent that state governments should help, and 64 percent that local governments should help. Stronger majorities, however, felt that businesses and corporations (72 percent), foundations (79 percent), and individuals (84 percent) should provide assistance. By 1992, one finds a shift with more people thinking that the federal government should help the arts (52 percent), and fewer thinking that state (48 percent) and local (43 percent) agencies should. The support for the arguments that businesses should help assist the arts dropped to 66 percent, and the proportion of those who believe that individuals should help assist stayed about the same.

More useful questions ask respondents to assess the "adequacy" of the current levels of arts funding relative to other (nonarts) government programs. These can be examined both as compared to other programs and in the economic political climate in which the question is asked.

Now I'd like to ask about some specific federal government programs. Again, for each, please tell me whether you feel spending for that program should be increased, decreased or left about
the same.) . . . Aid to arts and music . . . (If Increase/Decrease,
probe) Is that increased/decreased a great deal or somewhat?
(Survey Organization: ABC News/Washington Post)

1981	1986	1989	
4	4	7	Increase great deal
9	10	11	Increase somewhat
13	**14**	**18**	
41	**53**	**54**	Left about the same
22	14	15	Decrease somewhat
21	18	12	Decrease great deal
43	**32**	**27**	
2	2	1	No opinion
100	**100**	**100**	

(Listed below are various areas of government spending. Please
indicate whether you would like to see more or less government
spending in each area. Remember that if you say much more, it
might require a tax increase to pay for it.) . . . Culture and the
arts (Survey Organization: National Opinion Research Center)

1985	1990	1996	
4	2	4	Spend much more
10	10	11	Spend more
14	**12**	**15**	
39	**42**	**37**	Spend same as now
24	21	27	Spend less
15	16	17	Spend much less
39	**37**	**44**	
7	8	4	No opinion
100	**100**	**100**	

In both questions, less than 20 percent support any increase in federal funding for the arts in any of the six readings of public opinion.
However, only in the 1996 data do we see support for spending less
money on the arts. What is not clear is whether this increased opposition to federal funding is related to the NEA's political controversies, or
other budgetary and political concerns (for example, defense, saving social
security, and so on). Between 1990 and 1996, the National Opinion Research Center (in the GSS) also found support for increased welfare

spending dropping from 23 percent to 16 percent and spending for the environment drops from 72 percent to 61 percent, although it stays the same for education (71 percent and 70 percent). In any event it seems clear that there is no plurality—let along majority—support for increased arts funding. An arts advocate's best bet might be to support the status quo; an arts opponent's best bet might be to talk about federal dollars in terms of tax revenues.

American "Culture"

In this policy arena, the terms "arts" and "culture" are often used interchangeably. They can refer to very different things in popular thinking. Focus groups conducted by Louise Stevens (1997) suggest that the public defines culture as "an experience, something different and out of the norm," while "the arts are work that requires a willingness to be mentally engaged." (14) Furthermore, the arts are less "fun" than entertainment and usually require that you dress up. Some survey questions about "culture" beyond the arts include questions about American culture and/or the culture of another country notably Russia, China, and Japan. Do respondents think that cultural exchange programs are a good idea? Do they think that two cultures are too different for countries to get along? Do they like or dislike various aspects of another country's culture? Tied to these are questions that ask what makes American culture different, unique, or special in some way.

Other questions ask about the role of popular culture in influencing attitudes and behaviors with respect to sex and violence, particularly among teenagers. Current debates in American politics also raise questions about subcultures—ethnic groups, immigrant groups, and multiculturalism. Respondents are asked whether some specific people (for example, immigrants, different ethnic groups) should be encouraged to focus on their own heritage or to become more a part of the dominant culture.

The connections between popular culture and the arts have become central concerns in cultural policy discussions, including the American Assembly's. Key issues that emerged were (1) do "pop culture" and the "fine arts" complement or compete for people's time and money? 2) which activities complement or support other activities and how do their audiences compare? (3) how does the entertainment industry (for-profit arts) help nurture and sustain the nonprofit arts—and vice versa? (4) How do perceptions of "popular culture" activities compare with perceptions of the "fine arts"; 5) can these two areas learn from each other about how to generate and sustain support? 6) Is it appropriate to think of either or both as addressing public purpose and do they do so in the same way? 7) Do either or both have detrimental effects on public purposes?

Some survey data as well as focus group data have begun to address certain questions regarding popular culture,[14] such as the role of sex and violence in popular culture. These are generally framed in terms of the perceived impact of "popular culture" on children, conducted both by advocacy/interest groups and by news organizations.[15] Unfortunately, as yet there is little available data to examine how conceptions of popular culture compare with arts-related cultural activities.

For the purposes of this discussion, there are three significant aspects to "culture" beyond the notion of "the fine arts." Culture resides in those things that establish a common identity for a group of people—their mores/ethos/habits, their manner of dress, what they eat, how they signify special events in their lives. Culture also may be of the "popular" sort, as reflected in the ways we entertain ourselves and how we spend our free time. All of these things are part of the way in which we organize our life and give it meaning. As such they represent our common culture.

We explore some of these meanings of culture for Americans by looking at a diverse set of questions about culture. Evidence from the General Social Survey shows a surprising convergence around basic cultural themes. One of the major themes takes us back to Lippmann's land of Philistia.

American Culture: Evidence from the General Social Survey

The culture attitude questions asked in the 1993 General Social Survey (GSS) are particularly noteworthy—first, because of the care, sophistication, and thought that went into the questions; second, because of the multiple, cross-cutting questions that were asked; and third, because of the high quality of the national sample from which the data were derived. Due to the singular value of these data, we present in detail some of the generalizable and surprising conclusions they suggest.

The cultural attitude module was included as part of the GSS continuing in-person interviews with random probability samples of the U.S. population to monitor major trends in American public opinion. The General Social Survey is conducted by the National Opinion Research Center (NORC) of the University of Chicago, with long-range support from the National Science Foundation. The 1993 GSS question module focused on Americans' attitudes about culture and education, their leisure activities, music preferences, and other cultural topics and was asked of 1,606 adults, age eighteen and over. Unlike most commercial surveys of arts attitudes, the response rate was over 75 percent; moreover, many of the questions have been repeated in the 1998 GSS (see appendix, this chapter).

The 1993 GSS survey did identify substantial segments of the American public psychologically residing in Lippmann's Philistia. At the same time, the survey also showed the American people to be surprisingly more sensitive and tolerant in their artistic tastes than Lippmann might have dreamed of expecting. What is telling to a survey specialist is the large proportion of respondents who *disagreed* with many of these GSS culture questions, since the usual tendency for survey respondents is to agree with whatever questions are put to them.

Perhaps the main surprise is that majorities of the American public did not express hostility or smug indifference toward the arts. For example, most Americans of voting age do not believe that "Modern painting is just slapped on; a child could do it," indicating some respect for the skill represented in these works. Most also believe that classic works of literature should be taught in high school and college classrooms, and that the classics have something important to say to young people, even in today's technological age.

The GSS culture survey also suggests why it is conservative politicians who have led the movement to terminate the National Endowment for the Arts—even as the Endowment has greatly curtailed its support of controversial works, and even though the size of its budget is quite modest by federal standards. It turns out that people's attitudes about the arts are closely tied to their general political alignments, such as whether they consider themselves to be liberal or conservative, Republican or Democrat. Cultural orientations are also linked with their basic beliefs about economic opportunity, what it takes to get ahead in American society, as well as leisure activities and music preferences.

Philistines versus Cosmopolitans

The five 1993 GSS questions in the appendix to this chapter are rather varied in content but they tap a cohesive underlying cultural orientation that we have called the Cultural Cosmopolitanism; that is, answers to each individual question for each individual respondent are recoded and added together, and the resulting sum is a "score" on the Cultural Cosmopolitan Scale that we analyze below. The Cultural Cosmopolitanism Scale seems to differentiate people who are more sympathetic toward the arts and open to new forms of cultural expression from those who have little use for the arts or appreciate only homegrown and conventional forms of literature or art. Thus, people at the more

Cosmopolitan end of the continuum do not see much value in literary classics or modern abstract painting. Nor are they sympathetic to students' becoming fluent in more than one language; they reject bilingualism and think it "better for everyone if English is the only language used in the public schools." They believe that art is not for everyone; special knowledge and ability are required before one is qualified to make aesthetic judgments. At the same time, they tend to distrust the judgment of high school and college teachers who now decide what students should be reading. One could label respondents who shared more of these cultural attitudes as Philistines as Lippmann describes citizens of Philistia.[16] At the other end of this scale are those who share more open-minded cultural attitudes, labeled Cosmopolitans.

While considerable numbers of respondents endorsed the philistine positions, most U.S. adults did not. For example, when asked to agree or disagree that "students spend too much time reading 'classics' that have little relevance in today's world," 39 percent agreed that the classics were a waste of time, but 61 percent did not. An even larger majority—63 percent—said they trusted the judgment of high school teachers and college professors to decide what their students should be reading. Public opinion was more evenly divided on the matters of whether it would be better if English were the only language used in the public schools, and whether only a few people are qualified to judge excellence in the arts. Here again, however, slim majorities (52 to 48 percent and 51 to 49 percent, respectively) disagreed with these statements.

Who and Where the Cultural Cosmopolitans Are

People who gave more cosmopolitan responses tended to be younger and had more years of education than those who did not, although middle-aged baby boomers and offspring of the late Depression and war years were the most cosmopolitan. More cosmopolitan views were also expressed by the young adults of generation X. To illustrate, 47 percent of adults over 65 years of age agreed that modern painting is just slapped on, whereas 41 percent of those between 45 and 54 years, and 42 percent of young adults of ages 18 to 25 took that stance.

Differences by Education and College Major

Not surprisingly, the largest differences in cultural cosmopolitanism corresponded to the respondents' level of education. Thus, for example, 55 percent of adults with less than a high school education had a negative view of modern painting—in contrast to 31 percent of adults with college degrees, and 22 percent of those with at least some graduate education. Similar differences were found with respect to opinions on whether studying classic literature was a waste of student time.[17]

Geographic Differences

People living in nonmetropolitan areas of the country tended to endorse less cosmopolitan positions than people living in large central cities or their suburbs. Compared to other regions of the United States, people living in the Northeast tended to see things from a cosmopolitan perspective, whereas those living in the South were less apt to share this viewpoint. To illustrate, 49 percent of those living in nonmetropolitan areas believed that modern painting was just slapped on, as opposed to 31 percent in more urban areas.

However, these geographic differences were diminished notably after related factors, such as the age and education of respondents, were taken into account. After statistical adjustment for these demographic differences, the only places with notably higher concentrations of people with cosmopolitan outlooks were the New England region and the nation's twelve largest cities.

Differences by Occupation and Income

Cosmopolitan views varied greatly across occupational categories, being less evident among farming, forestry, and kindred workers. Blue-collar workers in production and transportation occupations and service workers were also relatively unsympathetic to the arts. White-collar workers, especially those in professional and technical fields, and administrators and managers, were more likely to espouse cosmopolitan views.

At first glance, people with higher family incomes were even more cosmopolitan in their outlooks than those with lower incomes. For example, the proportion of respondents who devalued classic literature was 48 percent among those with annual incomes below $15,000; 35 percent among those with incomes between $35,000 and $49,999; and 29 percent among those with incomes of $75,000 or more. But income is of course correlated with education, occupation, age, and other respondent characteristics. When these related factors were taken into account, the relationship between income and attitudes about the arts was not only weakened, the direction of the relationship was actually reversed. That is, higher incomes were now associated with less cosmopolitan attitudes. At least part of the explanation may reside in an association between higher income and a more conservative political orientation; the latter tends to be linked to philistine attitudes about culture.

Gender Differences

Although the differences on some of the items were not large, women tended to have more cosmopolitan attitudes than men. For example, 38 percent of women versus 41 percent of men thought classic literature a waste of time. Adjusting for the fact that more women are older and have fewer years of formal education made the difference in cultural attitudes more pronounced. In other words, women might be much more likely to be Cosmopolitan, if their education and age levels were equivalent to those of men.

Differences by Religious Affiliation

People's attitudes about the arts differed across the major religious denominations in the United States. Protestants were generally less cosmopolitan than Catholics, while Jews were the most likely to have a cosmopolitan outlook. Those with other religious affiliations or no affiliation were also relatively unsympathetic to artistic innovation. After taking educational differences into account, however, these religious differences were greatly reduced.

Differences by Race

Given their lower levels of formal education and historical exclusion from much of mainstream American culture, one might have expected African Americans to emerge as less cosmopolitan on these items than white Americans. In fact, the reverse was true (perhaps because of the antidiversity implications in some of the Cosmopolitan Scale questions).

Differences by Personal/Political Orientations

Higher Cosmopolitanism scores are associated with positive responses to other GSS questions. They are associated with more optimistic views of life.[18] Respondents who report having a happier life in general have higher Cosmopolitanism scores. Among both affluent and poorer respondents, how satisfied one is with one's financial status is associated with a higher Cosmopolitanism score (even after controlling for other predictors). The same is true for people who rate their income as "above average," no matter what their income level.

Even more pronounced are the relations with the GSS political questions. As might be surmised from the greater access to the White House by arts leaders and performers in Democratic times, those with Democratic Party identification have higher Cosmopolitanism scores. But the major political correlate is *ideological* identification. Self-defined liberals tend to be higher than either moderates or conservatives in their cosmopolitan responses.

Indeed the relation between cosmopolitan questions and ideological differences is among the highest of the more than one hundred politically relevant questions included in the GSS—higher than the differences between self-defined liberals and conservatives on international isolationism, support for government intervention on welfare issues, views on abortion, support for capital punishment, or policies on interracial busing.

Cosmopolitanism and Music Preferences

For GSS questions that more directly reflect cultural content, Cosmopolitanism has strong correlations with the eighteen types of music included in this GSS national study. In order to simplify the discussion, we focus on five major clusters of music preferences identifiable from these public ratings.[19]

The largest music cluster includes classical, opera, musicals, and big band music among others, and Cosmopolitans are far more likely than other respondents to say they liked all of them. Much the same is true for the other music dimensions but at a lower level. Thus, higher levels of Cosmopolitanism go along with greater liking of jazz and blues, rap and heavy metal, and with both older and newer generations of rock music. They also predict preferences for country music, but here the direction of the correlation is reversed in that higher cosmopolitan scores go along with less liking of country music—again, much as is true for more educated people. (Nonetheless, some 50 percent of the highest cosmopolitan scorers say they like country music—far higher than their liking for reggae, rap, or opera).

Activities and Lifestyle

Although it's not possible to separate cause from effect in these data, people with higher Cosmopolitanism scores are generally more active, and not just in "highbrow" arts activities. Thus, higher Cosmopolitanism scores are generally found not only among those who attend arts events or engage in cultural hobbies, but also among movie attenders, sports fans, campers, and dancers. Thus the scale predicts participation in both high culture and popular culture activities. These higher participation levels in camping, dancing, performing, and attending arts events remain significant with Cosmopolitanism after controlling for education, age, sex, and income. Thus activity and Cosmopolitanism are highly interrelated, suggesting a mind-set that goes along with more participation in the world outside the home.

The association is not universal. Lower Cosmopolitanism scores are found among those who participate in more so-called masculine activities like attending auto races or going hunting or fishing. And in terms of church attendance, it is moderate attendance that goes along with higher Cosmopolitanism, rather than either weekly attendance or no attendance.

As might be expected, more TV viewing is associated with lower Cosmopolitanism. However, viewing of more sophisticated programs (like the news or PBS) is not associated with higher Cosmopolitanism scores. Nor is more viewing of regular entertainment content related to lower Cosmopolitanism. It's not the content on the screen, but how much one watches that is relevant—rather than being more active outside the home.

Other GSS Cultural Scales

Two other cultural attitude dimensions emerged from the GSS cultural items, one is largely independent of Cosmopolitanism. The Ecumenicalism Scale assesses how broadly respondents define what it means to be artistic. Scores are computed according to the extent to which respondents agree with the following: (1) There is too much emphasis on politically correct art; (2) folk/popular art can share equal excellence with high art; and (3) the human element is what defines great literature. As respondents agree with more of these sentiments, they are scored as having a more ecumenical or universal cultural orientation. Ecumenicalism is also higher among college graduates and does relate independently with liking classical music and opera (but not jazz, rock, or country music).

A third GSS scale assesses Cultural Salience—the extent that respondents said that culture, creativity, intelligence and dynamism were very important factors in a close personal friendship. Cultural Salience has many of the same demographic correlates as Cosmopolitanism, particularly education and race. Like Cosmopolitanism, Cultural Salience is related to liking classical, opera, and jazz music, again independently of education, Cosmopolitanism, and Ecumenicalism. Salience is further related to activity participation, particularly attending arts events, music concerts, and dancing.

A final important set of questions in the GSS survey concerned the respondents' personal arts-education experiences. Among all of those who attended college, questions were asked about college major. The fine arts and literature were both tied for third place (with education) in terms of being one's major field of study while in college, behind business and science. About twice as many respondents—almost 10 percent of the overall sample—described one of the fine arts as their favorite course in high school, topped only by science and mathematics, Another 20 percent of the sample described literature or English as a favorite subject in high school, half again as many as those who mentioned science.

Thus, they may be a minority of the U.S. population, but those who had these arts-sympathetic education courses do represent a sizable number of the American citizens.

Thus, the GSS survey shows that how people feel about culture and the arts has a great deal to do not only with what activities they engage in and what music they like, but what they look for in their friends and how they orient themselves politically. In many ways, it reflects a healthier lifestyle, in that those higher in Cosmopolitanism seem to lead more active, positive, and happy lives. How much the arts themselves are responsible for this state of affairs cannot be inferred from these data, but the association provides some evidence of more vitality associated with the arts.

The cultural items from the GSS can be easily adapted to other surveys and do not require much survey time. They give us some valuable clues about what demographic groups are most likely to be mobilized to support the arts—not just college-educated professionals but younger adults, females, coastal/metropolitan residents, and African Americans. Significant numbers of them reacted positively to their arts and culture exposure in high school or college. It is important to keep in mind that income per se is not one of these correlates; those with more financial resources are not more sympathetic to the arts than the less affluent, once their greater years of education are taken into account.

"Culture" and Popular Culture

Studies of public opinion on popular culture overlap with studies of high culture or the fine arts in several significant ways, but there is an inherent tension as well. Questions about participation or activity are asked in both realms, but the tone is different. We ask who engages in arts activity with the hope of seeing that participation has increased and that more people, particularly young people, are being exposed to the arts. We ask about exposure to pop culture with the hope that people, particularly young people, are not being overexposed to sex and violence. The implied causal links between pop culture and deleterious effects, and the fine arts and beneficial effects, may or may not be valid. The point here is twofold: These assumptions are implicit in most contemporary discussions about the arts and culture, and the mass public seems to agree with these assumptions.[20]

There is a similarity in pop culture and the fine arts in the struggle with questions of freedom of expression, censorship and prior restraint, the impact of words and images on impressionable minds, the importance of having a cultural avant-garde, and the like. There is undoubtedly much more data available than we were able to explore here, particularly that found in marketing studies and audience surveys that are either inaccessible (most studies are proprietary and not easily attained) or narrowly focused (on one product, one event, one slice of the potential audience, and so on).

Issues for the Future

Several important key issues about the arts and arts policy have yet to be addressed in survey work. What contributions of the arts and culture to the quality of American life are recognized or acknowledged by its citizens? What do they see as the contributions of writers and artists to our national heritage, especially in relation to other professionals, like scientists, engineers, and doctors? How important do they feel the arts have been to the overall accomplishments and welfare of the country? As Filicko (1996) concludes, "we can ask individuals whether or not the arts have made their lives better. Beyond that, polling data can only give us the public perception of the necessity of the arts to the common good and their beliefs about the impact of the arts on our communities. . . . clarity about the public's understanding of what 'arts' refers to is a starting point as well. . . . [But is this something] on which should one base policy? Even in a democracy, the answer is not always obvious" (244).

On the more practical policy side, data are needed on the perceived importance of the arts as compared to other national goals; what does the public feel arts and culture spending levels should be in relation to science, medicine, and education?

Similarly, how important do they consider the arts in the school curriculum, compared to other courses? What is the level of public trust in artists, compared to other professionals? How close do ordinary people feel to artists in comparison to members of other occupations? Which arts activities warrant public funding, and which do not?

More generally, does the public see the arts as good for the country as a whole rather than for a few special interests or elites? Do they see the work of artists as addressing societal issues and problems as generating new ideas, or as just expressing their own personal problems or agendas? Do they feel that artists forecast societal issues and problems rather than focusing on what will sell in the market? More generally, do they see the arts as functioning to bring people and groups together or as dividing them?

On a more personal level, how important are arts or cultural issues in the lives of respondents? A national 1985 survey found 12 percent saying the arts were very important in their daily lives, 45 percent somewhat important, and 43 not important; however, a comparable question for music generated a 34 percent "very important" response. A more behavioral reflection of importance is how often people personally discuss or think about arts and culture. Have any works of literature or pieces of art helped them to solve or recognize problems, or to bring meaning or insight to their lives? How often are serious cultural programs or matters identified when questions are asked about their favorite TV programs or reading matter?

Most of these questions could be addressed in a single standard-length telephone survey. A wealth of data on arts attitudes have been collected by marketing companies and arts organizations that are proprietary and unavailable for public use. We are just beginning to gain access to these data sources, such as the Book Industry Study Group (which does regular proprietary surveys on the types of books Americans buy and are interested in), MTV, the Arts and Entertainment Network, the major TV networks, the Movie Association of America (which can tell us if John Wayne remains Americans' favorite actor) and the National Association of Broadcasters.

Public Opinion, Public Policy, and the Arts

Public opinion plays an important role in most, if not all, public policy discussions. Studies on the links between public policy and public opinion, particularly those done by Page and Shapiro, indicate that we can expect a fair degree of congruence between public opinion as expressed in polling data and public policy as seen in legislation.[21] In the long run, we would like to know how satisfied people are with the performance of government institutions with respect to the arts. Whom do they think should be held accountable? What services or programs are available to them, and what else would they hope to have made available to them? Policymakers and those interested in the arts must come to a better, more complete understanding of how Americans think about the arts.

The arts are often seen as a community resource—or at least as a potential community resource. The public does seem to support the idea that the arts are important and useful in a number of ways. We have found support for the arguments that education in the arts helps children develop certain skills; that art classes provide them with a more well-rounded education; that the arts help preserve our common heritage; and that exchanges of artists and works of art help us understand people who are different from ourselves.

As with any policy arena, there should be concern about the impact of government programs that are supported by the public as a whole and argued to benefit the whole polity. It is difficult and somewhat arbitrary to measure the impact of culture or the arts on any individual or on a community—though it is often attempted. Studies measuring economic impact or the literacy of the community do not allow us to assess what is arguably the central impact of the arts—to enlighten us and enrich our lives. It is not clear how one would even begin to ask public opinion questions that would assess the impact of the arts in this sense. However, survey questions can measure the perception of impact, particularly of schooling in the arts, and they can also allow us to characterize expectations about the impact of the arts. We can begin to ask respondents questions about their perceptions of the potential effects of arts exposure, on children, on their own lives, and on life in their communities.

Most citizens may be willing to leave most policy decisions to experts and political involvement to interest groups, only becoming involved when controversy or an event draws attention to the policy. Filicko (1997) has noted a potential danger with arts policy on controversial questions that is the experts or decision makers and the public often operate on very different assumptions. The question gets back to the complex question of who cares about the arts and culture and the public policies associated with them? We need to supplement our intuitive sense of when and why different people care with solid empirical evidence.

Appendix:
Cultural Cosmopolitans
versus Philistines

The following five questions from the 1993 General Social Survey form a scale that differentiates persons who are sympathetic toward the arts and intrigued by new and different forms of artistic expression (Cosmopolitans) from those who are uninvolved in the arts or who enjoy only homegrown or conventional styles of art or literature (Philistines).

"Do you strongly agree, agree, disagree, or strongly disagree with each of the following statements . . . ?"

1. High schools and colleges make students spend too much time reading "classics" that have little relevance in today's world.

Strongly Agree	Agree	Don't Know	Disagree	Strongly Disagree

2. Modern painting is just slapped on: a child could do it.

Strongly Agree	Agree	Don't Know	Disagree	Strongly Disagree

3. It is better for everyone if English is the only language used in the public schools.

Strongly Agree	Agree	Don't Know	Disagree	Strongly Disagree

4. Only a few people have the knowledge and ability to judge excellence in the arts.

| Strongly Agree | Agree | Don't Know | Disagree | Strongly Disagree |

5. I would feel comfortable inviting people I didn't know to my home.

| Strongly Agree | Agree | Don't Know | Disagree | Strongly Disagree |

Notes

1. A number of other policy questions might be dealt with at the state or local level, rather than the national level. State level public opinion on the various programs that might exist in the separate states has not yet been tracked.
2. As anyone familiar with the discussion of arts policy will quickly note, questions of censorship versus artistic expression/freedom of expression versus the protection and promotion of core values, and so on, and the possibility of and/or necessity of regulating the arts are also key policy questions. Most of these questions are specific to such controversies as those centered around the work of Mapplethorpe and Serrano, and the National Endowment for the Arts. The questions generally refer to particular artists, works of art, or political actors, and as such make it difficult to draw conclusions beyond the specific events, works, or artists. Readers interested in pursuing this topic are referred to Lang and Lang (1991) and the 1990 report from Research and Forecasts on "The American Public's Perspective on Federal Support for the Arts, and the Controversy over Funding for the National Endowment for the Arts."
3. There is an extensive literature on the history of polling and survey research, methodological problems and solutions, and so on. Readers interested in an introductory discussion of polling are referred to *Understanding Public Opinion* by Barbara Norrander and Clyde Wilcox (Washington: CQ Press, 1997); and to *The Voter's Guide to Election Polls* by Michael W. Traugott and Paul J. Lavrakas (Chatham N.J.: Chatham House, 1996).
4. The Surveys of Public Participation in the arts look at seven "benchmark" or core art forms. As given in the 1997 SPPA, the percentage of the sampled population that attended such events in the last year are as follows: classical music (15.6 percent), opera (4.7 percent), ballet (5.8 percent), musical plays (24.5 percent), jazz (11.9 percent), plays (15.8 percent), and art museums (34.9 percent). Other art forms include attendance at: other dance (12.4 percent), historic parks (46.9 percent), art/craft fairs (47.5 percent). In addition, 63.1 percent of the sample said they had read a work of literature in the last year. The 1997 survey also asked about exposure to the arts through TV, radio, videotapes, cassettes, and CDs, as well as about barriers to participation.
5. Those categories are: performing or rehearsing jazz music; playing classical music; singing any music from an opera; singing any music from a musical play or operetta; dancing ballet; dancing other dance such as modern, folk, or tap; acting in public in a nonmusical play; singing in public with a chorale, choir, glee club, or other vocal group; painting, drawing, sculpture, or printmaking; creative writing of stories, poems, or plays; composing music;

creating pottery, ceramics, jewelry, leatherwork, or metalwork; weaving, crocheting, quilting, needlepoint, or sewing; making photographs, movies, or videotapes as an artistic activity.

6. The full results of this study are reported in *Time for Life: The Surprising Ways Americans Use Their Time* by John P. Robinson and Geoffrey Godbey (University Park: Pennsylvania State University Press, 1997).

7. Filicko (1996) describes how:

We searched the archives of the Public Opinion Location Library (POLL) of the Roper Center for any and all questions on the arts. For a question to show up in our search results, the word "art" or some form of the word "art" had to show up in either the question or answer.

In addition to looking at the wording of the questions, we were also interested in seeing when the questions were asked (YEAR), by whom (SOURCE), for whom (SPONSOR), and of what kind of a sample. There were 885 separate questions.

Across this set of questions, the earliest question is one asked by the Roper Organization in 1939 of a national adult sample in personal interviews.... The most recent question was asked in telephone interviews of a national adult sample in April, 1996 by Princeton Research Associates for the Pew Research Center....

... A majority of the questions (64 3%) fall into one of the following categories:

PARTICIPATION (11.3% of the total questions; 100 questions)
ATTITUDES ABOUT PARTICIPATION (10.7%; 95)
CONTRIBUTIONS/VOLUNTEERING (5.2%; 46)
SCHOOLING/CLASSES (15.9%; 141)
FUNDING (15.5%; 137)
THE ROLE OF GOVERNMENT, POLITICAL LEADERS, AND INSTITUTIONS (5.7%; 50)

All other categories, with the exception of a MISCELLANEOUS category, represent under 5% of the total questions each. The Miscellaneous category includes 8.8% of the questions (78 questions). The smaller categories are:

THE ARTS AS A PROFESSION—4.7% (42 questions)
SPECIFIC ARTISTS—3.1% (27)
OBSCENITY IN THE ARTS—2.8% (25)
CULTURAL IDENTITY/CULTURAL EXCHANGE—2.6% (23)
GENDER AND THE ARTS—1.8% (16)
LIKES AND DISLIKES—1.9% (17)
CHILDREN AND THE ARTS—3.6% (32)
COLLECTING/INVESTMENTS—3.3% (29)
FACILITIES AND AVAILABILITY—1.8% (16)
THE ROLE OF CORPORATIONS—1.0% (9)

8. In a 1973 study conducted by Louis Harris and Associates for the Associated Councils of the Arts and Philip Morris, the following question was asked of a national (aged sixteen and older) sample of 3,005 adults (aged sixteen older) in personal interviews: "What does the word 'cultural' mean to you? Anything else?"

As reported in *Americans and the Arts*, the main responses offered by the respondents were:

The arts (music, theatre, dance, visual arts, museums, historical sites, etc.) ... 37%
Education, learning ... 19%
Life style, way people live, behavior ... 16%
Refinement, finer things, anything uplifting .. 14%

Historical background of people: customs and traditions . . . 12%

Progress, development . . . 9%

Making things beautiful . . . 8%

Things people enjoy doing: way they spend their time . . . 5%

Environment, beauties of nature . . . 4%

Any creativity used in work, home: talents . . . 4%

Good values: whatever is good in society . . . 4%

Understanding the sciences . . . 2%

Cultivation: farming: food and cooking . . . 2%

In 1990, Research and Forecasts asked the following for the People for the American Way Action Fund, as part of a study on *Federal Support for the Arts*:

To start, when I mention the word "arts" what comes to mind. Probe: What do you consider or include in the arts? Anything else?...

In telephone interviews of 1200 national adults, the main responses were:

Visual arts . . . 81%

Performing arts . . . 72%

Museums/art galleries . . . 17%

Literature/poetry . . . 9%

Movies . . . 6%

Architecture . . . 2%

T.V.(television)/radio . . . 2%

9. Full citations for these studies can be found in the bibliography.

10. J. Robinson (1989) showed Harris arts participation rates to be 15 to 20 percentage points higher than those in SPPA studies, thus raising concern that supportive arts attitudes would be biased in the same direction. Part of that bias is due to the high noncooperation rate in Harris surveys, which is typical for surveys conducted by commercial and public relation firms.

That may affect other responses from the Harris arts surveys, including evidence they contain of dramatic increases in work time and declines in the public's free time that would reduce their opportunity to participate in the arts. After reviewing Harris's results carefully, Hamilton (1991) concluded that: "There was no dramatic increase in 'work' between 1973 and 1985 nor was there a dramatic decrease in leisure. . . . The Harris workweek 'finding' appears to reflect changes in the methods used rather than any real change. The same conclusion appears justified with respect to his finding about (lower) free time" (354–355).

11. This relates to the discussion of public goods in Filicko (1997). Because the term "the arts" covers a wide array of activities, it can be difficult to tailor a question to assess what people know and feel about the arts. Nevertheless, it seems implicit in the Harris findings that if people are asked to pay admission or ticket prices, they are less likely to see a need for more of their money (in the form of tax dollars) to go to supporting those institutions. If some people have more access to the arts because they have more money (and can afford symphony or ballet tickets, for example), then it is difficult to argue that those organizations are providing a public benefit. Of course, to the extent that those organizations are seen to attract business to a community, they can be argued to provide an indirect benefit for all members of the community.

12. For example, Harris used the following preamble to questions to gauge support for the NEA:

The goal of the National Endowment for the Arts, also known as the Arts Endowment, is to foster professional excellence in the arts in America, to nurture and sustain them, and to help create a climate in which they may flourish so they may be experienced and enjoyed by the widest possible public. The Arts Endowment awards grants to individuals, state and regional arts agencies and nonprofit organizations representing the highest quality in the fields of performing and visual arts, folk arts, literature, film, radio, television and museums. Funding decisions by the Arts Endowment are made by diverse committees of citizens knowledgeable about the arts, drawn from across the country. Based on not just what you know is true but your impressions, expectations, or anything else you have read or heard about the Arts Endowment, please answer the next statements as to whether you strongly agree, agree somewhat, disagree somewhat, or strongly disagree.

13. The Harris questions used to measure support for specific arts curriculum are:

Some people think that classes in the arts for children should be taught in public schools, just like math or science or English. Other people think that classes like those should be given, but only after school or as a non-credit activity, and still others don't think they should be given at all. In your opinion, should the public schools in this area teach courses in . . . [INSERT ITEM] . . . for credit, should it be an after-school or noncredit course, or should it not be offered at all? (Survey Organization: Louis Harris And Associates)

Drawing, painting or sculpture

1980	1987	1992	
75	78	72	Teach for credit
22	19	24	After school non-credit
2	2	3	Not offered at all
1	1	1	Not sure
100	100	100	

Acting

1980	1987	1992	
59	61	n/a	Teach for credit
32	33		After school non-credit
7	4		Not offered at all
2	1		Not sure
100	100	100	

Playing a musical instrument

1980	1987	1992	
78	81	74	Teach for credit
19	16	24	After school non-credit
2	1	1	Not offered at all
1	1	1	Not sure
100	100	100	

Voice or singing

1980	1987	1992	
75	75	65	Teach for credit
22	21	32	After school non-credit
2	2	2	Not offered at all
1	1	1	Not sure
100	100	100	

14. There are likely to be many audience surveys, market surveys, focus groups, and so on, but most of these are not readily available to researchers.
15. See, for example, "Americans Despair of Popular Culture" by Elizabeth Kolbert in the *New York Times* (20 August 1995). The article reports some

of the more "newsworthy" results that support the thesis in the headline. The survey results are actually much more extensive than that which can be reported in a few charts for the Sunday paper. See also Jeffrey Cole, *The UCLA Television Violence Monitoring Report* (Los Angeles: UCLA Center for Communication Policy, September 1995).

16. The *Random House Unabridged Dictionary* defines a Philistine as "a person who is lacking in or hostile or smugly indifferent to cultural values, intellectual pursuits, aesthetic refinement, etc., or is contentedly commonplace in ideas and tastes." The dictionary defines a "cosmopolitan" as someone who is "free from local, provincial, or national . . . prejudices" and being "sophisticated, urbane, worldly." Another item related to this cosmopolitan end of the scale asks respondents if they would be open to entertaining strangers in their home.

17. Not only was the level of a person's education strongly linked to cosmopolitan versus philistine outlooks, so also were the types of high school and college courses the person took. Not surprisingly, respondents who reported enjoying literature and humanities courses most in high school were more likely to have a cosmopolitan viewpoint, as were those who remembered their science and psychology classes most fondly. Even larger differences were associated with courses taken at the college level. Those who majored in literature and the fine arts were more likely to have a cosmopolitan outlook than other college graduates. However, this was even more true among those who majored in psychological and political studies. In contrast, those who majored in business and vocational studies came out more on the philistine end of the scale. However, the least cosmopolitan college graduates in cultural outlook were engineering students; they were about as uncosmopolitan as high school graduates who had not gone to college.

18. The Cultural Salience items asked respondents about various characteristics of friends that were important to them; the higher they rated "intelligent," "cultured," and "creative" as more important characteristics, the higher the cultural salience. Thus, a cosmopolitan outlook is related to factors one looks for in choosing friends.

    The Darwinian worldview was mainly measured by questions about whether success in life is the result of genetic factors or of chance and by a general self-interest philosophy about helping others. A higher Cosmopolitan score goes along with a less fatalistic worldview, as well as one in which an active God plays a less important role.

19. In a separate analysis, the eighteen forms were more economically condensed into five dimensions or clusters: middle class (classical, musicals, big band, and so on), rural (country and bluegrass), urban (jazz and blues), novel (New Age, rap, heavy metal) and rock (contemporary and classic oldies). The major clustering in our category "middle class" includes not only classical music and opera, but also musicals, folk music, big band, and Latin as well. Respondents with higher Cosmopolitan scores are notably more favorable toward each of the music genres, even after education, age, gender, race, and region are taken into account. In addition to education, then, Cosmopolitan scores and these other variables continue to be significant predictors of liking these diverse forms of music.

20. Kolbert, ibid., notes that while most adults in a *New York Times* national survey report watching quite a bit of television and going to the movies, they have little to say about popular culture that is positive. They tend to support the use of warning labels, and they say they worry about the effects that popular culture will have on their children.

21. See especially Benjamin Page and Robert Shapiro, *The Rational Public: Fifty*

Years of Trends in Americans' Policy Preferences (Chicago: University of Chicago Press, 1992). Page and Shapiro examine whether or not policy changes follow changes in public opinion. They look at many policy areas and polling data over many years. They reach the conclusion that the government/policy makers do in fact seem responsive to the desires of the public.

KEVIN V. MULCAHY

6 The Government and Cultural Patronage

A Comparative Analysis of Cultural Patronage in the United States, France, Norway, and Canada

The American government is often viewed as a reluctant patron of culture with a parsimonious and puritanical bent. In contrast, the conventional wisdom sees European national governments as longtime, generous and unstinting benefactors of culture. Traditionally, both arts policy analysts and arts advocates have invidiously compared the reputedly deplorable condition of public support for cultural activities in the United States with an idealized conception of European public culture. As with most observations about comparative public policies, however, broad generalizations often disguise substantial exceptions. Three examples will suffice.

First, while it is certainly true that European governments substantially support a broad array of artistic endeavors, these subsidies have declined in recent years. Moreover, even if the aesthetic dimension of public policymaking is more apparent in many European nations than it is here, this aspect of public policy is not totally absent in the United States.

Second, the universe of funded art is very different outside the United States, as this includes support for what is primarily commercial here, such as film and most television products. However, recently many European nations are considering the reputed virtues of privatization and searching for alternative sources of arts support.

Third, while federal support for the arts in the United States has declined dramatically in the past decade, state and local arts councils have increased their composite support and demonstrated their institutional and political resilience in sustaining the nation's cultural infrastructure. In sum, the economically mixed and organizationally pluralistic character of arts support in the United States belies the most dire predictions about the decline and fall of public culture.

Most important, the role of the not-for-profit sector distinguishes the American case from that of other nations. To an extent unknown elsewhere, the American government through its tax code has delegated broad policymaking powers to private institutions in the pursuit of various eleemosynary goals. These areas of charity include religion, health, education, social welfare, the arts, humanities, and culture. The American system of cultural patronage is, in effect, much broader and stronger than may appear at first glance; similarly, the components of public culture in the United States are highly variegated and diversely supported. This chapter highlights these perspectives as the various cultural policies are compared.

Underlying much of the discussion is the theoretical assumption that a nation's political structures and public policies reflect the historical experiences and value systems that have characterized its societal development. The conceptual framework used here treats a nation's political culture—that is, an orientation toward politics involving general attitudes about the system and specific attitudes about the role of self in the system (Almond and Verba 1965, 13). With regard to the variety of institutions and policies that have been created to implement public culture, their organization, mode of support, and aesthetic values reflect the cognitions, feelings, and evaluations of the population. Public cultural policies, then, represent particularly sensitive barometers of macro-level consensus and conflict.

The variability in cultural patronage is rooted largely in different sociohistorical traditions, of which it is possible to delineate four ideal types: (1) a nationalist public culture that began in the latter part of the seventeenth century as part of the centralizing policies of dynastic states like the Bourbons in France; (2) a social-democratic public culture that emerged in the twentieth century in the trade union movements and socialist governments of the Nordic countries and the Netherlands; (3) a liberal political culture that created public and quasipublic cultural institutions as part of social and educational reforms in nineteenth- and twentieth-century capitalist societies; and (4) a libertarian political culture that is skeptical of sociocultural policies in general, but particularly

**Table 6.1. A Typology of Public Cultures and Systems of
Cultural Patronage**

MODE OF PUBLIC CULTURE	REPRESENTATIVE NATIONS	MODELS OF CULTURAL ADMINISTRATION	FORM OF CULTURAL FUNDING	TYPES OF CULTURAL POLITICS
Nationalistic	France	Statist	Subsidy	Hegemony
Social-democratic	Norway	Localistic	Entitlement	Redistribution
Liberal	Canada	Consociational	Grant	Sovereignty
Libertarian	United States	Pluralist	Tax Exemption	Privatization

those at the national level, preferring nonprofit cultural institutions and market allocations of cultural goods.

Among contemporary political systems, it is possible to associate each of the nations discussed here with a mode of political culture while recognizing that different cultures can coexist along with the dominant form and ideal types offer only generalized descriptions. Table 6.1 presents a typology of public cultures and the system of cultural patronage associated with each mode and its representative nations.

This chapter is an exercise in comparative cultural policy analysis—that is, an effort to systematically explore the varieties of ways in which cultural affairs are supported in France, Norway, Canada, and the United States. It is a broad overview of the patterns of public support for the arts with reference to administrative structures, funding policies, and cultural politics. Of course, any such broad, cross-national survey cannot do justice to the complexities and nuances of each nation's cultural policy. The goal is to provide comparisons that will highlight the different models that these nations employ in cultural administration, financing, and policymaking. Each nation will be discussed as it represents a particular mode of cultural policymaking.

Administrative Structures

As a general rule, the industrialized nations of the world have a recognizable and definable commitment to culture as a matter of public policy. On the other hand, the cultural policies and institutions created to implement public culture differ significantly. "This variety reflects not only differing national traditions in the organization of public functions and the delivery of public services, but differing philosophies and objectives regarding the whole area of culture and the arts" (Cummings and Katz 1987, 4). Cultural policies are an expression of national identity, and public cultural policies are concerned in various ways with maintaining a distinctive cultural identity. Depending on their cultural heritages, governments vary in the ways in which cultural affairs are administered.

One model, for example, is that of a country with a tradition of centralized administration and a highly developed cultural patrimony with an accompanying ideology of art and the state. This can be juxtaposed against an equally idealized cultural marketplace in which private institutions and individual values determine the cultural institutions that are needed without government involvement. Of course, these ideal types are tools for analysis rather than a prescription for a realizable, or desirable, outcome.

France is the nation typically viewed as most closely approximating the royalist, but also Jacobin and Napoleonic, traditions of a highly centralized state bureaucracy and in cultural affairs, a paramount ministry of culture. Following the centralized, administrative-state tradition, the Ministry of Culture established by the de Gaulle government in 1959 was characterized by an "extreme Parisianization." The first minister, the writer and intellectual André Malraux, was responsible for the restoration of several important national monuments and the creation of *maisons de la culture* (literally, "houses of culture"—cultural centers) in the provinces. Although the aesthetic emphasis was changed under Jack Lang, the equally forceful Socialist minister of culture in the 1980s and early 1990s, Malraux's twofold orientation continued to inform French cultural policymaking.

One aspect of French cultural policy has been an obsession with *grands travaux* (great works), such as the Pompidou Center and the Musée d'Orsay, conceived in the 1970s: "Even in the periods of budget restrictions and austerity, government seems irresistibly attracted to grand projects . . . and the will of the prince is always a determining factor. Every French President wants to associate his name with a large project" (Gildea 1996, 351). This was especially true for François Mitterand, who in his fourteen years as president transformed the face of Paris as no one has since Baron Hausmann in the reign of Napoleon III. Mitterand's monuments include the pyramid and the newly renovated Louvre, the Bibliothéque Nationale, La Défense, the Institut du Monde Arabe, the Opéra Bastille, and the new Ministry of Finance. The second aspect of Lang's cultural "new look" transformed Malraux's dream of creating cultural centers as "modern-day cathedrals spread across the countryside" into a policy based on regional cultural development and administrative decentralization. *L'état culturel* (the cultural state) is now a more pluralistic and localized administrative structure than the traditionally unitary ethos of the French state would have allowed.

Norway has only existed as an independent nation since 1905, when it peacefully seceded from Sweden; and before 1814, it was in union with Denmark for four hundred years. With only 4.2 million people, Norwegians constitute a small potential audience for any art and, with the country's inhabitants scattered over a vast area, the cost of providing arts activities is very high. Nonetheless, Norway's social democratic governments after 1945 have been committed to quite extensive support of the arts and, in particular, have supported a policy of fostering the decentralization and democratization of culture and cultural goods.

As Marit Bakke of the University of Bergen has observed, "Democracy and decentralization have always been, and still are, basic elements in the government's cultural policy" (Bakke 1994, 115). This has required a two-pronged approach: supporting national cultural institutions such as the National Art Gallery, the Norwegian Opera, and the Norwegian Broadcasting Corporation; and making concerts, theater, films, and art exhibitions available to those outside of Oslo and to peripheral social groups through public touring institutions. Since 1991, Norway has had a separate Department of Culture, which replaced the Department of Culture and Science (1982) and an earlier division of culture within the Department of Church and Education (1946–1981).

Canada established its equivalent of the Arts Council of Great Britain, the Canada Council for Encouragement of the Arts, in 1957. Originally, funding for the Canada Council's grants to artists and arts organizations came from an independent foundation formed from the death duties of two of Canada's richest industrialists, who rather fortuitously died within the same year. In addition to the Canada Council, there are related cultural agencies such as the National Film Board, National Arts Centre, National Archives, National Gallery, and the Canadian Broadcasting Corporation which, in its English- and French-language programming, has been a bulwark of Canadian cultural identity. The Department of Canadian Heritage is the federal agency responsible for policies and programs related to the arts and humanities, broadcasting, cultural industries, Canadian identity, multiculturalism, national parks and national historic sites, official languages, and sports. Under the Department's aegis are the Canadian Conservation Institute, the Canadian Heritage Information Network, the Cultural Property Export Review Board, and the Historic Sites and Monuments Board of Canada.

The basic responsibility for cultural affairs is not in Ottawa, however, but in the ten provinces that make up the Canadian federation. Provincial supremacy in matters of culture and education is particularly significant in the case of Quebec, where the centrality of the French language defines the unique cultural identity as a distinct society. Always protective of its political privileges, Quebec, since the "quiet revolution" of the 1960s, has developed a self-conscious and outward-looking cultural awareness and strong, local cultural institutions such as the Place des Arts in Montréal and the Musée de la Civilisation in Quebec City. Indeed, a newly created Ministère de la Culture actively supported the *épanouissement* (blooming) of Québecois arts and literature during this period. Since 1993, Quebec has administered its grants for artists and arts organizations through the Conseil des Arts et Lettres, which, like the Canada Council, is administered according to the "arm's-length principle," that is, through the use of an intermediate and autonomous body to allocate grants on the basis of expert advice (Chartrand and McCaughey 1989, 43–80).

There is no ministry of culture in the United States, that is, a Cabinet-level department responsible for comprehensive cultural policymaking and for administering a wide range of artistic activities. With the exception of some limited programs during the New Deal, the United States has eschewed the idea of establishing an official culture in which the national government would act as an influential patron of the arts (Park and Markowitz 1992, 131). In the United States, government support for cultural affairs is typically associated with the National Endowment for the Arts (NEA), established in 1965. The National Foundation on the Arts and Humanities Act of 1965 outlines the NEA's functions as providing:

> matching grants to States, to non-profit or public groups, and grants to individuals engaged in the creative and performing arts for the whole range of artistic activity. . . . A major objective of this legislation is to stimulate private philanthropy for cultural endeavors and State activities to benefit the arts. . . . The term "the arts" includes, but is not limited to, music (instrumental and vocal), dance, drama, folk art, creative writing, architecture and allied fields, painting, sculpture, photography, graphic and craft arts, industrial design, costume and fashion design, motion pictures, television, radio, tape and sound recording, and the arts related to the presentation, performance, execution, and exhibition of such major art forms. (Public Law 89–209, 1965, 1)

However, the NEA is only one of a number of federal agencies responsible for the nation's cultural affairs. For example, the NEA's administrative companion, the National Endowment for the Humanities (NEH), provides support for scholarly studies and public programs in the following disciplines: history, philosophy, languages, linguistics, literature, archeology, jurisprudence, history and criticism of the arts, ethics, comparative religion, and those aspects of the social sciences employing historical or philosophical approaches.

The cultural programs of the federal government are highly fragmented, located in a variety of administrative agencies, overseen by various congressional committees, supported by and responsive to a variety of interests, and articulating the policy perspectives of discrete segments of the cultural constituency. This institutional fragmentation reflects both the diffuse nature of artistic activity in the United States and a fear of the effects that a unified cultural bureaucracy might have on artistic expression. Among the other federal agencies and departments involved in cultural affairs besides the NEA and NEH are the Federal Council on the Arts and Humanities (which has been sporadically active in coordinating federal cultural policies), the National Gallery of Art, and Smithsonian Institution (which includes federal museums such as the Hirshhorn, Sackler Gallery, Freer Gallery, Museum of American History, Air and Space Museum), the Library of Congress, the Corporation for Public Broadcasting, and the Institute of Museum and Library Services. The Department of the Interior supports Native American arts and crafts as well as overseeing the allocation of funds dedicated to historic preservation. The federal government also supports the Kennedy Center for the Performing Arts and several other cultural affairs programs in the District of Columbia. The United States Information Agency supports various cultural and educational programs abroad (Cherbo 1992, 40).

Table 6.2. details the expenditures of the various federal cultural agencies with an estimated total of $1.3 billion in expenditures for FY 1999. (This table is not a comprehensive listing of all federal programs funding the arts and humanities; many others are imbedded in agencies seemingly unrelated to public culture. Also, several cultural agencies listed could be included in both the arts and humanities agencies.) Of this, the 1999 NEA budget of $98 million is a very small part and is likely to remain so as part of a political compromise to preclude further attempts by congressional conservatives to abolish the agency. While the symbolic importance of the NEA in the cultural world is clearly greater than its monetary resources, it needs to be underscored that the NEA is not the sum total of the federal government's cultural activities. The federal government is a decidedly minority stockholder in the business of culture (Mulcahy 1992a, 9). In sum, public culture is a much broader concern than simply arts policy and administration.

Furthermore, the American arts organization is typically a private, not-for-profit entity supported by earned income, individual and corporate donations and government grants; it is neither a public agency nor one that is largely supported by public funds. The indirect public sup-

Table 6.2. Select Federal Support for the Arts and Humanities, Fiscal Year (actual funding in millions of dollars)

SELECT FEDERAL ARTS SUPPORT

Program	Appropriated Funds
National Endowment for the Arts	99
Smithsonian Institution	318
National Gallery of Art	54
Institute of Museum and Library Services	22
Kennedy Center for the Performing Arts	12
Institute of American Indian and Alaskan Native Culture	6
National Capital Arts and Cultural Affairs Program	6
Total	516

SELECT FEDERAL HUMANITIES SUPPORT

Program	Appropriated Funds
National Endowment for the Humanities	110
Corporation for Public Broadcasting	260
Library of Congress	208
United States Information Agency, cultural and educational affairs	190
Historic Preservation Fund	37
Advisory Council on Historic Preservation	3
United States Holocaust Council	32
Woodrow Wilson International Center for Scholars	6
Total	846

SOURCE: *The Budget of the United States, Fiscal Year 1999.*

port provided by tax-exempt charitable deductions is the crucial element in sustaining the nation's 8,000 museums, 2,000 local preservation commissions, 351 public television stations, 548 public radio stations, 7,000 community theaters, and 1,800 symphony orchestras among other components of the nation's cultural infrastructure (PCAH 1997, 2). This organizationally pluralist system, supported by mixed funding and largely outside the public sector is the distinguishing characteristic of the American cultural condition.

The NEA is buttressed by fifty-six "little NEAs," the state arts agencies (SAAs) and special jurisdictions that receive yearly, formula-driven grants amounting to 40 percent of the NEA's budget. Of these SAAs, half are independent agencies and half are located within other departments of state government such as departments of education, economic development, and state. Every state arts agency is governed by a part-time advisory council, usually appointed by the governor and approved by the state legislature. These governing bodies review grant recommendations, set agency policy, and determine the goals of public support of the arts in their state or territory. The arts agency staff is typically headed by a professional executive director who is accountable to the council. Total state spending to their arts councils were $305 million in 1997, of which about 85 percent was in legislative appropriations.

Nearly half of the states have some form of decentralization program through which part of its funds are regranted to artists and arts organizations by local arts agencies (Mulcahy 1992b, 60–63). It should also be noted that the American states support a range of cultural institutions in a manner similar to the federal government. There are state historical museums and commemorative sites, state-funded television and radio stations and arts and humanities programs in public schools and universities that are line items in addition to SAA appropriations. Each state has a humanities council which is often organized as a not-for-profit organization. States also promote movie production, market cultural tourism, and legislate on historic preservation. Many states (and localities) have developed inventive tax exemptions and incentives to encourage cultural production.

A local arts agency (LAA) is defined as a not-for-profit organization or an agency of city or county government that primarily provides programs, services, financial support, and community-wide cultural planning for a variety of arts organizations, individual artists, and the community as a whole. In its "Local Programs Guidelines," the National Endowment for the Arts defines a LAA as either a nonprofit, 501(c)(3) corporation designated to operate on behalf of its local government, or an administrative unit of city or county government. Three-fourths of all LAAs are private not-for-profits; among the largest LAAs, two-thirds are agencies of state or county governments. There are approximately 3,800 local arts agencies throughout the United States and territories, of which about 1,000 operate with a professional staff. LAAs serve 80 percent of American communities and are found in 90 percent of the largest cities; overall, 49 percent of local arts agencies are urban, 30 percent are rural, and 21 percent are suburban. Total spending by local arts agencies in 1997 was estimated at $700 million—most of which was raised from local sources.

While grant-making is the most common activity, 87 percent of LAAs manage festivals and art exhibitions; and over 70 percent provide services such as advocacy, volunteer referral, arts calendars, and newsletters; 57 percent collaborate with convention and visitors bureaus, and one-third administer programs for art in public places. In addition, other funds are available to the arts from other local agencies such as parks and recreation departments and downtown development districts. In effect, the local arts agency is a catalyst that brings together a range of

Table 6.3. Models of Cultural Administration in Comparative Perspective

NATURE OF PUBLIC CULTURE	ROLE OF CENTRAL GOVERNMENT	
	Direct	*Indirect*
Strong	France Statist	Canada Consociational
Weak	Norway Localist	United States Pluralist

community organizations (public and not-for-profit) to serve a public cultural purpose.

Table 6.3 summarizes schematically the four major models of arts administration that have been discussed with reference to two variables: whether the role of the national government in the administration of cultural affairs is either largely direct or indirect, and whether the public culture is weak or strong, that is, the degree to which a self-conscious and articulated policy of governmental responsibility for cultural affairs is present.

In the case of France, state responsibility for culture is a national policy commitment of long standing. Various regimes—royalist, Jacobin, Napoleonic, republican, as well as Vichy—have been substantial patrons of the arts; and not just the high arts but crafts and the decorative arts as well. While the Ministère de la Culture has operated in its present form only since 1958, French cultural patronage actually dates from the creation in the late seventeenth century by Louis XIV of the great French institutions devoted to the performing arts: the Comédie Française, the Opéra, and the Opéra Comique (Dorian 1964, 135).

Norway has been an independent nation only since the beginning of the twentieth century. Because it was a provincial dependent of Sweden and, earlier, of Denmark, its national cultural institutions have developed only relatively recently. Norwegian culture survived locally, and its local governments are now the major providers of cultural services. Also, as a "small language" culture Norway (like other Scandinavian countries and the Netherlands) promotes extensive instruction in English while also encouraging Norwegian-language cultural industries and local arts activities.

Canada, as it emerged from colonial status by the British North American Act of 1867, is constitutionally and administratively a strong federal arrangement; indeed, the extent of the policymaking powers possessed by its provincial governments suggest more a Canadian confederation than a federal structure. In a system designed to accommodate disparate societies, as well as Quebec's "distinct society," strong powers on matters concerning identity (including culture and education) are exercised by the subnational governments. Canada is, in effect, a consociational society that is, one that must accommodate its national cultural policies to recognize the special status of a large and historically recognized region with its political system (Lijphart 1977).

The United States represents a unique model of cultural policymaking with its reliance on pluralism in administration and funding. There is no public agency that approximates a ministry of culture. First, responsibility for public culture is spread among a variety of federal agencies; among these the National Endowment for the Arts may be *primus inter pares*, but it is not paramount. Second, in support for the arts, the NEA's efforts are dwarfed by those of state and local arts agencies. Third, and most important, American culture is largely composed of commercial enterprises in film, music, design, theatre and publishing as well as not-for-profit cultural industries (Netzer 1992, 174–175).

Funding Policies

Nations fund cultural activities by a variety of mechanisms and for different public policy purposes. In particular, three modes will be examined here. First, and most common, is the direct appropriation of subsidies or grants to underwrite the operations of cultural institutions. Second are a growing number of alternative sources of revenue other than the direct appropriations that are increasingly popular as sources of support for culture in the United States. Third are governments outside the United States that have long provided indirect subsidies to a variety of cultural industries that are judged important for these nations' cultural policy objectives.

Direct Funding

The preponderant form of support for the arts in Western Europe and Canada is an appropriation by the government to a public cultural agency (national, regional, municipal) or a grant to an arts organization (museums, orchestras, opera houses, theaters, dance companies). Arts organizations are usually public institutions subject to the government's cultural policy although their artistic fare tends to be more independent. While tax incentives for philanthropy often exist, their share of funding remains quite small. Similarly insignificant is earned and commercial-type income (Zimmer and Toepler 1996, 186). On the other hand, these nations also provide significant indirect subsidies to their private cultural industries.

France is the exemplary patron state, with a presidentially directed cultural policy characterized both by a strong sense of cultural mission and, particularly during the epoch of François Mitterand (1981–1995), visible political significance. The stated goal of his minister of culture, Jack Lang, was a cultural budget of one percent of the total national spending. By and large, this goal was closely approximated especially with the inclusion of spending for the *grands travaux*, which may be Mitterand's most enduring legacy. If we include this spending, the French cultural budget is about one percent of total spending; excluding the *grands travaux*, spending on the arts has stayed steady at .79 percent after an initial jump from .45 percent to .74 percent in the period 1981–1982 when the Socialists assumed power (Perret and Saez 1996, 24).

This should be recognized as a significant commitment to culture in a nation that takes itself very seriously in cultural matters. On the other hand, the design of French cultural policy is not the exclusive preserve of its formidable ministry of culture. The most recent (1993) available data indicate that the subnational levels, especially the cities, have an importance equal to the national level. Of the total public spending on culture, about 40 percent was by communities, 10 percent by regions and departments, and 50 percent by the nation, of which only about 20 percent of the national total was from the Ministère de la Culture (*Le Monde*, 12 June 1996).

Norway is a social-democratic state with a well-articulated policy of cultural democratization and a strong emphasis on promoting maximum feasible accessibility to its national cultural heritage. To further this goal, various Socialist governments in the postwar era established four national touring companies in the areas of theater, film, music, and the visual arts to distribute cultural goods on a local basis. Government support for these national touring institutions required: creation of a local administrative unit to serve as a link between the central administration and the locality, professional status for the touring companies, an established record of public-private partnership, and commitment to the highest aesthetic standards.

Funding for culture in Norway is rooted in a social-democratic ideology that views government as the primary actor for providing social goods. "The welfare state's task is to make sure that the goods are present, meaning that they are created or made, and that the goods are distributed equally among the population' (Bakke 1994, 124). To further this redistributionist end, the Norwegian government gives the counties and municipalities general block grants leaving to the regional and local councils the determination of how to spend the money. The share of total public spending on culture by each level of government is: 38 percent national, 6 percent counties, 56 percent municipalities.

Canada is a liberal state that maintains an arm's-length approach to arts administration along with a commitment to cultural pluralism; while Ottawa supports important national cultural institutions, the arts are a provincial responsibility in the Canadian confederation. Furthermore, Canada has no tradition of private support for the arts, since its history has included neither royal or princely patrons nor the industrial robber barons who often so generously endowed American cultural institutions. Finally, Canada has also suffered from problems of cultural identity. While possessed of a highly literate population and an advanced economy, Canada has faced three obstacles to cultural development: a long history of cultural dependence on Britain in the anglophone community; a high degree of antagonism between the francophone and anglophone communities, especially as regards Quebec's cultural distinctiveness; and the problems with cultural definition for a nation of twenty-seven million (twenty million of whom are anglophones) living in the shadow of two hundred seventy million Americans with a particularly seductive and pervasive popular culture.

The Canada Council, originally created in 1957, was to make grants in support of the arts from an independent endowment of $50 million provided by a windfall inheritance tax. However, this amount has proved to be completely inadequate for providing sufficient grants to arts organizations (Kleberg 1987, 289). Today about 90 percent of the Council's funds comes from an annual parliamentary appropriation. Like education, culture has been a provincial prerogative and one that is zealously guarded especially by Quebec (Meisel 1989, 88). And, if the costs of running the bilingual Canadian Broadcasting Corporation (with its highly regarded radio programming and news reporting) are considered separately, provincial and municipal appropriations for cultural affairs are extensive. Whether Ottawa or the provinces should play the decisive role in cultural policy is a controversial issue in Canada, where the appropriate balance between the center and periphery is still being defined. Cultural matters are often central to debates on political and constitutional arrangements.

Alternatives to the regular appropriation to a public culture agency do exist in Europe, but in distinctly limited cases. For example, Denmark has allocated part of the proceeds from its national football pool for support of the arts, as Canada has done with lottery money. And, while tax laws in Great Britain and Canada encourage philanthropy, less than 5 percent of arts organizations' incomes come from private support. J. Mark Davidson Schuster has observed, "The differences in levels of private support are due less to differences in national tax legislation than to differences in historic patterns of patronage and volunteerism and differences in the modern importance of the public sector in support of artistic activities . . . Many taxpayers express the opinion that because they view the arts as a public sector responsibility they have already given through their taxes and will not give more through donations" (Schuster 1989, 32–33).

Comparisons between the United States and other nations in cultural spending are notoriously difficult. This reflects a basic structural difference: In the United States support for the arts is diverse, pluralistic, and mixed; outside the United States, cultural activities are typically funded and often produced directly by the government with little private philanthropy and few, if any, not-for-profit arts organizations. Also, the United States makes distinctions between the not-for-profit arts and the for-profit entertainment industries and deals primarily with the not-for-profit as recipients of public funding. Outside the United States, profit-making entities are funded when these cultural industries are deemed important to the nation's cultural policy goals, which often entail economic concerns.

The United States government promotes cultural philanthropy, support to private and nonprofit arts organizations through several tax measures. For example, like all nonprofit 501(c)(3)s, arts organizations benefit from provisions allowing corporations, foundations, and individuals to deduct the full amount of charitable contributions made to them. Total donations to the arts, culture, and humanities sector of philanthropy amounted to $10 billion of the $143.8 billion contributed to all charities. Eighty percent of cultural philanthropy came from individuals, 13 percent from foundations, and seven percent from corporations (PCAH 1997, 18). Also, nonprofit arts organizations generally do not pay local property taxes or federal tax or local sales taxes on income that is related to their mission. Nonprofits also receive substantial subsidies through preferential postal rates; for example, nonprofits receive a 60 percent discount off the third-class base rate (Cummings 1991, 39–41).

There has been little public patronage by the U.S. government on the European scale given the absence of monarchical or aristocratic traditions. However, the U.S. government is the proprietor of several fine-arts collections in the Smithsonian complex and a world-class portrait gallery; also, through its commissioning of public buildings and the associated decoration, the government is an architectural client and art buyer. This is also the case with the increasing number of commemorative memorials. State governments are somewhat more modest public collectors, curators, and clients.

The most conventional form of public support for the arts is an annual appropriation to a public cultural agency. Total federal government appropriations for cultural agencies amounted to about $1.3 billion in

**Table 6.4. Total Arts Spending by Level of Government, 1992 and 1997
(funding in millions of dollars)**

	1992	1997
National Endowment for the Arts	132	98
State arts agencies	213	305
Local arts agencies	600	700

SOURCE: *Executive Budget of the United States, 1999*; NASAA 1998, *State Arts Agencies Legislative Appropriations*; Research Division of Americans for the Arts, 1998.

1997, and the NEA appropriation was a very small portion of the intergovernmental total. Moreover, as table 6.4 shows, using 1992 and 1997 as points of comparison, the states and localities are the major-league players in public funding with total spending on the arts of $305 million and $700 million respectively. Indeed, as federal funding has declined from a high point in the early 1990s, state and local arts councils have become increasingly the more important public patrons of the arts.

The local arts agency is largely a community creation that depends on mixed funding from public, private, and earned-income sources. Overall, LAAs received 50 percent of their funds from public sources (primarily local governments), 31 percent from earned income, and 19 percent from the private sector as corporate and individual contributions. However, there are marked differences between the private, not-for-profit agencies (more typically found in small communities) and public agencies (more typical in urban areas). Where public LAAs receive 87 percent of their funds as governmental appropriations, private LAAs have a more even distribution of revenue sources: 38 percent from the government, 38 percent from earned income, and 24 percent from private sources (see tab. 6.5).

The government is a distinctly limited partner as a source of support for arts organizations in the United States. For the performing arts, government accounts for about 6 percent of their budgets, compared to 36 percent from philanthropy and 58 percent from earned income; for museums, this is about 30 percent, which reflects a greater degree of public ownership and long-standing public-private relationships. Philanthropy and earned income account for 23 percent and 47 percent respectively (see tab. 6.6).

Alternative Funding (United States)

To support an increasing responsibility for public culture, state and local governments have devised some creative mechanisms for supporting the arts. The information presented here is a gen-

Table 6.5. Sources of Support for Local Arts Agencies in the United States (in percentage)

	GOVERNMENT	PHILANTHROPY	EARNED INCOME
All LAAs	50	19	31
Not-for-profit LAAs	38	24	38

SOURCE: Americans for the Arts 1998, *Local Arts Agency Facts.*

eral overview of alternative methods of supporting the arts (NALAA 1995, 65–93; Rafool and Loyacono 1995 13–29).

Hotel/Motel Levies. So-called bed taxes are generally a fixed tax on any-one who rents a hotel or motel room in a local jurisdiction. These may also be extended to a surcharge on restaurant meals. These taxes are es-pecially popular with voters who prefer that the city tax visitors rather than local residents. However, the tourism industry is highly suscep-tible to fluctuations in the economy, leaving these revenues somewhat unstable as a long-term system for support of the arts. Also, such a tax may be opposed by the hospitality industry unless the arts are regarded as playing a significant role in the local tourism industry.

For example, the city of San Francisco gets over $30 million to sup-port the arts from the hotel tax. The Greater Columbus Arts Council re-ceives 25 percent of a 6 percent hotel/motel tax for distribution to its arts program.

Special Property Taxes. Specialty property taxes to support the arts have had some success in prime real estate areas such as Aspen, Colorado. As a form of revenue, it can be lucrative but subject to fluctuations in property values and is often opposed by the real estate and business communities.

In 1971, St. Louis, Missouri, and its surrounding suburbs established the St. Louis Zoo–Museum District able to levy a property tax to sup-port designated "arts" institutions. (The inclusion of the zoo was cru-cial to securing approval.) In 1991, this "cultural" property tax district yielded $27 million to support the zoo, the art museum, the botanical gardens, the science museum, and the historical museum. Part of the justification for such a large level of support is that all the recipient in-stitutions have free-admission policies.

Sales Tax. Although sales taxes are generally regarded as unpopular (es-pecially among local retailers), they have been effective in certain places,

Table 6.6. Sources of Support for Arts Organizations in the United States

	GOVERNMENT	PHILANTHROPY	EARNED INCOME
Performing arts	6	36	58
Museums	30	23	47

SOURCE: Research Division of Americans for the Arts, 1997.

notably Denver, Colorado. In 1987, 75 percent of the electorate voted to add .01 percent to the sales tax in the six-county area that was expected to produce $13 million for local cultural institutions. The funds are distributed according to a formula that allocates 65 percent of the total to major institutions (such as the Denver Art Museum, the Museum of Natural History, the Botanical Gardens, and the Zoo) and 35 percent to local organizations.

Admission and Entertainment Taxes. Entertainment taxes can take a variety of forms, such as levies on movie tickets and video rentals, license fees on cable television franchises, and, more typically, taxes on admissions to commercial theater and music productions and sporting events. The attractiveness of such taxes is that, since commercial entertainment industries historically weather fluctuations in the economy better than other sectors, the revenue generated is fairly stable. Also, since attendance at movies, sporting events, and other forms of commercial entertainment cuts across a wide segment of the population, such a tax is fairly equally borne. (Some argue that the not-for-profit arts industries provide the research and development for commercial entertainment and are only recouping some of their investment.)

Sin Taxes. These are the revenues gained from special taxes on alcohol and gambling-related activities. State-sanctioned gambling operations that allocate a portion of the proceeds to cultural institutions are a controversial mechanism of support, and not just on moral grounds. Gambling revenues cannot be guaranteed and very often are used to replace, rather than supplement, general revenue allocations.

Gambling Proceeds to Cultural Programs (South Dakota) began after state residents voted to amend the state constitution to allow gambling within the city limits of Deadwood. The proceeds—after Gaming Commission expenses—go toward the historic preservation of that city. In 1996, Huntsville, Alabama, put a 10 percent tax on liquor and earmarked a portion for the Arts Council and a new civic center.

Tax Checkoffs. The U.S. Conference of Mayors reports that about 5 percent of state taxpayers use checkoffs to make contributions to various causes including, in some states, specifically being able to earmark a portion to support the arts. San Diego County allows several arts organizations to solicit donations on its property-tax bill.

Percent-for-Art Programs. A percent-for-art program requires that a certain portion of a city's capital expenditures be set aside for the purchase of public art and that a method of allowing artists to compete for the commissions be established.

Live/Work Ordinances. This process involves modifying the existing zoning and building codes to allow for artists' housing and studio facilities. These ordinances are applied in areas where revitalization efforts for blighted neighborhoods include an emphasis on the arts.

The city of Providence, Rhode Island, has transformed one square mile of its downtown area into an arts and entertainment zone, established in 1996. Artists and performers from the district pay no state income tax on what they sell; their customers pay no sales tax on what they buy. And, in what city and state officials say is key to examine redevelopment in the area, the city offers tax breaks to property owners who convert old, unused buildings into residential units.

Miscellaneous Revenues. In several localities, a portion of the sales taxes and major public events are used to support the arts. There is a provision for earmarking funds for the arts through a checkoff on income tax returns. Three states have lotteries with proceeds used in support of the arts.

Trust Funds. Ten states have created independent cultural trusts through some kind of dedicated revenue stream. Such trusts may also receive industrial and corporate contributions. Tennessee instituted a fee from the sale of vanity license plates, and Florida increased its corporate annual report filing fee (from $25 to $35) to create a trust fund to support the state's major cultural institutions.

The Missouri Cultural Trust receives partial funding through legislation that allocates 50 percent of the Missouri state income tax paid by nonresident performers and athletes working in the state. The Arizona Arts Trust Fund was created in 1989 through an increase in the annual filing fee for the sixty-thousand profit-making corporations doing business in the state. It is administered by the state's Commission on the Arts and covers anywhere from 5 to 10 percent of the audited operating income of major cultural institutions and emerging organizations. One requirement is that all these organizations have a board of directors representing the ethnic diversity of their communities.

A related development is the number of suggestions for transforming the NEA into what is essentially a private endowment. Joseph Zeigler has proposed remodeling the NEA as a true endowment with a $6.5 billion fund that at a rate of 6 percent could earn $360 million annually. Following Alice Goldfarb Marquis's (1995) suggestion, he proposes that a one percent federal tax be levied on commercial entertainment and professional sports over a three-year period that would gross $6 billion in combination with a private campaign from foundations, corporations and individuals which would leverage another half billion dollars (Zeigler 1996).

Many of these alternative funding mechanisms have achieved some degree of success in states and localities across the country. However, no one of these can be judged to be the optimal solution. Each must be evaluated in terms of its feasibility in relation to the economic and political climate of the given locality. No one should be considered a panacea to cure the fiscal ailments of any arts community. Given the site-specific nature of these alternative forms of revenue, it is incumbent on an arts agency to ascertain which methods are appropriate and possible given the nature of its state and local tax laws as well as the community's private resources. In addition, successful public funding must also address issues of greater equity within the arts community and be able to justify the return on the tax dollar to the average citizen. Finally, public funding for the arts should consider the need for access by the culturally underserved and be sensitive to minority and marginalized art forms within the community.

Indirect Subsidies (Western Europe and Canada)

European nations are extremely active in providing a variety of indirect support (benefits other than direct appropriations) for their "cultural industries"—profit making, private enterprises involved with film, books, television and radio, sound and video recordings, and the press. In France, the Ministry of Culture has become "a sort of ministry of cultural industry in which the cultural policy is integrated into a total strategy of the French government" (Saez 1996, 135).

These subventions of the cultural industries take two basic forms: a reduction of all or part of the value-added tax, and other incentives for the production and promotion of certain artistic endeavors.

Books

The oldest subvention for some European cultural industries has involved the publication and distribution of books. This public support is primarily for literature (poetry, novels, plays), scientific works and art books (including exhibition catalogues) as well as translations, books for the blind, and works in minority languages and those of regional, ethnographic, and folkloric interest. Numerous kinds of subsidies make up some of the losses involved in the publication and distribution of specialized books with limited market appeal. These include preferential taxation rates, purchase of copies for public libraries, preferential loans to bookstores, and contributions toward the cost of transportation of these books. Overall, the public policy goal is to enlarge the market for books deemed essential to the national cultural interest by keeping the sale price low. Twelve European nations have some form of subsidy for books (Rouet and Dupin 1991, 235–255).

Norway is a good example of how different modes of support are provided to the book industry. The Norwegian program has three elements: First, books published in Norway are exempted from the value-added tax, which reduces the price about 16 percent. Second, the state buys a thousand copies of books within designated categories where the press run is three thousand. This provides a reduction of 10 percent. Third, the state pays the author the royalties of 10 percent on the first three thousand copies. This reduces the price another 25 percent. The result is a reduction of over half of the book's retail price (Schuster 1989, 11).

Videos and Recordings

In twelve of the European countries, support is given to the production of certain types of music, such as those with a nationalistic or folkloristic character and works by young artists. Five of the countries provide further assistance by aiding in the promotion of recorded music through general advertising and cultural festivals. Sweden, Belgium, and Denmark help small recording companies with distribution. These measures both promote the domestic music industry and mitigate the dominance of American popular music.

In aiding the video industry, most governments use product-specific taxes to generate funds for their efforts; they tax videotapes, both prerecorded and blank. The three most typical types of assistance are for production, distribution, and technical support. Production assistance is mainly provided for low-budget films; aid for distribution is provided through copying services and exhibition at cultural festivals (Rouet and Dupin 1991, 257–263, 293–296).

The taxes on videos and recordings are generally high on the grounds that they are luxury goods for which the demand is indifferent to price. Similarly, pornography is taxed heavily in France not so much as a sin tax as a ready source of revenue, given the relative inelasticity of demand (Schuster 1989, 31).

Film

Most European countries provide a variety of assistance for the making of feature films. The emphasis is usually on films with a cultural or artistic content, the works of independent/experimental filmmakers, short films and documentaries, and films that have a national character. In Germany, aid policy for filmmaking distinguishes between "cultural aid" and "economic aid." Support usually includes preproduction help in the writing of scripts and funding for studio production as an advance against future revenues. All European nations support the dubbing of films and their distribution and promotion through festivals (Rouet and Dupin 1991, 277–292).

In France, the government has concerned itself with the condition of French cinema since the 1930s. State intervention was reinforced after Liberation with the creation in 1946 of the National Cinematography Center (*Centre National Cinématographique*—CNC), the principal governmental policy instrument in this sphere, and of the Fund to Aid the Cinematographic Industry, which became in 1953 the Cinema Industry Development Fund. The financial aid given by the government to the cinema industry stems from a tax on the movie tickets purchased and is administered by the CNC. Thus, funding availability is closely allied to the behavior of cinema audiences. The government's financial contribution also takes other forms: production subsidies, technical help, public events (like the Cannes Film Festival), or education (Institute of Advanced Cinema Studies), advances against future sales, subsidies for distribution, building or modernization of movie theaters (Andrault and Dressayre 1987, 24).

In Norway, there are grants to various institutions and activities concerned with film. For example, the Norwegian Film Institute is state financed. In addition, subsidies are given to documentaries, children's films, the import of valuable foreign films, the writing of scripts; there is also one state-owned film production company, Norsk Film A/S. Apart from the grant to the state production company, the basic principles of this design may be described this way: On the basis of a script, a cost estimate, and a financial plan, a special committee appointed by the Ministry, evaluates the project. Based on this evaluation, the Ministry may grant state support of up to 55 percent of the anticipated gross revenue.

In addition to this general support, the Ministry may give state loan guarantees to meet production costs, up to complete financing. Practically all feature films are dependent both on support and on guarantees. In fact, because of rising production costs and declining revenue, practically all films are close to being fully financed by state guarantees or loans (Berg 1987, 167).

It might be noted that many nations are protectionist in their support for national film industries. The fear of American "cultural imperialism" is particularly strong in France and Canada where Hollywood movies dominate viewership. For a small country, like Norway, a few native-language films are important manifestations of cultural prestige.

Radio and Television
The earliest and until relatively recently, only broadcasting medium was a state-run activity in the European countries and Canada. In a way similar to that of the self-financing of French film production through a tax on admissions, television license fees support the British Broadcasting Corporation and the French public stations. The Canadian Broadcasting Corporation has been a jewel in the crown of the Confederation's cultural life.

Among other things, the Broadcasting Act specifies that the Canadian broadcasting system should "safeguard, enrich, and strengthen the cultural, political, social, and economic fabric of Canada," and that the programming should be of high standard, "using predominantly Canadian creative and other resources." It specifies, for instance, that 60 percent of each day's programming on Canadian television must be Canadian. Still, if all English-language TV stations are taken together, it is found that of all the time Canadians spend on television during the day, 65 percent is devoted to American shows. The corresponding figure for the evening hours is 75 percent. The CBC has tried to make up for this and has produced some highly successful Canadian shows, but the production costs prevent enough of these being made to give Canadian viewers a real choice between domestic and American television (Meisel and Van Loon 1987, 294).

France, with its long tradition of centralized government and a strong national cultural identity, provides an extensive system of subsidies for the arts throughout the country and direct management of national cultural institutions in Paris. France may be the preeminent patron state with its placement of culture as a part of the definition of its national identity.

For Norway, also a generous national provider of cultural financing, culture is more a matter of an individual social right than an element of national prestige. In this sense, broad access to cultural activities is as integral an entitlement of the social welfare state as is health care or housing. Cultural affairs are delivered largely on the local level with a strong emphasis on popular participation.

Canada, unlike France and Norway, is a strongly federal system that allocates control over domestic affairs to its provincial or territorial governments. The administration of cultural affairs is an important provincial privilege. The Canadian government, however, does subsidize a number of national museums and historical sites and the Canadian Broadcasting Corporation. Moreover, the Canada Council, modeled on the British Arts Council, is a semiautonomous (arm's-length) entity within the Department of Canadian Heritage that makes grants to artists and arts organizations on a nationwide competitive basis.

The United States represents the great exception in the funding of public culture, with its extensive reliance on tax exemptions for charitable deductions and on not-for-profit, 501(c)(3) organizations. There are certainly subsidies for some cultural institutions in Washington, like the Smithsonian and the Corporation for Public Broadcasting, as well as grants awarded though an arm's-length panel system by the National Endowments for the Arts and Humanities. What makes American arts unique is the extent to which the indirect mechanisms of tax exemptions are a means by which the government empowers private institutions and individuals to address a public purpose.

For example, the Metropolitan Museum of Art is a not-for-profit organization; like other such arts organizations, it can receive tax-deductible donations and may operate profit-making enterprises that are, in part, exempt from sales taxes. In exchange, the Metropolitan maintains and displays a depository of art-historical treasures that is the single most visited site in New York City and the keystone of its attractiveness for cultural tourists. "To a degree unparalleled elsewhere, the nonprofit sector in the United States is enshrined in constitutional law, instrumental in the delivery of many social services, and inextricably bound up with broad social processes of change and governance" (Clotfelter 1992, 1).

In sum, the persistent notion that the United States lacks a significant public commitment to culture must be adjusted to take into account the role of not-for-profit sector. Cultural activities in the United States may not be directly as well funded as in other nations, but the government's role is hardly negligible given its provision of tax advantages for the cultural organizations and their contributors. Whether a highly privatized system of subsidy best promotes the public interest in cultural development is another issue (see tab. 6.7).

Table 6.7. Forms of Arts Funding in Comparative Perspectives

	ROLE OF NATIONAL GOVERNMENT	
NATURE OF PUBLIC CULTURE	*Direct*	*Indirect*
Strong	France subsidies	Canada grants
Weak	Norway entitlements	United States tax exemptions

Cultural Politics

In Canada and France, the policies concerning public culture have been hotly debated among political elites and the general public. In both cases, public culture is related to questions of political culture—that is, with issues of national identity and social cohesion. Culture wars have also raged in the United States over questions of public support for controversial art and, more broadly, the continued existence of the NEA and support for the arts by the federal government.

What is most notable about Canada's cultural policy, and may account for the seriousness with which it is engaged in the public arena, is the relationship between cultural identity and political identity. For the Canadian Royal Commission on National Development in the Arts, Letters and Sciences, chaired by Vincent Massey from 1949 to 1951, it was an article of faith that there was an identifiable Canadian culture that would serve as a unifying principle of national identity (Litt 1992, 3–7). For the members of the Massey Commission and its disciples, opposition to American mass culture was the basis of a Canadian cultural identity (Meisel 1989, 82–83). As Seymour Martin Lipset has put it, "Canadians are the world's oldest and most continuing un-Americans" (Lipset 1990, 53). Indeed, many English-speaking Canadian intellectuals mobilized to fight the Canada–U.S. Free Trade Pact because they saw it as a threat to their national culture and distinct Canadian values. However, an unanticipated consequence of the Massey Commission's emphasis on a distinctive Canadian culture—the creation of a national culture distinct from Britain and the United States—may have been to encourage artists and intellectuals in Quebec to want to become a "distinct society"— to assert the distinctiveness of their francophone culture. (See Mulcahy 1995a, 335–362; Mulcahy 1995b, 225–249.)

This cultural crisis mentality has persisted in Canada, where 70 percent of radio air time, 80 percent of magazines sold, 75 percent of prime time television, and 96 percent of movie screen time are dedicated to foreign (mainly U.S.) products. Deputy Prime Minister and Heritage

Minister Shelia Copps has been particularly outspoken on the subject of U.S. cultural domination. She declared Canada prepared "to use all the tools in our arsenal to fight the decisions that restrict our capacity to build our own culture" (*Los Angeles Times*, 18 February 1997). The context of Copps's remarks concerned a World Trade Organization ruling on a Canadian tax intended to prevent the proliferation of Canadian editions of U.S. magazines. In recent years the United States and Canada have also clashed over Canadian efforts to ban U.S.-owned broadcast networks from Canadian cable systems, to prevent U.S.-controlled bookstores from expanding into Canada, and to levy a tax on blank audiotapes to raise money to support Canadian performers and producers. In 1998, Canada convened a meeting of nineteen ministers of culture (and pointedly did not invite American representatives to participate) to discuss measures that could be taken to protect their national cultures from the escalating threat from Hollywood and the American popular entertainment industry (*New York Times*, 1 July 1998).

French intellectuals frequently position themselves as the last exponents of high culture and artistic taste, especially as these are under attack by the popular-culture, mass-entertainment industry. In particular, it is American popular culture, or as Jack Lang liked to put it in the early 1980s, American "cultural imperialism," that is seen as the enemy of aesthetic excellence (Gildea 1996, 158). The French government sets a quota of 50 percent for films of French origin; and, in 1993, the French government successfully lobbied the European Commission to secure an exemption for cultural products from the GATT agreement on free trade (Gildea 1996, 159). This was widely interpreted as an effort to defend the French film market from increasing competition from Hollywood; for example, the French share of its film market has fallen from 50 percent to 34 percent while the share for American films rose from 29 percent to 55 percent. The French government also sets a quota to give French songs 40 percent of time devoted to popular music on French airwaves (Gildea 1996, 163).

Furthermore, support for culture in France is also seen as an element of social policy with the government funding bookstores, libraries, movie theaters, and musical cafes in the working-class and immigrant housing projects in the suburbs of Paris and other French cities. In transforming these "territories of exclusion" into "places of creation," the then minister of culture, Philippe Douste-Blazy, saw the arts as playing an important role in reconciling the "social fracture" (*Le Monde*, 18 January 1996). What may be most important to note here is that the French see culture as an essential part of what constitutes the *sens civique*— that is, a sense of civic solidarity that has traditionally been regarded by the French as a distinguishing characteristic of their society, especially when compared to the "Anglo-Saxon alternative" (Konig 1995, 95–106). Although there is a constant debate about the structure of French cultural policy "at least there are cultural policies, at least there is public patronage of the arts, both national and local, at least the French remain self-conscious about their creative genius" (Gildea 1996, 232).

In Norway, cultural politics takes a different form than the other nations considered here. In a country with a small, homogenous, affluent population; a common cultural heritage; and a strong social-democratic ideology, debates about public culture concern the scope of state intervention and the best mode of implementation. There are no emotional debates about cultural imperialism; nor is there a cultural region with claims to autonomy as a distinct society. Norwegian governments in the post–World War II era have accepted responsibility for public culture as a logical extension of the welfare state. "The welfare ideology implied that 'cultural goods' should be fairly distributed throughout the country, and that the population should have extended influence upon decisions affecting the cultural life of its own community" (Mangset 1995, 68). The welfare principle also applies to the artists' right to economic security and recognizes that cultural activities—the crafts as well as the fine arts—are "a national resource for social and economic development" (Kangas and Onsér-Franzén 1996, 19). Since cultural administration has been largely decentralized to the municipal level, the questions have been how best to realize a socially oriented cultural policy.

In the United States, the political controversy involving the NEA and its support for exhibits of photography by Robert Mapplethorpe and Andres Serrano called into question the fundamental assumptions underlying public support for a commitment to culture at the national level. The degree of public scrutiny far surpassed the magnitude of the public expenditure involved and the rarity of controversial grants from among the totality of those that have been awarded. What should have been a political side show that the NEA could have routinely survived developed into a kind of Kulturkampf, that is, a struggle over the legitimacy of public support for the arts and the NEA as a public arts agency (Wyszomirski 1995c, 1–48). Unfortunately, many members of the cultural community were content to dismiss criticisms of the NEA as simply atavistic. However, the range, intensity and impact of such criticism has been too great to be dismissed as solely a delusion of the ideological fringes. In the minds of many moderate citizens and their elected representatives, the NEA became labeled as one of the nation's promoters of pornography. In fact, an underlying issue with many controversial grants has been the absence of an accepted public purpose in the

**Table 6.8. *Types of Cultural Politics in Western Europe and
North America***

	ROLE OF NATIONAL GOVERNMENT	
NATURE OF PUBLIC CULTURE	*Direct*	*Indirect*
Strong	France hegemony	Canada sovereignty
Weak	Norway redistribution	United States privatization

NEA's grant-making decisions (Mulcahy 1991, 5–27; Mulcahy 1995b, 205–228).

The NEA moved toward administration by public purpose in 1995 when its disciplinary panel structure was abolished and its grantmaking activities reorganized into four divisions: heritage and preservation; education and access; creation and preservation; partnership, planning, and stabilization. Unfortunately, this belated response to its friendly critics did little to assuage unfriendly criticism. As recently as April 1997, House Speaker Newt Gingrich was still denouncing the NEA as a purveyor of pornography and an elitist frill that would be best supported privately (*New York Times*, 11 April 1997). More substantively, Senator Spencer Abraham (Republican, Michigan) has proposed the creation of a privately supported, not-for-profit foundation to take over existing federal responsibility for support of the arts and humanities. In essence, the goal would be to terminate the national government's commitment to culture through privatization of the grant-making process. By 1998, Republican opposition had tempered as threats to abolish the NEA gave way to a continued reduced appropriation with guarantees against grants for pornography and with guidelines about the distribution of grants in a more localistic (that is, non–New York) fashion (*New York Times*, 22 July 1998).

Table 6.8 summarizes the major cultural policy concerns that engage the four nations compared in this study as these relate to the national government's role and the nature of the public culture that is supported.

French cultural policy has been a long-standing high profile issue of national debate. Both right and left in France accept the principle of *l'état culturel* whatever the differences in programmatic emphases. The hegemonic status of French culture, that is, the claim of its language, literature, philosophy and fine arts to represent a model worthy of emulation, is a widely accepted principle of political discourse. Whether a

Malraux in a conservative government or a Lang in a socialist government, ministers of culture have often employed aggressive policies to promote these hegemonic claims such as the *maisons de la culture* at home and the *Alliance Française* abroad. Of course, it is anglophone culture, particularly American popular culture, that has displaced French preeminence as a cultural hegemon. For many French intellectuals, EuroDisney was not just a theme park, but a cultural Chernobyl.

The politics surrounding cultural policymaking in Canada has been inextricably intertwined with issues of national sovereignty. As a former English colony, Canada has established identifiably Canadian cultural institutions only in this century. Coupled with the politics of self-determination left over from British colonialism, Canada has also sought to insure its cultural sovereignty in the face of "American cultural imperialism." Exacerbating the problem of creating a distinct Canadian identity is the recognition of francophone Quebec as part of this larger national identity. The accommodation of Quebec's status as a "distinct society" has entailed a large measure of political autonomy and cultural regionalism.

Norway and the United States are in some respects at polar opposites on matters of cultural politics. Successive Socialist governments in Norway in the post–World War II era have engaged in redistributionist policies generally; this has included extensive cultural programs at the local level as an entitlement of citizenship. In the United States, by contrast, there has never been a national consensus about the appropriateness of public support for the arts, especially by the federal government. The emphasis has typically been on local initiatives, particularly by not-for-profit cultural organizations. As the decline in federal government support for the arts has accelerated in recent years there has been an increasing localization and privatization of public culture in the United States.

The State of Public Culture

It is as difficult as it is risky to offer even the most tentative generalizations about comparative public policymaking. Cultural policies are particularly enmeshed with national histories and political cultures. However, it does seem possible to outline three broad developments that generally characterize the state of public support for the arts in the four nations discussed in this chapter and that suggest the structural arrangements, funding policies, and policy debates of the foreseeable future; and to present some general observations concerning the prospects that increasing privatization and market economics present for cultural development.

First, there appears to be a clear movement toward the decentralization of government support for cultural affairs. In federal systems, such as that of Canada, this is a long-standing administrative practice; in the Canadian case, the provinces—led by Quebec—have long asserted virtual autonomy in matters of local government, including education and culture. Even France, a model of the centralized state since the seventeenth century, has pursued a strong policy of cultural decentralization over the past fifteen years. As noted earlier, the municipal governments, not the ministry, administer the largest share of the cultural budget. In the United States, where support for the arts has traditionally been a community initiative, state and local arts councils are assuming ever greater responsibility for cultural affairs as the presence of national government has diminished in both funding and policy direction.

This is not to suggest that there is not an important federal role in cultural policymaking in the United States. In a "new cultural paradigm" (Wyszomirski 1995b, 80–81), the National Endowment for the Arts could still function with existing funding as the arbiter of broad cultural standards and evaluator of public cultural programs in the states and localities. The state arts councils could, with enhanced cultural block grants (perhaps from a federally sponsored, independent foundation), assume broader responsibility for the coordination of large initiatives within their jurisdictions particularly support for major, standard-setting arts organizations and arts-education programs. The local arts councils, with enhanced funding from appropriations, philanthropy, and alternative funding sources, could be the primary providers of cultural programming at the community level, emphasizing public accessibility through arts development and support for individual artists. Even if a restructured national arts policy were to rely ever more heavily on the state and local arts agencies, there is nothing in this arrangement that belies the importance of the federal arts agency and the national interest in public culture.

Second, the increasing importance of local arts administration and local funding responsibility is paralleled by the increasing salience of localistic cultural concerns. This cultural particularism can take two forms. For a cultural leader like France, cultural protectionism takes the form of an often ritual opposition to "American cultural imperialism." For the French, the fear is less of the penetration of their culture by American popular culture (although that is a frequent complaint among some French intellectuals) than of the displacement of *la civilisation française* as a viable alternative to the American model of social and cultural organization. For Canadians, by contrast, proximity to the United States presents a pervasive reminder of the American omnipresence in television, film, books, magazines, and popular music. Exacerbating the question of maintaining a cultural identity in the shadow of the United States is the necessity to construct a Canadian national culture that can accommodate francophone Quebec.

Overall, there has been a trend toward the devolution of responsibility for cultural affairs to local levels of government. This may be a reflection of the cultural nationalism of regional minorities or an expression of identity politics among marginalized social groups. For many, public culture is associated positively with community and heritage, with how people define their arts and see themselves in the world and in history. An arts policy that would appear to offer the best opportunity for public support would position itself as part of a broader sense of cultural heritage, including the humanities, historic preservation, public broadcasting, and arts education. This ideal cultural policy would provide a sense of communal continuity and definition while continuing to promote aesthetic discourse and artistic creativity.

Third, there is a seemingly inexorable demand that the arts carry their own weight rather than rely on a public subsidy to pursue art for art's sake. This cultural Darwinism is most pronounced in the United States, where public subsidy is limited and publicly supported arts are expected to demonstrate a public benefit. Non-American cultural institutions are less constrained by the need to maintain diversified revenue streams that include ticket sales and individual and corporate donations as well as government appropriations. On the other hand, all cultural institutions are increasingly market-driven in their need for supplementary funds and a source of justification. European and Canadian cultural institutions are actively seeking alternative revenue streams such as corporate sponsorships and increasingly looking to the American model of mixed funding for guidelines.

There is much to recommend the mixed-funding formulas of not-for-profit arts agencies and cultural institutions; on the other hand, a completely privatized arts world would be less likely to address questions of aesthetic diversity and public accessibility. The corporate sector may be concerned about distributional equity in its investment in cultural products; but, it is, at root, market driven and necessarily concerned with profitability (Yudice 1995, 1–26). In a system of mixed funding, the public arts agency can nurture the arts groups and cultural activities that contribute to individual self-worth and community definition even if accounting for less in the corporate bottom line. In effect, the public arts agency can offer the means for achieving greater cultural equity, that is, the right of every citizen to participate in some form of cultural activity and to experience the diversity of a nation's cultural heritage.

Underlying this argument is an assumption that cultural agencies would be well advised to adopt a "latitudinarian approach" to public culture, that is, one that is aesthetically inclusive and broadly accessible. In conceiving of public policy as an opportunity to provide alternatives not readily available in the cultural marketplace, public cultural agencies would be better positioned to complement the efforts of private institutions rather than duplicate or challenge their activities. Such a public cultural policy could remain faithful to the highest standards of aesthetic excellence while providing the broadest possible access to people from different geographic locales, socioeconomic strata, and educational backgrounds (Mulcahy 1992, 22–24). Similarly, cultural agencies could promote community development by supporting aesthetic preferences and heritages that are at a competitive disadvantage in a cultural world that is increasingly privatized and market-driven. The real issue is not whether a public cultural agency should exist, but what its role should be in a funding triad comprised of individuals and private institutional philanthropy, earned income, and grant funding. Every nation has a public interest in cultural matters. Whatever the government role in cultural patronage, it will be largely determined by each nation's history and political culture.

Note

Special thanks should be accorded to my assistants, Chad Long and Adam Ducote, for excellent research and editorial assistance as well as to my student-workers, James Hebert and Joshua Harvey, for unstinting wordprocessing.

PART III

Perspectives from Arts Subsectors

ANN M. GALLIGAN
NEIL O. ALPER

7 The Career Matrix
The Pipeline for Artists in the United States

This chapter provides an overview of the career patterns of individual artists—how one becomes, exists, works, prospers, and retires as an artist in the United States. Using data derived from various sources, we seek to establish a baseline profile of who and how many artists there are; how they prepare for their careers as professionals; where and by what means they make a living as practitioners at a variety of art forms in both the profit and the not-for-profit sectors; and how they compare to similar nonarts professionals; and other select issues.

While the individual artist is the primary focus of this study, this is only part of the profile. A secondary aim is to develop the concept of a matrix comprised of individuals and organizations that function as a dynamic and interactive system encompassing the talent and capacity to create, promote, support, distribute, and preserve both the commercial and not-for-profit arts. The ensuing picture details the experiences of artists as they develop professionally, along their career paths.

There are three major assumptions at work in shaping this profile: First is the premise that the individual artist is part of a distinct arts sector—similar to health or education—encompassing a broad array of art forms and outlets for their dissemination. The American Assembly has grouped artists in this sector into three main categories. The first two are identified by the arena in which they work—that is, as employees or as freelance artists in either the commercial or the not-for-profit parts of the sector. The third group operates outside the scope of traditional labor market categories and can best be described as representing avocational or citizen-based artists. Second, there is a matrix of individuals and organizations involved in supporting and sustaining artists throughout their careers. This system of support serves commercial, non-for-profit, and avocational constituencies in various ways, including education, health care, and other forms of direct and indirect benefits such as privately and publicly sponsored grants and tax incentives. Third, while it is true that each of these sectoral groups has its own unique identity—often with different (and sometimes conflicting and competing) motivations, values, and interests—the dichotomy between the not-for-profit arts and the entertainment industry, the commercially based system of cultural production represented by entities such as Disney or Hollywood has made it very difficult to see the career matrix and pipeline for artists that flows across the commercial, not-for-profit, and avocational worlds. By focusing on the individual artist over time rather than concentrating solely on the venue in which the artistic creation occurs, we can present a more comprehensive picture of lifelong artistic behavior and a more vivid portrait of the arts sector at work in the United States.

Data on Artists

Who are artists in the United States? Where do they live and work? What do they do to earn a living? How did they become artists? And what kind of support is available to assist them in achieving their professional goals given the context of a segmented but interrelated arts sector? No one qualifier alone defines an individual as an artist. For the purposes of this study we will include artists' categories as those defined by the National Endowment for the Arts as well as those internationally defined within the broader context as "the Culture Industries," for example, radio, film, television, cable, and so on (UNESCO 1996, 1980).[1] There are many ways of examining the data on artists—for example, either by artistic occupations, stages of artists' professional life cycle such as education, the workplace, and their involvement in organized forms of support such as unions, foundations and government agencies. The bulk of this study we focus on occupations. However, we broaden the discussion by including the larger field, peers and institutions that are the gatekeepers of each artistic discipline, when we consider issues related to the structure and role of the underlying matrix of support. It is not our intent to comment on the art forms themselves, or on their audiences. While both may have significant impact on how artists operate, our primary focus is on the individual artist and the profile that emerges as s/he interacts over time with a wide range of arts-oriented organizations and how this constitutes both a conceptual and operational matrix.

The Data Sets

Three main sources of information have been used to develop this picture. The first, and in many ways the best source, is the information collected from national studies and other surveys. The second source is specifically designed surveys of artists and specific artists' groups. The third source is records from various arts organizations, especially unions, that collect information on their members.

National Studies. The largest and most widely used source of national information is the decennial census of the United States. This count of the population, required by the Constitution, has expanded over the decades to include the collection of a wide range of socioeconomic data on households, families, and individuals. Its strengths lie in several factors: (a) Its size permits detailed examination of artists in various occupations; (b) since the same categories of information are collected across occupations, comparisons to nonarts occupations are possible; (c) even given the difficulties associated with the definitions and information used in the Census, it provides the most accurate count of artists; and (d) since it is regularly repeated every ten years, it enables an examination of trends over time.

The major limitations of the Census information are: (a) The definition of "artist" is too broad; that is, it includes florists among the designers, palm readers among the artists "nec" (not elsewhere classified) occupation, and an elocutionist among the actors; (b) it misclassifies some artists, who are more likely than other workers to be multiple job holders, by basing the occupational classifications on the activity in which the individual spends the most time during the survey week; and (c) it ignores the uniqueness of the labor market experiences of artists, especially their multiple job-holding within and outside the arts, and its impact on their economic and artistic well-being.

Less extensive national household surveys, such as the Current Population Survey (CPS) and the National Science Foundation's 1993 Survey of College Graduates, tend to utilize the same definitions as the Census, and, therefore, they perpetuate the problems that are associated with it. In addition, they often are too small to provide reliable information on the various artist occupations.

Specially Designed Surveys. The major strength of specially designed surveys is their ability to focus on distinctive aspects of artists' careers and experiences, such as multiple job-holding within and outside the arts and its impact on their economic circumstances. They do address some of the deficiencies of the government's national surveys; however, a major drawback to the specialized surveys is that they are not obtained through a national or a random sampling process, so that the findings are not necessarily representative of the population of artists as a whole, but are limited to those who were able or willing to be surveyed. For example, the New England artists' study referred to throughout this chapter was based on a sampling of artists from various lists obtained from: artists' membership organizations, including unions (for example, Actors' Equity), and professional organizations (The League of New Hampshire Craftsmen); New England colleges and art schools (the New England Conservatory of Music); directories of artists (the Directory of American Poets and Writers); performing arts businesses (the Boston Ballet); and various arts associations throughout the region (the Worcester Craft Guild). Even though the lists of artists used for a specialized survey such as the New England study may seem comprehensive, they are likely to exclude groups of artists at various points in their careers due to a variety of reasons, including a change of residence, absence of professional association or union membership, or a school affiliation outside the sample parameters.

Studies Based on Association Records. The studies of artists based on the records from arts associations, especially unions, add a level of detail that cannot be readily obtained from any other source. For example, the studies based on the Writers' Guild of America West provide detailed industry- and firm-specific information on the earnings of writers in the television and film industries. The major drawback of this and similar studies is that they are limited to the information that the artist and the employer are required to provide. This is generally information regarding only earnings and working conditions from employment that is covered by the union contract. This information is needed to guarantee union minimums and other standards, and for participation in union-based health and benefit programs. Information on other aspects of employment is generally not available, nor is information on the socioeconomic characteristics of the artist and his/her family. Studies based on the records from arts associations, unlike special surveys, can be undertaken on a regular basis, allowing for comparisons over a time period that is likely to be more frequent than the ten-year span between censuses.

Who Are the Artists

The number of people identified by the Census as artists has grown considerably since 1970 (see tab 7.1). The data for the eleven Census occupations selected by the NEA to define the artist population show that the number of artists in the experienced civilian labor force has more than doubled.[2] The overall growth rate for the period was 127 percent. The number of artists in the labor force grew from approximately three-quarters of a million people in 1970 to 1.7 million in 1990. Using a somewhat less restrictive definition of the labor force, which included those who identified themselves as having worked as artists over the last five years but who were not currently working at present, the 1990 Census identified almost two million people as artists, out of a total U.S. civilian labor force of almost 125 million people.

The growth in number of artists was not uniform across artistic occupations (see tab. 7.1). Authors grew the most over the twenty-year period, an increase of almost 300 percent. The number of post-secondary-school art teachers actually declined by almost 50 percent over the same period. Where art teachers once accounted for 5 percent of all artists, they now account for only one percent. In comparison, the growth rate for artists was more than double the growth rate in the labor force as a whole, and was almost 50 percent higher than the growth rate in all the remaining nonartist professional occupations. This rapid growth in the number of people working as artists increased the proportion of artists in the overall labor force from just under one percent in 1970 to 1.37 percent in 1990 (Alper et al. 1996).

As a result of the differences in growth among different artist occupations, there has been a change in the composition in the overall artist occupation. Some of the most dramatic changes are in the relative size of the various artistic disciplines (see tab. 7.1). For example, the musicians and composers decreased in relative size since 1970 by almost 50 percent. On the other hand, those occupations that increased in relative size were the actors and directors, with a tripling in their share of artists. The largest group of artists, whose relative size grew very slightly over the twenty-year period, was designers. They continue to comprise about one-third of all artists.

Demographics

In 1990, the artistic workforce was 47 percent female, 10 percent nonwhite, and 3 percent Hispanic (see tab. 7.2). Artists are overwhelmingly white (87 percent). Blacks were underrepresented in the arts. They comprise just under 5 percent of the experienced civilian artist labor force while representing just over 10 percent of the total labor force.

Table 7.1. Artists in the Experienced Civilian Labor Force: 1970, 1980, 1990

	1970	1980	1990	GROWTH RATE
All artists	736,960	1,085,693	1,671,278	126.8%
Percent of labor force	.92	1.05	1.37	
Actor/director	39,969	66,782	109,573	174.1%
Percent of labor force	.05	.06	.09	
Percent of artists	2.1	2.2	6.4	
Announcer	25,942	46,986	60,270	132.2%
Percent of labor force	.03	.05	.05	
Percent of artists	3.3	4.5	3.4	
Architect	53,670	107,693	156,874	192.3%
Percent of labor force	.07	.10	.13	
Percent of artists	7.6	10.3	8.6	
Art teacher	42,000	28,385	21,393	-49.1%
Percent of labor force	.05	.03	.02	
Percent of artists	5.0	2.7	1.2	
Author	27,752	45,748	106,730	284.6%
Percent of labor force	.04	.04	.09	
Percent of artists	3.9	4.4	6.3	
Dancer	7,404	13,194	21,913	196.0%
Percent of labor force	.01	.01	.02	
Percent of artists	1.0	1.3	1.4	
Designer	232,890	338,374	596,802	156.3%
Percent of labor force	.29	.33	.49	
Percent of artists	33.3	32.5	35.9	
Musician/composer	99,533	140,556	148,020	48.7%
Percent of labor force	.13	.14	.12	
Percent of artists	14.5	13.5	9.4	
Painter/sculptor	86,849	153,162	212,762	145.0%
Percent of labor force	.11	.15	.17	
Percent of artists	12.8	14.7	12.6	
Photographer	67,588	94,762	143,520	112.3%
Percent of labor force	.09	.09	.12	
Percent of artists	12.8	14.7	12.6	
Artist nec	53,131	49,653	93,421	75.8%
Percent of labor force	.07	.05	.08	
Percent of artists	7.0	4.8	6.1	
Professionals	8,800,210	12,275,140	16,647,688	89.2%
Percent of labor force	10.99	11.80	13.53	
All workers	80,051,046	104,057,985	123,044,450	53.7%

SOURCE: D. Ellis and J. Beresford, *Trends in Artist Occupations, 1970–1990* (NEA, 1994), tab. 1–12, and authors' calculations.

The proportion of artists who are foreign-born and who are not citizens has grown. For example, in 1990, slightly more than 10 percent of artists were born outside the United States, and about 5 percent were not citizens.[3]

There are considerable differences in the demographic characteristics between artistic occupations (see tab. 7.2). Sixteen percent of architects and 80 percent of the dancers were female in 1990. Blacks comprised 9

Table 7.2. Demographic Characteristics of Artists by Occupation, 1990 (percent)

	MALE	FEMALE	WHITE	BLACK	HISPANIC	NATIVE AMERI- CAN	ASIAN AMERI- CAN	AGE (YEARS)
All artists	53.1	46.9	85.8	4.6	2.9	0.5	3.2	39.1
Actor/director	57.7	42.3	85.3	7.5	2.7	0.4	1.7	37.9
Announcer	78.2	21.8	85.6	9.3	1.9	0.9	1.5	31.9
Architect	84.1	15.9	90.6	2.9	3.4	0.3	4.8	40.4
Art teacher	45.0	55.0	90.6	5.1	2.0	0.8	2.3	43.1
Author	49.7	50.3	94.7	2.9	1.2	0.5	1.6	44.5
Dancer	21.7	78.3	84.3	7.2	4.4	1.7	4.8	28.5
Designer	41.3	58.7	90.4	3.3	2.8	0.4	3.8	39.2
Musician/composer	65.4	34.6	87.3	8.2	2.3	0.5	1.9	40.1
Painter/sculptor	45.4	54.6	91.2	3.5	2.7	0.9	2.6	40.2
Photographer	66.4	33.6	89.2	5.9	2.6	0.6	2.4	37.2
Artist nec	49.8	50.2	84.5	5.6	6.6	0.8	5.6	37.8
Professional/tech.	46.6	53.4	86.2	3.0	2.2	0.5	3.9	40.1

Source: Tabulations from the 1990 Census PUMS.

percent of the announcers but only 3 percent of the authors and architects. Hispanics, who comprised almost 3 percent of all artists, were only 1.2 percent of the authors but 4.4 percent of the dancers.

While the average age of artists at thirty-nine years has not changed much over the last twenty years, and was only slightly less than that for other professional/technical workers, there are considerable differences between the disciplines. The youngest artists, on average, were the dancers, at just over twenty-eight years old. In contrast, authors were the oldest artists, with an average age of just over forty-four years, and musicians had the greatest variation in age of any arts occupation.

Education, Training, and Retraining of Artists

One of the myths underlying the subject of the artist's education is the perception that it occurs outside the standard educational pathways; this is both correct and not correct. Artists may start training for their professions at very young ages. Like professional athletes who start their training through Little League, Pop Warner football, and community-based soccer programs, artists often follow a similar path. The average age at which artists started both their formal and informal artistic training was fifteen (Wassall, Alper, and Davison 1983, 24, tab. 2). Not only are there "soccer moms" there are "dance moms," too.

In the study of New England artists, the performing artists started training at the youngest ages. This was especially true for dancers and musicians. The average age at which the musicians started learning their art was just over nine, with female musicians starting approximately a year and a half earlier than males. One explanation is tied to elementary school performing arts programs. Students generally are invited to learn to play musical instruments when they enter the fourth grade. Choreographers, composers, and playwrights (a single occupational group in the New England study) started their training at about age ten, and the dancers at around age eleven. In both these occupations the female artists started learning their skills at a much younger age, almost six years earlier than their male colleagues. Private lessons may account for this gender variation. The exception to this pattern of early training was in the case of actors, who were found to start their training at about seventeen.

The Early Pipeline: K–12

Another myth about artists is that as a group, they are innately creative and have acted on their talents since birth. As psychologist Ellen Winner has documented in her study of gifted children, the arts do have early geniuses, but those going on to achieve adult mastery in a particular art form are not limited to child prodigies (Winner 1996). It requires more than talent to become a creative professional artist. Gifted children must develop the necessary discipline to make their mark upon a field. Many individuals who are not defined early as being gifted succeed as professional artists because they possess this drive. Thus, the deeper question is: What forces influence the success or failure of aspiring artists?

Formal and Informal Training

Career paths for artists must be understood as a blend of formal and informal training and support. The arts were cut back in traditional middle and high school curricula during the 1970s and 1980s. This may have increased the importance of specialty programs such as performing arts schools and extracurricular summer programs and private lessons. The vast majority (85 percent) of artists in the New England survey indicated that not only did they participate in specialized arts training as part of their formal education, but over three-quarters also participated in training outside the formal education system (Wassall, Alper, and Davison 1983, 24, tab. 3). Almost 98 percent of dancers received outside training, and even two-thirds of all writers and poets, who were the least likely to have received nonschool training, did so as well.

Young people training to become artists have a broader set of opportunities as part of their formal schooling than do those who are interested in becoming professional athletes. Athletes can, and do, participate in organized sports offered by their schools, but these opportunities tend to be extracurricular in nature. Young artists, on the other hand, can receive artistic training in a formal school environment in a variety of ways, often as an integral part of their academic programs. One option is public or private secondary schools specializing in the arts. In fact, almost 10 percent of the artists in the New England study said they had attended such schools (see tab. 7.3). Broken down by disciplines, almost 20 percent of dancers, and 15 percent of painters and sculptors, attended schools specializing in the arts. Only 3 percent of writers and poets surveyed attended. Those most likely to major in art during their secondary schooling were musicians, painters, and sculptors. While most secondary schools may not offer arts majors, they generally do offer students some courses and extracurricular arts activities such as drama club or band. More than one-fourth of the artists participated in the arts while attending high school. The only artistic occupations in which fewer than 20 percent had artistic training as part of their secondary school education were dancers, writers and poets.

Dancers constitute a unique group because of their early entry into the artistic pipeline: They are the youngest group with the least amount of formal education. The window of opportunity for entry into the profession is very short and occurs at a very young age, usually between fourteen and eighteen. Formal training at institutions can be expensive. For example, annual tuition, including room and board, at the School of American Ballet (SAB) in New York City is approximately $10,000. This includes partial tuition at a professional children's school (PCS) which itself can cost up to $14,000. Until 1991 there was no formal academic requirement at SAB. Currently, the school recognizes New York State law and mandates participation in some academic program until the age of sixteen. Those who do not attend a PCS are required to participate in home schooling or a correspondence program. Other artists enter the pipeline at later points, and a growing number of recognized artists receive their training outside the traditional educational pipeline, such as outsider artists, native artists, some folk artists, as well as artists in prisons and institutions such as hospitals and asylums (Zolberg and Cherbo 1997).

Higher Education

At the college level, a much wider range of training possibilities exists. This includes art schools that are either independent institutions, such as Juilliard and the Rhode Island School of Design, or

Table 7.3. Artistic Training as Part of Formal Education

	SECONDARY LEVEL			UNDERGRADUATE LEVEL			GRADUATE LEVEL		
	ART SCHOOL	ART MAJOR	NON-MAJOR	ART SCHOOL	ART MAJOR	NON-MAJOR	ART SCHOOL	ART MAJOR	NON-MAJOR
All artists	9.7	8.6	25.8	40.9	23.8	14.3	47.2	17.4	5.8
Actor	7.8	6.9	22.6	23.7	32.3	20.4	39.0	17.1	7.3
Choreographer, composer, playwright	9.7	8.6	30.1	23.6	40.4	24.7	47.5	34.4	3.3
Craft artist	8.9	6.9	21.9	35.8	19.2	16.0	36.3	21.1	6.6
Dancer	18.6	0.0	16.3	35.1	13.5	27.0	50.0	16.7	5.6
Media artist	4.0	3.6	22.7	31.5	19.2	16.0	36.1	20.0	8.2
Musician	8.8	12.9	40.6	58.2	19.7	10.8	63.7	10.6	5.5
Theater production personnel	7.8	12.1	36.2	38.4	39.3	10.7	50.7	26.0	2.7
Visual artist	14.3	9.8	24.0	53.3	24.7	9.3	59.1	15.4	3.7
Writers and poet	2.7	5.4	16.6	8.5	25.7	24.8	18.5	17.6	10.1

SOURCE: G. Wassall, N. Alper, and R. Davison, *Art Work: Artists in the New England Labor Market.* (Cambridge, Mass.: New England Foundation for the Arts, 1983), tab. 4, p. 27.

are an integral part of a college or university that has a wide range of academic programs, like the College of Fine Arts at Carnegie Mellon University. Forty percent of artists in the New England survey who went to college attended an undergraduate art school (see tab. 7.3). Almost 60 percent of the musicians did so, yet only 10 percent of the writers and poets did (understandable, given the inclusion of literature with standard academic programs). Almost one-quarter of those artists surveyed who attended college majored in an arts discipline as an undergraduate. Another 14 percent said they minored in an artistic field. Only 20 percent of the artists surveyed who attended college neither attended an art school nor majored in an artistic field.

A more recent survey of college graduates done in 1993 (NSCG) found that almost 28 percent of artists with a bachelor's degree majored in a visual or performing art. At the postbaccalaureate level, the proportion of artists majoring in an art field was higher. Slightly more than one-third of artists with a master's degree majored in an arts field, and more than half those with doctorates did as well.[4] The survey also found that of those artists who reported having completed a second major or minor as part of their bachelor's degree, almost 20 percent did so in an art field. For the master's degree and the doctorate, those taking a second major or minor in an arts field were 24 and 26 percent, respectively.

According to the 1990 Census, artists were well educated (see tab.

Table 7.4. *Highest Level of Educational Attainment of Artists by Occupation, 1990 (percent)*

PROF.	KG	1–4	5–8	9–12	HS	SOME COLLEGE	ASSOC. DEG.	BA	MA	OTHER DOC.
All Artists	0.3	0.2	1.1	5.7	16.0	25.1	9.3	30.7	9.1	1.1	1.5
Actor/Director	0.1	0.1	0.3	3.2	13.2	24.6	6.4	42.1	11.6	1.1	1.1
Announcer	0.7	0.2	0.1	0.3	10.2	18.6	37.2	8.7	21.0	2.3	0.1
Architect	0.1	0.1	0.2	0.3	4.7	10.9	4.9	51.3	19.2	0.7	7.1
Art Teacher	—	—	—	0.2	3.6	11.6	2.9	20.5	46.7	12.2	2.3
Author	0.2	—	0.2	1.6	4.8	15.8	3.8	43.3	21.1	6.4	3.0
Dancer	0.8	0.3	2.5	18.0	30.5	27.5	3.8	13.8	2.7	0.1	0.4
Designer	0.3	0.3	1.4	6.4	19.8	25.9	12.4	28.3	4.5	0.2	0.7
Musician/ Composer	0.7	0.4	1.9	7.3	16.3	28.9	5.1	24.2	13.1	1.3	0.9
Painter/ Sculptor	0.3	0.2	0.8	4.9	16.2	27.5	12.1	29.7	7.3	0.4	0.7
Photographer	0.3	0.1	1.0	7.0	21.1	30.4	9.7	25.9	3.6	0.3	0.6
Artist NEC	0.4	0.3	1.9	8.4	18.6	27.9	8.4	21.4	9.2	2.3	1.1

SOURCE: Tabulations from the 1990 Census PUMS.
NOTES:

KG: Kindergarten or less	HS: High school diploma/GED	MA: Master's degree
1–4: First through fourth grades	Some College: Attended college	Doctoral degree
5–8: Fifth through eighth grades	Assoc. Deg.: Associate's degree	Prof.: Other
9–12: Ninth through twelfth grade, no high school diploma	BA: Bachelor's degree	professional degree

7.4). More than three-quarters had formal schooling beyond a high school diploma, and more than 40 percent had completed a bachelor's degree or higher. Dancers were the exception with respect to formal education, as more than half the dancers had a high school diploma or less. In every other artistic occupation, fewer than 30 percent did not go beyond high school. Seventeen percent of dancers had a bachelor's degree or better, compared with 56 percent of the actors and directors. Given the greater amount of academic training necessary, architects and post-secondary-school teachers had a bachelor's degree or better.

Additional Training

Not only do artists start their artistic training at a young age, but many continue to receive education and training throughout their careers. The New England survey found that approximately 40 percent of the artists had participated in an organized class or training program with the purpose of improving their professional abilities (Wassall, Alper, and Davison 1983, 29, tab. 5). The artists' participation was across the board, but not uniform Slightly more than 70 percent of dancers and only about one-third of writers and poets had done so. Those artists who participated in a program averaged a little more than eleven hours per week and almost seventeen weeks during the year in additional training. Dancers spent most of the year in such classes, a little more than thirty-two weeks, but they spent fewer than nine hours per week. Craft and media artists spent the most time per week, about seventeen hours, but the fewest weeks, only about nine, in a training program.

According to the NSCG, many artists continue their formal education as well. Even after completing their highest degree, more than 40 percent enrolled in additional arts courses. Additionally, the NSCG found that half the college-educated artists had participated in a work-related workshop or seminar during the past year.

Apprenticeships and Internships

In many arts disciplines, working is very much tied to membership in some form of professional organization or union. In the New England survey more than half of the artists were members of a professional association (Alper and Wassall 1984).[5] Not surprisingly, membership was particularly high among performing artists and writers whose unions play an important role in inducting new members into the field. The performing arts for which traditional union-based apprenticeship programs have existed used to be found among those unions that organized "below the line" workers, or the nonperforming technical workers, in the industry. The training function of on-the-job apprenticeship tended to be through hands-on work experience, such as that of an apprentice grip.

In the last few years, training has moved outside the unions and has been academized, moving to film and television schools or preprofessional programs in colleges, where skills for the technical crafts and the talent fields now are subject to educational policies and practices as well as those of the workplace. According to a recent study of unions in the arts and entertainment industry, most apprenticeship programs have been eliminated due to "frustration of potential industry entrants, the disgruntlement of employers over labor supply conditions, and the introduction of new production technology" (Christopherson 1996, 108). In addition, over the years there has been a blurring of the various roles in the industry—labor, supervisory, and management—that has created problems for the traditional union structures, including apprenticeship programs. While union-based programs have decreased, college-based internships and state and local arts agencies-sponsored apprenticeship programs have expanded across the arts sector.

Postprofessional Concerns: Retraining

All art forms have active professional stages, with some longer than others. Once this active stage is over, because of natural cycles or due to injury, most performing artists are faced with issues of retraining for a job outside their original career track. Nowhere is this issue as crucial as in the field of dance, where practitioners begin at a relatively young age and eschew formal academic training, compared to other artists. One of the most common aspects of retraining is to move into a niche related to the original art form, as evidenced in the *Dancemaker* study of the career paths of choreographers (Netzer and Parker 1993), where the majority of the respondents had turned to choreography after careers as dancers.

There are issues of retraining within most art forms as well as issues of training for entry into completely different arts or non-arts field. In the field of dance, a number of support groups have been formed to assist in retraining. Performing arts unions such as the American Guild of Musical Artists (AGMA) have been particularly active in assisting artists such as dancers to reinvent themselves professionally. In addition, in 1985, Agnes de Mille founded Career Transitions for Dancers, in conjunction with other ballet and musical-theater dancers (with the support of the unions). Career Transitions's mission is to offer career seminars, skills assessment, and support through retraining grants. One unexpected and positive consequence of this effort has been the creation of an informal support network of dancers who have been recycled into the nonarts workplace. A similar program, the International Organization for the Transition of Professional Dancers, was created in 1993, with nineteen member countries. Private scholarship funds also exist to assist older dancers and academically oriented programs such as Dance On funnel younger dancers into General Education Degree (GED) programs and college courses on their way to other careers. As artists in other art forms tend to have more formal academic training than dancers, issues such as high school equivalency are not as crucial for them as are career retraining programs.

There are myriad reasons that such varied educational training is needed, including mastery of the knowledge base and skills involved in each arts discipline; artistic and academic credentialing; and socialization into the formal and informal norms of the arts fields.

One justification for formal education for artists is the belief that increased education will result in greater monetary remuneration; that is, the more degrees, the more dollars. Evidence both supports and challenges this notion. The view from the Census data, which does not differentiate among sources of earnings, suggests that artists' education plays an important role in career advancement and economic success. Several studies have concurred that additional years of formal schooling significantly increase earnings and that the return to the artist is worth the investment (Alper and Wassall 1994, tab. 2–30; Filer 1986a). Yet the New England study, in which a distinction can be made among three sources of earnings, finds that formal education had a positive impact on career advancement and economic success when artists worked at jobs related to their art, such as teaching, but not necessarily when they worked in their art form. The lack of formal education of many successful artists suggests that it is not a barrier to career advancement. However, education is a must for some artistic fields and can be an important avenue for entry into the professional pipeline for other artistic fields.

Where Artists Work

Artists live and work throughout the country. This can be examined relative to a number of dimensions, including geographic location, the industry, and the type of business. It also can be tracked by the art forms they work in as well as by the industries that employ them. The geographical distribution of workplaces for artists clearly reflects, in part, the relative size of the market for their work in a particular location. While some artists, particularly the visual and graphic artists, have more options due to such factors as the physical and technological flexibility of their art forms, for others, particularly those who perform live and onstage, location plays an important role in their career possibilities.

Geographical Location: The Top Ten States

Ten states account for 60 percent of the workplaces for artists in 1990. The same ten states also account for approximately 54 percent of total artistic employment in the United States, indicating that artists are somewhat overrepresented in these states. The largest number of artists worked in California: more than 260,000 artists, or almost 17 percent of all artists. New York had the second largest number of artists: almost 180,000, or slightly more than 11 percent. Texas was next, with almost 90,000 artists, almost 6 percent of the total. Yet Texas, along with the remainder of the top ten states, had significantly less artistic employment than California and New York combined. Following Texas, in decreasing order, were Florida, Illinois, Pennsylvania, Ohio, Michigan, Massachusetts, and New Jersey.

Within different artistic disciplines there are some interesting anomalies in the top ten places of work. The state of Washington was among the favorite places of work for architects. While it is no surprise that California is by far the most popular place of work for actors and directors (with more than 25 percent working there), Washington, D.C., was also among the ten top places for them to be found. Among the top ten places of employment for announcers was Georgia, home of CNN. Authors, like actors, found Washington, D.C., a popular place, but they found working on the west side of the Potomac River in Virginia just as congenial. Certainly reflective of employment opportunities for dancers is the finding that Nevada is the fifth most popular place of work. There is little mystery as to why Tennessee, as the center of the country music industry, is one of the top ten spots for musicians, but it is more of a challenge to explain why Indiana and Minnesota are among the top ten locations of employment for post-secondary-school art teachers.

Top Industries for Artists

Artists work in a variety of industries. Artists are found in all thirteen major industry groups used by the Census.[6] Perhaps surprisingly, the industry with the largest proportion of all artists in 1990 was not the entertainment and recreation services industry, but the professional services industry, which employed one quarter of all artists. In part this is an artifact of the federal government's industrial classification scheme, which places "establishments primarily providing services, not elsewhere classified, such as authors . . . , songwriters . . . , writers, and artists working on their own account" in this industry, along with artists who work in colleges museums, architectural firms, and religious organizations (*Standard Industrial Classification Manual* 1987, 406). The second largest industry of employment for artists was retail trade, with almost 16 percent of all artists employed there. (Included in this industry were nightclubs, restaurants, bars, and florists.) Then came entertainment and recreation services, providing employment for 13 percent of all artists. The fourth largest was business and repair services, which included commercial photography art and graphic design firms, advertising, and interior decorating and designers, which represented more than 12 percent of all the artists. The industry that employed the fewest artists in 1990 was the finance, insurance, and real estate industry, which employed only one percent of them.

Closer examination of the industries in which artists were employed reveals findings that reflect the breadth of the artists in practice. For example, the second largest employer of architects, after architectural firms, were businesses in the landscape and horticulture service industry, with construction being the third largest employer. Authors were highly concentrated, with more than half in the miscellaneous professional services industry, for reasons just discussed, with the next three industries being the printing and publishing industry, excluding newspapers, theaters and motion pictures, and colleges and universities. The two industries that were the most likely to employ designers were the retail florist industry and the business services "nec" industry, followed by printing and publishing, with 5 percent of the designers. Almost half of the musicians were employed in the theater and motion picture industry, but surprisingly almost one-quarter were employed by religious organizations, making them the second largest employer of musicians. About 6 percent worked in eating and drinking establishments, the third largest industry for musicians' employment. There were no surprises for actors and directors. Employment in theater, motion pictures, television, and radio account for the vast majority (83 percent), with colleges and universities next, accounting for 5 percent of their employment. Miscellaneous professional services industry was the largest place of employment for painters and sculptors, and accounted for 31 percent of the painters. Dancers were essentially found in three industries. One-third were employed in miscellaneous entertainment and recreational services, which includes dance studios and other leisure activities. Another third were employed in the theater and motion picture industry, while cne-quarter were employed in eating and drinking establishments. The artists in the "nec" category were primarily employed in theaters, miscellaneous entertainment, and schools at all levels.

Workplace Venues

Artists are found working in a variety of different environments. They can be employees of either private for-profit businesses, private not-for-profit organizations and businesses, or governments at the federal, state, or local levels. They may choose to be self-employed—that is, working for themselves in their own unincorporated or incorporated businesses[7] or they can work as volunteers.

While the American Assembly has divided the arts sector into three parts—commercial, not-for-profit, and unincorporated or avocational—the Census divides artists into four similar, but not parallel sectoral groups. They are: the private for-profit or commercial sector, the private not-for-profit sector, the government sector, and the self-employed sector. The Census's self-employed designation encompasses artists who are freelancers and can work in either a commercial or a not-for-profit organization and possibly for an unincorporated group. Unfortunately, as the Census does not distinguish the source of earnings, the exact labor market alignment of these artists in any particular part of the arts sector is unknown. Therefore, based on the results of specially designed surveys such as the New England study conducted to date, freelance artists can best be described as "crossover" artists who have the greatest potential to shed light on the movement of artists between the commercial and the not-for-profit parts of the arts sector (Galligan and Alper 1998).

Given this caveat, the majority of artists according to the 1990 Census (more than half) worked as employees of a commercial business (see tab. 7.5). Slightly more than one quarter of the artists were self-employed; the majority of the writers, more than one-third of the visual artists and musicians, and approximately one-quarter of the photographers, architects, and artists "nec." Just under 7 percent of all artists were employees of not-for-profit concerns, a surprisingly low figure given the visibility of the not-for-profit sector. Nearly one-third of the musicians and almost one-quarter of the post-secondary-school teachers were employed in the not-for-profit sector. The only other artist occupations in which more than 10 percent of their members were employed in the not-for-profit sector were the dancers, actors, and directors. Among the 25 percent of the artists who identified themselves as self-employed, many may work in the nonprofit sector. This may account for the relatively small percentage of artists who fall within this sector according to the Census count. The government was not a significant place of employment for artists, with the exception of art teachers. Overall, slightly more than 6 percent of all artists were government employees, with almost half employed by state governments.

The Myth of the Starving Artist

There are two characteristics of artists' work experience that have become almost apocryphal and are directly tied to the starving-artist myth. The first is that all artists drive taxicabs or wait on tables when they are not working as artists, and the second is that they are working at both jobs at the same time in order to survive. Like most stories, there is at least a grain of truth to both. Census data and similar surveys are unable to address these issues because respondents are asked to identify only their chief job or business activity in the week prior to the survey week. The CPS has only recently started asking, on a regular basis, whether a person holds more than one job at a time, but it does not identify work that the artist may have done at other times during the year. The specialized artist surveys have provided the best, most consistent information on both these matters.

The New England survey asked artists to distinguish three types of work they may have participated in: work as an artist; work in an arts-related job, such as teaching art or working as an arts administrator; and work in a non-arts-related job, such as driving a taxi or waiting on tables. Only 24 percent of the artists indicated working solely as artists (Wassall,

Table 7.5. Employment Venue of Artists by Gender, 1990 (percent)

	EMPLOYEE—COMMERCIAL	EMPLOYEE—PRIVATE NOT FOR PROFIT	SELF-EMPLOYED	GOVERNMENT	ALL (NUMBER)
All artists	55.0	6.9	30.9	6.4	1,988,186
Male	54.6	6.0	32.0	7.0	1,055,113
Female	55.5	8.0	29.8	5.5	933,073
Actor	60.4	13.1	19.3	6.8	127,601
Male	61.0	11.5	20.9	6.4	73,613
Female	59.7	15.4	17.0	7.1	53,988
Announcer	83.0	5.8	7.6	3.4	68,348
Male	83.0	5.0	8.8	3.2	53,417
Female	82.9	8.7	3.3	4.3	14,931
Architect	581	1.2	33.0	7.4	170,470
Male	57.0	1.2	34.5	7.0	143,413
Female	63.5	1.4	24.6	9.3	27,057
Author	25.5	6.6	58.0	8.3	125,460
Male	25.8	5.9	59.0	8.2	62,333
Female	25.2	7.4	57.1	8.4	63,127
Dancer	67.9	11.7	18.1	2.0	28,103
Male	50.9	25.2	21.5	2.1	6,107
Female	72.6	8.0	17.1	1.9	21,996
Designer	70.4	1.8	24.2	2.6	713,533
Male	72.3	2.0	21.1	4.2	294,740
Female	69.0	1.7	26.4	1.6	418,793
Musician	24.6	32.1	37.3	5.6	186,913
Male	28.8	19.9	45.0	6.1	122,205
Female	16.7	55.3	22.7	4.9	64,708
Photographer	54.2	3.0	34.5	7.6	172,482
Male	49.0	3.1	38.9	8.6	114,558
Female	64.5	2.9	25.9	5.5	57,924
Teacher (postsecondary)	17.6	24.7	0.0	57.2	24,661
Male	15.2	23.5	0.0	61.3	11,109
Female	19.6	25.6	0.0	54.8	13,552
Visual Artist	44.4	2.9	46.9	4.7	250,067
Male	45.9	2.9	44.9	5.5	113,572
Female	43.1	2.9	48.5	4.0	136,495
Artist nec	43.4	9.9	26.8	19.2	120,548
Male	45.1	9.1	29.0	16.3	60,046
Female	41.6	10.8	24.6	22.0	60,502

SOURCE: Author's tabulations from the 1990 U.S. Census PUMS.

Alper, and Davison 1983, 32, tab 7). The remainder indicated that they had held at least one of the other types of jobs during the year. Those artists who were most likely to work during the year outside their artistic occupation were choreographers, composers, and playwrights (90 percent), musicians (86 percent), and dancers, writers, and poets (84 percent). Those most likely to work only as artists and hold no other job during the year were visual artists (27 percent), craft artists (34 percent), and actors (37 percent). Similar patterns were found in other surveys of artists in the United States and throughout the world.

More than half the artists in the New England study had held an arts-related job at some time during the previous year. The choreographers, composers, and playwrights were the most likely to have held arts-related jobs (almost 80 percent). Two-thirds of the dancers and musicians also spent time doing arts-related work. The actors and the crafts artists were the least likely to have done this type of work, approximately 40 percent of both groups. The vast majority of the artists, almost 80 percent, who did arts-related work, taught their art. This could have been in a formal school environment or in the form of private lessons. Almost 10 percent worked in arts management, and 6 percent had other professional and technical jobs in the arts field (Wassall, Alper, and Davison 1983, 34, tab. 8).

Slightly more than one-third of all artists surveyed worked in a non-arts-related position. The writers were the most likely to do this, while dancers and actors were only slightly behind in holding such a job. Approximately one-third of musicians, visual artists, and crafts artists held nonarts jobs. The choreographers, composers, and playwrights were the least likely, probably because most of them were already working in an arts-related job along with their artwork. The primary occupation for these jobs was not waiting on tables, as only 14 percent of the nonarts jobs were service ones, nor was it driving a cab, as only 5 percent held those jobs. The most commonly held non-arts-related occupations were nonteaching professional and technical occupations, for example, working as lawyers, doctors, or computer programmers, at 20 percent. Nonarts teaching was the next most likely occupation, followed by clerical worker, and sales and managerial jobs.

With all these artists working outside their artistic occupation, a reasonable question to ask is: Why? Not surprisingly, the primary reason given in the New England study for taking on other work was economic (Wassall, Alper, and Davison 1983, 37, tab. 11). More than 60 percent worked outside their art because it paid better. Almost half indicated that their nonarts job provided better job security. Half indicated they took on other work because there was not enough work available in their

Table 7.6. New England Artists—Labor Market Crossovers

	ACTOR	CCP[a]	CRAFT ART-IST	DANCER	MEDIA ART-IST	MUSI-CIAN	THEA-TER[b]	VIS-UAL ARTIST	WRITER/ POET	ALL ART-ISTS
Weeks worked:										
Art	27.4	26.9	37.6	27.3	37.7	32.9	34.7	39.7	33.6	36.1
Art-related	12.3	27.8	12.3	23.5	13.8	26.3	23.7	15.6	16.6	17.3
Non-art-related	10.6	8.1	10.6	11.3	13.0	12.8	9.1	11.5	15.5	11.8
Total	38.5	44.7	46.1	43.1	46.2	46.1	46.0	46.8	46.2	46.0
Income/earning (1981 dollars)										
Arts earnings	15,597	4,053	6,166	5,249	8,691	6,453	9,127	6,037	3,947	6,420
Art-related earnings	1,632	10,763	2,839	3,214	3,420	6,000	6,102	4,632	5,828	4,743
Non-arts-related earnings	2,433	2,230	2,403	2,942	3,949	3,515	1,997	2,444	4,182	2,916
Total income[c]	22,032	18,495	12,820	11,445	18,137	16,934	18,681	14,588	16,501	15,644

SOURCE: G. Wassell, N. Alper, and R. Davison, *Art Work: Artists in the New England Labor Market.*
(Cambridge, Mass.: New England Foundation for the Arts, 1983), tab. 13, p. 39, and tab. 22, p. 55.
NOTES:
[a] Choreographers, composers, and playwrights
[b] Theater production personnel
[c] Total income includes all earnings from work (artistic, art-related, and non-art-related earnings) and nonlabor income (e.g., interest, Social Security, and welfare).

artistic field. Only 4 percent indicated that they actually preferred their nonarts work to their work as artists, while almost 40 percent indicated that they worked outside their art because they felt it complemented their work as artists.

The Artist as Job Juggler

With all this work effort on the part of artists, the question remains: Where do artists find the time? The answer is very simple; many of them work more than one job at the same time. Multiple job-holding is not unique to artists, but it is a behavior that is more likely among artists than other occupations. Based on the May 1991 CPS, the federal government's national household survey used primarily to obtain monthly unemployment statistics, the multiple job-holding rates for artists were 25 percent higher than for other professional/technical workers (Alper et al. 1996, tab. 17, p. 42). Almost 11 percent of all artists were simultaneously working at more than one job during the survey week. The artists with the highest multiple job-holding rates were the post-secondary-school teachers at 25 percent, followed by authors (21 percent) and musicians (21 percent). Those with the lowest rates were architects

Table 7.7. New England Artists—Artistic Crossovers (percent)

	ACTOR	CCP[a]	CRAFT ART-IST	DANCER	MEDIA ART-IST	MUSI-CIAN	THEA-TER[b]	VIS-UAL ARTIST	WRITER/ POET	NO SECOND OCCU-PATION
Actor	17.6	2.9	1.0	1.0	2.0	8.8	13.7	2.9	6.9	43.1
CCP[a]	6.6	5.5	0.0	12.1	1.1	22.0	11.0	3.3	5.5	33.0
Craft artist	0.4	0.4	10.1	0.2	1.8	0.7	1.3	15.5	2.4	67.2
Dancer	4.8	38.1	0.0	9.5	0.0	4.8	4.8	4.8	2.4	31.0
Media artist	0.0	1.0	2.5	0.0	11.3	1.5	1.0	10.8	3.0	69.0
Musician	1.4	7.4	1.4	0.7	0.2	58.1	0.7	1.2	2.1	26.9
Theater[b]	11.4	11.4	3.5	0.9	0.9	3.5	31.6	7.0	3.5	26.3
Visual artist	0.6	0.4	9.1	0.1	3.3	1.5	0.1	27.1	1.9	55.9
Writer/Poet	1.0	4.9	1.9	0.0	3.9	1.9	1.9	4.9	23.1	56.5

SOURCE: G. Wassall, N. Alper, and R. Davison, *Art Work: Artists in the New England Labor Market.* (Cambridge, Mass.: New England Foundation for the Arts, 1983), tab. A-3, p. 184.
NOTES:
[a] Choreographers, composers, and playwrights
[b] Theater production personnel

and photographers, both around 6 percent. Looking at the average number of weeks worked in each type of job in the New England study, the total number of weeks worked averaged sixty-six, which can only be due to multiple job holding (see tab. 7.6).

Another work-related characteristic that distinguishes artists from other professional/technical workers is that many work in more than one artistic occupation. For example, there are painters who sculpt, actors who write, and dancers who choreograph. Many of the artists in the New England study indicated that they worked in at least one other second arts occupation during the year—for example, ballet dancers who also perform in another dance form such as jazz or tap (see tab. 7.7).

Artists' Working Conditions

The Census provides information on how much time artists spend working. Unfortunately, it does not distinguish between the many activities they may participate in during the year. In 1990, the vast majority of artists (70 percent) were characterized as full-time workers. Typically, they worked at least thirty-five hours per week. A smaller proportion of artists (60 percent) would have been characterized as working a full year of fifty weeks. Architects were by far the most likely to have worked full-time and full-year, with almost three-quarters having achieved that status, and an additional 17 percent worked full-time for less than the full year. Dancers were the least likely to have worked full-time and full-year, only 20 percent.

The Glass Ceiling in the Arts: Issues of Gender, Race, and Ethnicity

There are some differences in the artistic work environment related to gender, race, and/or ethnic background. The major gender differences are that female artists were more likely to have been employed in not-for-profit businesses than males by about one-third, and that male artists were about 50 percent more likely to be self-employed than females. With regard to race and ethnic origin, black, Hispanic, and Asian American artists were all more likely than white artists to be employees of private for-profit businesses and less likely to be self-employed (see tab. 7.5). Native American artists were less likely to work in a commercial business than white artists and more likely to be employees of a not-for-profit concern. Blacks were also slightly more likely to be employed in a private not-for-profit business than any other group.

In some arts occupations there were considerable differences in the amount of time female artists worked. The largest difference was among musicians, among whom the proportion of women working full-time was only 60 percent that of male musicians. Among the post-secondary-school art teachers the difference was only slightly better, with the proportion of women working full-time being 63 percent of that of male teachers. For most of the remaining occupations the proportion was between 70 and 80 percent. On a positive note, among architects, actors, and directors, the proportion of women working full-time was approximately 90 percent the proportion of men. The comparison between men and women working full-year shows much greater similarity. In the majority of the occupations the proportion was between 80 and 85 percent. Finally, women artists were much less likely to work full-time and full-year than males, 40 percent compared to 60 percent of the men.

Health Insurance and Other Benefits

Of the many benefits that artists should expect from the workplace, quality of life issues are essential (Jeffri, Hosie, and Greenblat 1987). Eighty-two percent of all respondents in this study had some medical coverage, 44 percent had life insurance, 43 had a retirement plan. Fifty-one percent had been exposed to work-related occupational hazards. Coupled with the fact that almost 6 percent of artists had some form of physical disability that restricted their ability to work, health care is clearly an important workplace issue for artists, as it is for all workers. In 1993 a task force formed by the Boston Mayor's Office of Cultural Affairs, The Artists Foundation, and Boston Health Care for the Homeless concluded that artists were being excluded from the national health care debate and were not being viewed as a unique constituency with unique needs (Artists' Foundation, and Boston Health Care for the Homeless 1994, 11). A 1991 national study by the American Council of the Arts concluded that 30 percent of all performing, literary, and visual artists in large cities are without health insurance, almost twice the national average. Of those without insurance, 55 percent were between thirty-six and forty-five. The study found that artists who derived more of their income from their artistic endeavor were less likely to have insurance than those whose primary source of earnings came from their nonarts employment. Fifty-seven percent of the artists with insurance were covered by a plan through an employer, government, or parent. Complicating this profile, artists tend to be categorized as a high-risk population by many insurance companies because of the perception of a high incidence of HIV and AIDS, fluctuation in incomes, and/or low income, and the occupational hazards associated with working with potentially toxic materials.

Poverty Among Artists: Does the Winner Really Take All?

In any discussion of the working conditions of artists it is important to discuss the topic of their economic status. What follows is an overview. A detailed discussion can be found in the recent NEA report on artists in the work force from 1970 to 1990 (Alper et al. 1996). The average total earnings for artists in the experienced civilian labor force in 1989 (from the 1990 Census) was $23,992, which was approximately $7,200 less than the average for all professional and technical workers. In 1990 dollars, architects had the highest average earnings of approximately $40,000, and dancers the lowest, $12,200. In between, in order of decreasing average earnings, were actors, authors, designers, photographers, art teachers, announcers, artist "nec," and musicians. The estimated hourly wage earned by artists in 1989 was $16.76 compared to $17.31 for all professional and technical workers. This suggests that much of the observed earnings difference between artists and other professional/technical workers was the difference in the number of hours worked, not in how the market compensated their work.

Aggregate earnings figures mask the answer to two important questions regarding economic well-being. One is: How widespread is the problem of poverty among artists? In this instance, is the starving-artist myth reality or fiction? Poverty status is determined by the federal government based on standards established by the Social Security Administration in 1963 using the U.S. Department of Agriculture's least costly, nutritionally adequate food plan as the basis, along with annual adjustments for inflation. Poverty is a family concept, so the income from all family members, not simply the artist's, is taken into account. Slightly more than 7 percent of artists were in families that were officially poor. In comparison the poverty rate for all professional/technical workers was less than half the artists' rate, at a little more than 3 percent. The New England study determined that there are two factors that fend off poverty for artists. One is that without working outside the arts occupation, it is likely that artists' economic status would be much worse. It was found that artists' earnings from working in their field was only 40 percent of their total income (Wassall, Alper, and Davison 1983, 55, tab. 22). Earnings from arts-related work accounted for one-third their earnings, with the remainder from working in nonarts jobs. The second factor is that without other members of the family working, poverty would have been much more pervasive among the artists. While artists' income was, on average, almost 60 percent of their family's income, the absence of the other family members' earnings would have had a serious impact on their well-being.

The other half of the question is: Does the winner really take all? How risky is it to enter and attempt to thrive in an arts occupation? One answer (as in the case of professional sports), is that there are some artists who are very successful, and the chance of being among the select is sufficient to attract many people to the field. Interestingly, one of the reasons cited for a decrease in the popularity of ballet as a career option is the lack of existing big stars to attract new members.[8] An examination of the variation in earnings from the 1990 Census is revealing. It shows that nine among the top fifteen professional occupations with the highest variability in earnings were arts occupations. Greater variability in earnings means that there are relatively few artists at both extreme ends of the earnings distribution, but that there also exists a great difference between the extremes and the average earnings. While athletes showed the most variability, the next six occupations in order of decreasing variability in earnings are: musicians, announcers, authors, artists "nec," and visual artists. Photographers are ninth, dancers twelfth, and designers fifteenth. In plain language, this means that when artists, such as musicians, make it, they make it big relative to the average musician, though few ever reach such heights.

The Matrix of Support for Artists

A 1995 *Washington Post* article, "The Winners Take All," noted that there is a widening gap in a growing number of fields between winners and losers, including the arts (Pearlstein 1995). Three main factors are involved in creating this phenomenon in the arts: the growth in global markets especially for stars; shifting creative capital, which effects artist occupations; and changing patterns in arts patronage. To understand this phenomenon, it is imperative to explore the career path of the individual artist in relation to the larger matrix of individuals and organizations that function as an interactive system which creates, promotes, supports, distributes and preserves the commercial, not-for-profit arts, and amateur arts.

The Arts Go Global

According to Robert Frank and Philip Cook, the authors of *The Winner-Take-All Society* (1995) what distinguishes the modern economy is the degree to which small differences in talent (and luck) can equal great difference in status and financial reward. They argue that what distinguishes the new global economy is not simply that the supply and demand for skills has changed, but that labor markets now balance supply and demand in different ways that favor top performers. According to Frank and Cook, technology and market conditions created by the modern global economy are largely behind the paradigm shift. Artists no longer perform in the Opera House on Main Street but in the "Cyber Cafe" of the Global Village, standing the traditional relationship between suppliers and customers literally on end. Ramifications of this movement are evident in the arts arena from "canned music in the pit" to Brad Pitt at the international box office. Driving this new paradigm is the power of networks, and the power of individuals and institutions to capitalize on global advances in information technology and rapidly changing business strategies. As in the case of union-based apprenticeship programs, technology was a major factor in shifting training outside unions and into more academic settings thus altering the pipeline for new entrants. Currently the reverse is occurring in the film industry, where technology and the immediate demand for technically savvy designers is driving the search outside the traditional academic pipeline.

Yet successful acts of creativity, even in the global marketplace, cannot be understood by focusing on changing and technological market conditions alone. Equally important in the implementation of these advances is accreditation from professionals in the field. Mihalyi Csikszentmihalyi speaks to this phenomenon. He defines creativity as encompassing any act, idea, or product that changes an existing domain (or discipline) into a new entity (1996, 28). Artistic creativity results from the interaction of a system or matrix composed of three elements: a culture that contains symbolic rules, a person who brings novelty into the symbolic domain, and a field of experts who recognize and validate the innovation (6). A domain cannot be altered without the explicit or implicit consent of a field of experts responsible for it, (that is, its gatekeepers). It is a given that one of the primary roles of educators, mentors, and their respective institutions is to assist individual artists in mastering the content and skills of their discipline in gaining what Bourdieu (1984) has termed "cultural capital." Yet an equally important role for the field is defining the norms and protocols for induction and acceptance of new members.

Shifting Creative Capital

According to Csikszentmihalyi, in order for an artist to achieve creativity, there must be "surplus attention available," or time for the artist to experiment and "play" with ideas and master art forms (8). Jane Picker Firstenberg, director of The American Film Institute, describes the accelerating pace of technological change as having a major impact on training resources and on overall cultural literacy as well.[9] Noting both a current shortage of digitally savvy artists as well as a long-term crisis in funding and nurturing artists made worse by cutbacks in K–12 arts education, she laments a drop in cinematic literacy. "While independent American films and filmmakers have become the equivalent of rock stars today, the horizon of most young filmgoers has contracted."

The American Film Institute report concludes, "The arts and arts education are rooted in aesthetics and craft, whatever the tool." Support for better access to the tools made possible by new technologies is outpacing the support for arts education and overall aesthetic literacy. The accompanying explosion of new media has opened new career paths in the arts, but it poses new challenges for artistic mastery. One possible implication of this shift is that academic institutions will be forced to reconsider their role as gatekeepers to the profession. The primary focus of the first part of this study has been on artists' direct earnings and related issues concerning their individual welfare. We need to reconsider what constitutes a conducive climate for artists to flourish in American society. What will allow artists the time to learn requisite skills—both technical and aesthetic—to experiment, and to extend the boundaries of their disciples? The role of income in the form of fellowships, grants, and residencies must be considered in this regard.

Changing Patterns of Artist Patronage

Perhaps one of the most significant changes in the profile of the matrix of support for individual artists over the past four decades has been the shift in institutional patronage, both public and private (Galligan 1993). A significant catalyst has been the cutback of funding for individual artists from the NEA.

The Federal Response: The NEA

During the 1990 Reauthorization Hearings, both the NEA and Congress recognized the positive aspects of funding individual artists. Yet a growing debate ensued over the appropriate means of achieving these objectives. Prominent individual artists such as Andres Serrano, Karen Finley, Holly Hughes, and others challenged America's sensibilities, and drew the wrath of congressional and social critics. Pressure was brought to bear to end federal funding to individual artists. Federal programs involving fellowships and commissions were subsequently phased out, with the exception of those designated for writers. In addition, the cuts had a direct negative impact on some state and regional programs such as the Artists Projects Regional Initiatives (APRI) and some regranting programs such as the Regional Visual Artists Fellowship Program. In the subsequent five years the NEA was forced further to a limited role with respect to direct support to individual artists. Due in part to the political impetus behind these cuts, the NEA reorganized many discipline-based to thematic grants-making structure.

As federal funding available to individual artists shifted, many foundations found themselves in the position of reevaluating their role. In 1995, the Artists Projects Regional Initiatives (APRI) and the National Artist Advocacy Group (NAAG) authorized a study to detail the impact of the NEA cuts to individual artists and to assess its impact on the other funders. A major impetus for this study was the Rockefeller Foundation's move that year to end its ten-year commitment to APRI. One of the original goals of the APRI/NAAG study was to map the funding terrain of support for individual artists in order to assess the feasibility of alternative funding approaches such as a trust for artists, which would be instituted to pick up the slack caused by the pullout of the NEA and Rockefeller funds.

Much to the surprise of all, *Financial Support for Artists: A Study of Past and Current Support, with Reflections on the Findings and Recommendations for Future Action* (Focke 1996), did not recommend the creation of such a trust. Nor did it find patterns of retrenchment on the part of nonfederal funders. In fact, the study found that while recent losses of support were significant and real, they were more limited than expected. There were actually more programs either in existence or in the planning stages than those that had been cut or eliminated. Statistics were not available as to whether the dollars associated with these new programs would equal the support lost through NEA's retrenchment. Artists' earnings from grants ranged only from $2,433 to $3,690 annually (Jeffri, Hosie, and Greenblat 1987, 112). The nominal dollar amount suggests that the significance of these awards might be primarily symbolic. These dollars are needed; their importance may be in their ability to provide the time for "surplus attention."

The APRI/NAAG study identified forms of existing and new support for artists. Many of the programs were "fundamentally different" than those lost due to NEA cuts. They include: writers' royalties, and composers' checks from BMI and ASCAP based on copyright protections; the "percent for art" programs on the state and local levels, cooperative galleries; support from artist colonies and other forms of sponsored fellowships and sabbatical leaves; as well as legal and health care collaboratives. Contrary to popular perception, many state and local programs actually maintained or even expanded their existing policies toward individual artists during the same period that the NEA and some foundations were scaling back their programs.

The funding perspective from the state level is a particularly telling example of how adoptable the arts matrix system is. According to the most recent 1994 *State Arts Agency Profile* (Wax and National Assembly of State Arts Agencies 1995), grants to individual artists were awarded in all fifty states, the District of Columbia, and Puerto Rico. Forty-eight (of the fifty-two entities) also offered fellowships to individuals, and more than half provided assistance in the form of workshops, conferences, technical assistance, and support for travel and works-in-progress. Fourteen states also offer additional types of funds to individuals, ranging from career development programs to assistance for the creation of new works.

While many programs targeting individuals artists were phased out on the federal level in the early 1990s, only ten states reported similar program cuts during this period (in many cases, reflecting a reduction in budget or staff, or the end of an earlier initiative). Thirty-seven reported the initiation and/or expansion of programs designed to assist individuals. In terms of the origin of the funds for these programs, the 1994 *State Arts Agency Profile* reported that forty-six received state moneys, while forty reported receiving funds from federal sources, and thirteen received private dollars as well. Many forms of new support came with conditions or limits to their use, and others were administered through various regranting channels. For example, Missouri made funds available indirectly through special projects; Oregon and New York allocated money for individual fellowships via such entities as the New York Foundation for the Arts regrant program. Other state and local initiatives supported artists through indirect means. For example, municipalities such as Providence, Rhode Island, in an effort to create a conducive environment for artists, began instituting programs ranging from tax breaks and housing incentives; developing economic partnerships with state and local government, and businesses (both commercial and not-for-profit); to linkages to institutions of higher education.

In the fall of 1996, the Alliance of Artists' Communities held a symposium on the nature of creativity and the need for increased collaboration for artists' survival.[10] Its goal was to support and encourage collaboration among members of the field, provide leadership, discuss professional standards while raising the visibility of artists' communities and other organizations promoting philanthropy in the arts. At approximately the same time a group of artists in Hollywood formed the Creative Coalition, an effort designed to unite individual artists across creative fields. In adopting a "united we stand, divided we fall" approach, players across the arts field—individuals, unions, government agencies, foundations, and corporations—are all experiencing new avenues for dialogue across sectoral boundaries. These efforts can work to make more explicit the interconnectedness of the arts matrix.

Policy Implications and Future Research Agenda

Katrina Trask, the founder of Yaddo, one of the largest artists' colonies in the United States, had a vision that someday artists would walk through her pine woods, "creating, creating, creating" (Csikszentmihalyi 1966, 37). But the creative process involves more than solitude and escape; it requires a conducive climate for artists and the arts to flourish. This relates to the importance placed on the role of artists and the arts in American society. The American Assembly called for a reexamination of the broad purposes served by the arts and the ways in which they meet the needs of the nation.

While the main focus of this study has been on individual artists and their career paths, our point of departure from previous research is in employing a broader lens in considering artists as they exist in the commercial, not-for-profit, and avocational parts of the arts sector, moving toward a more inclusive approach. The first step in achieving this goal is to devise better means of collecting data. Three important data-oriented initiatives are suggested: The first is a national survey of artists that has the integrity of the Census and that is designed to provide consistent and reliable information relevant to what has been learned about artists' education, training, work, and support mechanisms. Without this information, those surveys that show a picture of the artists' experiences will be overlooked as not entirely representative of the entire arts sector. That said, the Census is presently incapable of capturing the breadth and depth of the artists' conditions. New methods of developing a more accurate profile of artists in America are definitely required.

The second initiative called for is the initiation of a longitudinal survey of artists' experiences. This would provide us with a much better understanding of the transitions and issues that artists encounter during their careers. Among the issues that could be examined are: the role of life-long learning, occupational choice; paths to success; how artists come to realize that they should pursue an artistic occupation; how they make career transitions; the rate and pattern of movement into and out of the commercial, not-for-profit, and self-employed areas; the difficulties faced by new entrants into an arts field; and the effects of changes due to social forces such as globalization, shifting creative capital, and changing patterns of patronage.

Knowledge is power: we need to better understand the role of artists as productive members of our society. A better portrait of artists and their careers, as well as of the substance and the structure of the support matrix, is the first step in developing a framework for informing policy concerning artists in America.

Notes

1. UNESCO has recognized the definition of an artist as " . . . any person who creates or gives creative expression to, as an artist, or recreates works of art, who considers his [sic] artistic creation to be an essential part of his life, who contributes in this way to the development of art and culture and who is or asks to be recognized as an artist, whether or not he is bound by any relation of employment or association" (UNESCO 1980, 5).
2. NEA occupational categories include; actors and directors; announcers; architects; post-secondary-school teachers; authors; dancers; musicians and composers; painters, sculptors, craft artists and artistic printmakers; photographers; and all other artists not elsewhere classified or artist "nec," those artists who do not easily fit into any other artistic category and include: acrobats, circus performers, puppeteers, and so on. The experienced civilian labor force included individuals not in the military who were working as artists or who had worked as an artist in the recent past and were currently unemployed.
3. In addition, almost 6 percent of artists had some form of physical disability that restricted their ability to work (these proportions were slightly higher among artists than among the other professional/technical occupations). More than 8 percent of the authors had some work-related disability, almost 8 percent of the musicians and composers, as did visual artists and craftspeople. Architects were the least likely to have disabilities that affected their ability to work.
4. Detailed analysis of the artistic occupations is not possible with the NSCG data because artists, with the exception of architects and post-secondary-school art teachers, were aggregated into one occupational category.
5. With the merger of the Screen Extras Guild into the Screen Actors Guild (SAG), there are now six major performing arts unions (see Gray and Seeber 1996, tab. 1.1): Actors Equity Association (AEA), American Federation of

Musicians (AFM), American Federation of Television and Radio Artists (AFTRA), American Guild of Musical Artists (AGMA), and American Guild of Variety Artists (AGVA). There are three major nonperforming unions: Directors Guild of America (DGA), the Writers Guild of America (WGA East and West), and the Society of State Directors and Choreographers. Over the period from 1988 to 1994 some of the unions have lost considerable membership, in part reflecting the changes in markets. The largest decline has been in the AFM, where a recent 27 percent decline followed a decline of almost 40 percent from 1979 to 1984. Others like AFTRA, SAG, DGA, and WGA had increases in membership

6. The major industry groups are: agriculture; construction; manufacturing; mining; transportation, communications, and public utilities; wholesale trade; retail trade; finance, insurance, and real estate; business services; personal services; entertainment and recreation services; professional services; and public administration. In this study agriculture and mining were aggregated into one industry group, and durable and nondurable manufacture were treated separately.

7. This classification should not be confused with the "unincorporated" category used by the American Assembly to describe those individuals who "reflect a range of citizen-based, often avocational, arts in the many manifestations" (1997, 1).

8. Interview with Carol Landers, director of research, New York City Ballet, 22 March 1997.

9. Jane P. Firstenberg, response to the American Assembly questionnaire, March 1997.

10. The Alliance of Artists' Communities is a national service organization with a membership of over twenty-seven leading not-for-profit colonies and thirty-seven associate individual members.

CHARLES M. GRAY
JAMES HEILBRUN

8 Economics of the Nonprofit Arts
Structure, Scope, and Trends

This chapter provides a general overview of the economics of the nonprofit arts, identifying contributions that economists have made to our knowledge of nonprofit arts organizations, as well as noting related questions and issues awaiting answers or at least clarification.[1] In this effort, we take a microperspective of the structure of nonprofit arts organizations, a macroperspective of their overall performance in the economy, and, for good measure, an intermediate perspective on market structures in the nonprofit arts. We regard all three perspectives as vital to an understanding of the sector.[2] We first establish the boundaries of our effort, lest we be tempted to pursue every interesting avenue that an endeavor of this nature inevitably offers.

The nonprofit arts account for only a very small part of the national economy. We estimate that as of 1997, the nonprofit arts constituted well under two one-thousandths of gross domestic product, or about $11.9 billion.[3] On the other hand, it is also true that this particular measure of nonprofit arts activity has been growing faster than the economy as a whole. Due perhaps in part to its small size, only in the last two decades has an "economics of the arts" literature emerged, as economists sought to gain a better understanding of the nonprofit arts and to share that understanding with policymakers, arts administrators, and other stakeholders.[4]

Historically, nonprofit organizations (NPOs) have presented a challenge to the economics profession, which ordinarily assumes profit-maximizing behavior on the part of firms. NPOs are of course prohibited by law from distributing any surplus earnings (or profits) to "owners." The difficulty is that such organizations cannot be squeezed easily into the dominant neoclassical economic model. Even though most nonprofit arts organizations earn revenues, profit maximization is typically inconsistent with their missions. So not only are the nonprofit arts a relatively small component of the economy; they are also not "well behaved." We believe nonetheless that economic tools and concepts will enhance our understanding of this sector.

We define the nonprofit arts industry as comprising art museums as well as the live performing arts of theater (excluding Broadway and Broadway road companies, which tend to be for-profit), symphony orchestras, opera, and dance (including both ballet and modern). We treat the live performing arts as an internally coherent group because they are organized on a not-for-profit basis and also because they share a common production technique: A performance is put on in a venue to which the audience must come, and the performance can be repeated in exactly the same form as often as may be desirable. We will not here be analyzing art museums or the publishing industry. Their economic situations are so different from the performing arts that it is impractical to deal with them in a relatively short essay. Art museums are, however, included in our overall estimate of the size of the nonprofit arts sector. Table 8.1 positions this sector, "high culture," in the larger economy, with comparisons to both the for-profit organizational form and the nonprofit, nonarts sectors of the economy.

Among the performing arts, the included categories are traditional forms sometimes referred to—as we have done—as "high" art, while the excluded ones—motion pictures, broadcasting and cable, and rock, pop, and jazz concerts—are forms described as "popular" or "mass" culture. The competition for audiences between the former and the latter is much on the mind of those associated with the high arts, especially when the share of the entertainment dollar going to the high arts may be declining.

Whatever its defects, this definition of the sector does correspond to the one adopted by most economists who have worked in this field, and it closely, if not precisely, corresponds to the seven "core" arts identified in the NEA's Survey of Public Participation in the Arts.[5]

We begin our exploration with a look at the NPO, or "firm," itself, including elements of what is called the architecture of the organization.[6] We then apply economic models of industry structure to the arts, using specific examples from one geographic region, and then segue into the overall size and significance of the sector. We next take a national perspective, presenting updated trends in several of the performing arts. Finally, we draw some conclusions and offer an agenda for discussion

Table 8.1. *"High Culture" in the Economy*

| | | ORGANIZATIONAL FORM | |
		Nonprofit	*For profit*
Industry sector	Arts	"High culture"	Pop music, Broadway, movies
	All other goods and services	Health care, social services	Manufacturing, retail, finance, etc.

and future research. While seeking to avoid needlessly obscure jargon, we do draw upon current economics and management usage as appropriate.

The Nonprofit Arts Firm

Economists have historically treated the business firm as a profit-maximizing production function. Managers, as agents for the organization's owners, or "residual claimants," would seek to create the greatest excess of revenues over costs. They would do this in part by selecting and purchasing such inputs as capital equipment, labor, and supplies in competitive markets; combining them as efficiently as possible; and selling the product in competitive output markets. All revenue is derived from product sales in competitive markets, costs are incurred during production, and output itself is a technical result of the combination of capital and labor.

The nonprofit sector labors under the widespread perception that it is inherently inefficient: "Residual claimants are crucial actors in any society characterized by extensive specialization and exchange. Institutions that do not have residual claimants do not, by and large, function as effectively as those that do.... Nonprofit institutions by definition have no residual claimants. That is why they so often behave in such clumsy ways.... The buck stops nowhere" (Heyne 1997, 268–269).

If clumsy means inefficient, then this distinctive organizational form may inherently exacerbate the "cost disease" first identified by Baumol and Bowen and subsequently explored by Felton and others.[7] The cost disease characterizes those industries, including the live performing arts, where output (performances) per work hour rises more slowly than in manufacturing and similar industries, which can more easily incorporate advances in technology. This means that labor costs in the performing arts increase disproportionately, contributing to the problem of financing the performing arts, especially if earned revenues fail to keep pace.

Neither traditional microeconomic theory nor the managerial economics customarily taught to prospective business managers has treated the nonprofit sector as more than a curiosity or an afterthought.[8] It has been left to two separate but interrelated strains of economic research and conceptualization to provide insights into the operation of the non-profit sector, including arts and cultural institutions. The first of these is the behavioral approach to the economics of organizations pioneered by Cyert and March, who stated their "articles of faith": "We believe that, in order to understand contemporary economic decision making, we need to supplement the study of market factors with an examination of the internal operation of the firm—to study the effects of organizational structure and conventional practice on the development of goals, the formation of expectations, and the execution of choices."[9] Hence a complete understanding of decision-making within and among organizations, including NPOs, would be enhanced by the tools of economic analysis.

The second strain is exploration of the nonprofit model by economists who have found nonprofit activity inconsistent with the neoclassical model, yet important enough to merit focused inquiry.[10]

Organizational Governance and Structure

Coase was the first to point out that firms (including NPOs) exist because of "transactions costs," including the costs of securing information, making decisions, monitoring performance, and carrying out other activities related to conducting business (Coase 1937; Williamson 1989). Imagine a dance performance developed and offered under the following circumstances: A group of dancers, desiring to generate income from the use of their skills, decides to present a dance concert. Each of them contracts with the others to combine their efforts; each contracts separately with a choreographer, who will create a dance for the group and perhaps also direct the performance, and with a business manager, who will see to rehearsal and performance space rental and take care of other details. Then each independently solicits payment from potential audience members.

The number of separate contracts required to make this event happen approaches the mind-boggling. And failure to perform by just one participant could result in multiple contract breaches. Far better for a dance company to employ a choreographer, a business manager, and dancers, and perhaps vertically integrate to own both rehearsal and performing space, to offer the event and sell tickets to patrons. The number of independent transactions is reduced substantially.

All of the organizations that "produce" the high arts bear strong resemblance to traditional for-profit firms. They sell tickets to performances or exhibits, secure resources to offer such events, and incur the costs of

Figure 8.1. Structure of arts organizations

those resources. They also seek to raise funds by other means and, in many instances, they participate in financial markets as borrowers or as investors. They are structured as hierarchies, with a governing board which establishes policy, a chief executive officer who oversees policy implementation, and separate artistic and administrative staffs. The typical nonprofit arts organization has the general structure depicted in figure 8.1. Variations on this prototype abound. The artistic director may be the executive director, especially in smaller organizations. In organizations which encourage—wisely or unwisely—collective decision making, staff members may also serve on the governing board.

Organizational leadership and staff may not be marching to the same drummer. For example, the artistic director may seek to maximize his or her reputation among peers by creating the finest possible artistic experience, regardless of cost, while the managing director seeks to balance revenues and costs to ensure the long-term viability of the organization. These disparate goals are examples of incentive conflicts that can impair organizational success and require effective decision management and control on the part of the governing board. Difficulties are compounded in arts organizations, since it is not uncommon for the artistic or executive director to be a member of the board. Although the nonprofit organization form is said to reassure donors that their funds will be used for the purposes stated, there have been many instances of personal gain and aggrandizement at the expense of organizational quality and efficiency within the nonprofit community.[11] Clearly, we would benefit from more case studies and focused research on organizational structure and behavior in the nonprofit arts.

Speaking of the larger nonprofit area, Milgrom and Roberts (1992,

524) note: "A chief characteristic of charitable activities is that those who provide money to support the activities find it difficult to ascertain if their money has been well spent.... This fact means that the monitoring that occurs naturally in a normal market . . . cannot be nearly as effective in disciplining the providers of charitable services. This problem is compounded by the fact that, like most service activities, performance by the charitable services "business" is often very difficult to measure."

Nonprofit Purpose

Cultural organizations are established as nonprofits because, like other NPOs, they are deemed to serve a larger social purpose; they are said to be mission driven rather than profit motivated. The existence of this larger social purpose is said to justify public subsidy of the arts. However, lacking the clear market valuations of worth common to the for-profit sector (that is, stock value, discounted net cash flows, and so on), the arts have struggled with the issue of demonstrating their value to policymakers and politicians. Arts advocates have sought to use "economic impact" studies to demonstrate that the arts create jobs and incomes and contribute to state and local tax revenues. Despite their surface appeal and seeming widespread acceptance, many of these studies have been ill conceived and improperly conducted, and they are controversial sources of support for arts subsidies.[12] Far more promising might be "contingent valuation" studies whose methodology, borrowed from environmental economists, consists of surveys designed to ascertain citizens' willingness to subsidize the arts out of public funds (Heilbrun and Gray 1993, ch. 11). Such studies have been conducted in Australia by Throsby and Withers (1983), in Denmark by Hansen (1997), in the United States by Thompson, Berger, and Allen (1998), and in several other countries,

The Artistic "Product"

Markets for the products of nonprofit arts organizations are characterized by what is known as "asymmetric information" (Easley and O'Hara 1986). This means that one side of the market—in this case, the consumer—lacks adequate information about product quality prior to purchasing the product. More specifically, it is said that the arts are experience goods, meaning that the consumer will not perceive the quality of, say, a dance performance until after viewing it.[13] Furthermore, it is widely argued that enjoyment of high culture—opera as a premier example—requires investment in "consumption skills." Without appropriate education or training, the consumer is unlikely to enjoy a performance as fully as possible (Stigler and Becker 1977). To the extent that this may lessen the demand for the product, it may also jeopardize longer-term survival of the provider.

Summary[14]

- Nonprofit arts organizations lack residual claimants (owners) who might enforce "efficiency" in operation. This might give rise to operating inefficiencies that exacerbate the "cost disease."
- The structure, or architecture, of nonprofit arts organizations may compound internal conflicts.
- Despite their presumed higher purpose, nonprofit arts organizations may have a difficult time demonstrating their social value according to objective measures.
- Markets in artistic products entail "asymmetric information," in that enjoyment is enhanced by costly investment in consumption skills.

The Nonprofit Arts Industry

Here we take a closer look at prototypical market structures and their application to nonprofit arts organizations. Examples are drawn from the Twin Cities of Minneapolis and St. Paul, one of the nation's most culturally rich metropolitan areas. The art forms and companies selected as examples represent only the larger and more notable among the many organizations which constitute the Twin Cities cultural community. Some would surely argue that these particular examples ignore a few of the most innovative groups; we would not disagree.

Economists argue that market structure has implications for organizational behavior and performance. In practice, each nonprofit arts organization operates in a local or regional market. While some may tour regionally, nationally, or even globally, even the largest are tied to a specific locale. Economists have identified four prototypical market structures and organizational behaviors characteristic of firms within those markets. The structures are monopoly, oligopoly, monopolistic competition, and perfect competition. The last of these consists of countless small firms dividing up a market, none having any influence on market price, but achieving maximum overall efficiency. This is a benchmarking structure with no examples extant among the arts, so it is not considered further. The other three structures are considered below, with illustrations specific to the Twin Cities of Minneapolis–St. Paul.

Monopoly

A monopolist is a single producer dominating a product/geographic market. Monopolists are regarded as having the ability

Table 8.2. Twin Cities Classical Music and Opera

COMPANY	BUDGET OUTLAYS, 1996–1997
Minnesota Orchestral Association	$24,874,349
St. Paul Chamber Orchestra	8,648,521
Minnesota Opera Company	4,828,807

SOURCE: Minnesota Council on Nonprofits.

to maximize their profits (or minimize losses) through pricing decisions, with no regard to the reactions of rivals. If the product is defined as regional theater, then a single company—the Guthrie Theater in the Twin Cities, the Arena Stage in Washington, D.C., or Actors Theater in Louisville—may dominate (if not entirely monopolize) a market. But even a monopolist in such circumstances does not have complete pricing freedom. After all, patrons do have other entertainment or cultural choices.

Oligopoly

This structure is characterized by a few relatively large and strategically interdependent firms operating in a market, traditionally exhibiting highly rivalrous behavior. Table 8.2 depicts the classical music and opera market in the Twin Cities, dominated by the "big three" indicated in descending order of budget size. No other classical music organization in the area has a budget even approaching a million dollars.

Presumably one could analyze and predict the behaviors of market participants with noncooperative game theory, a staple of economic market analysis.[15] And, to be sure, the organizations depicted are strategically interdependent. Neither the Minnesota Orchestra nor the St. Paul Chamber Orchestra (SPCO) can be totally unmindful of the practices of the other, including pricing and programming. They do in fact compete for patrons as well as public and private gifts and grants.

In the face of the very obvious competition, there happens also to be a great deal of cooperation as well. All three companies perform at least part of their seasons in St. Paul's Ordway Music Theater; SPCO musicians often join the pit orchestra for the Opera; and the SPCO performs portions of its various series in Orchestra Hall owned by the Minnesota Orchestra.

Monopolistic Competition

In this market structure, numerous firms of varying sizes, with somewhat differentiated products, serve part or all of a given

Table 8.3. Twin Cities Dance Companies[a]

COMPANY	BUDGET OUTLAYS, 1996–1997
Ballet Arts Minnesota	$519,806
Ballet of the Dolls	222,872
Ethnic Dance Theater	114,453
James Sewell Ballet	287,700
Jawaahir Dance Company	84,097
Hauser Dance Company and School	122,011
Zenon Dance Company and School	306,373

SOURCE: Minnesota Council on Nonprofits.
[a] This does not include a number of smaller, unincorporated, and often transitory troupes.

market. If the market is broadly defined as dance, then several modern, ballet, jazz, folk, and ethnic dance troupes may compete for the audience. Table 8.3 lists alphabetically the larger dance companies in the Twin Cities. In the strictest sense these companies do compete with each other for audience and funding, and their very names indicate a degree of "product differentiation." But they also cooperate: Dancers move somewhat freely among choreographers; the dancers and companies jointly support a "trade" organization, the Minnesota Dance Alliance; and companies frequently join together to present a dance season series.

Table 8.4 reflects the relative sizes of some of the more notable nonprofit theater companies in the Twin Cities. While the Guthrie is the flagship company, the others have established niches of their own in order to differentiate their products. For example, Jeune Lune offers original works or unique adaptations of existing works, Penumbra is one of the nation's premier African American theater companies, and Mixed Blood is known for "color-blind" casting. Again, while the companies compete for the audience dollar, they also collaborate in their offerings, and they share directors, actors, skilled support personnel, and performing space.

Obviously, the nonprofit arts exhibit pricing choices, product strategies, and other rivalrous behaviors characteristic of traditional market structures. But they also exhibit open and explicit cooperation, which begs additional research and case studies to enhance understanding. In this era of ever tightening budgets, cooperative ventures both within and outside of local markets look increasingly attractive. In reference to Washington's well-known Arena Stage, the *New York Times* reported that "more than half of the Arena's shows this year are co-productions of some kind; that is, the shows are being put together or underwritten in cooperation with other nonprofit theaters" (Weber 1997). The Minnesota

Table 8.4. Twin Cities Theater Companies[a]

COMPANY	BUDGET OUTLAYS, 1996–1997
Children's Theater Company and School	$5,815,949
Guthrie Theater	9,966,453
Illusion Theater Company	1,077,323
Jungle Theater	817,766
Mixed Blood Theatre Company	1,164,255
Park Square Theatre Company	598,250
Penumbra Theater Company	1,668,935
Red Eye Collaboration	169,566
Theatre de la Jeune Lune	1,044,722
Theatre in the Round	212,085

SOURCE: Minnesota Council on Nonprofits.

[a] Companies included are among the largest and most notable of some two-score companies.

Opera's 1998 production of *Aida* drew upon a great deal of local talent, but the lead performers, set, and costumes will travel to other midsized companies throughout the United States.

Nonprofit Arts in the National Economy

Having looked inside the firm and the local market, we now turn our attention to a larger, national perspective on the arts, addressing the overall performance of the arts sector. Then we examine trends in arts growth over the past several years in an effort to support a tentative statement of the outlook for the nonprofit arts. Although we offer an estimate of overall sectoral size, our discussion of specific art forms is meant to illuminate performance issues rather than subsectoral magnitude.

Performance

Using the definition of the field described at the beginning of the chapter, we estimated the size of the nonprofit arts sector in 1990 as $6.660 billion (Heilbrun and Gray 1993, 7–10). Since we may have underestimated private giving to the arts, which is an important component of the sector's revenue, $6.660 billion might reasonably be regarded as a lower bound, or conservative estimate.[16]

In 1990 the nation's gross domestic product stood at $5,743.8 billion. Thus the nonprofit arts sector amounted to only a little more than one-thousandth of GDP, or, to be more precise, .116 percent. According to Department of Commerce data, consumer spending for admission to the live performing arts, which is a major component of our size estimate, increased 78.3 percent from 1990 to 1997, while GDP rose only 40.7 percent. If other sources of support for the arts rose as fast as consumer spending, the field would have grown to $11.875 billion by 1997, or .147 percent of GDP. Even if that is an underestimate, one cannot avoid the conclusion that the nonprofit arts industry, as defined here, is very small in relation to the U.S. economy.

However, size is not the only measure of significance; the arts in the United States are immensely important to the nation's self-image. The founding of the NEA and NEH in 1965 was a declaration that we in the United States take the arts and humanities very seriously. We are the nation not only of Henry Ford and Thomas Edison, but also of Martha Graham, Jackson Pollock, and Tennessee Williams.

The Growth of Consumer Spending on Admissions

We all know that the nonprofit arts industry in the United States—whether measured by employment, number of institutions, size of audiences, or amount of revenue—enjoyed rapid growth in the 1970s and the first half of the 1980s. Since that date, growth appears to have slowed, but not stopped. We will examine these trends in some detail while at the same time explaining the data by which trends in the arts can be judged.

The longest continuous data series is the figure on consumer spending for admissions to the live performing arts, which is estimated annually by the Commerce Department as part of the National Income and Product Accounts. This series runs all the way back to 1929 and also has the advantage of appearing only six months after year's end. It is a component of Spectator activities in the Recreation sector of Personal Consumption, which allows us to compare trends in the live performing arts with trends in Spectator Sports and Motion Picture attendance at theaters, as well as with Recreation as a whole. Table 8.5, covering 1970 through 1997, shows the consumer spending data both in dollar amount and as a percentage of Disposable Personal Income (DPI). The ratio of spending for admissions to DPI is a good measure of trends in the performing arts industry because dividing through by DPI gives us a measure free of the effect of a rising general price level.

Table 8.5 indicates that spending for admission to the live performing arts began to increase as a percentage of DPI after 1975 and has risen almost without interruption since then. A sort of milestone was passed in 1985: before that date, and running back many years, the dollar amounts of spending on admission to motion pictures and to spectator sports had exceeded consumer outlays for the live performing arts; af-

Table 8.5. Consumer Spending on Admission to the Performing Arts

YEAR:	1970	1975	1980	1985	1990	1997
	Spending as a percentage of disposable personal income					
Recreation, total	5.92	6.08	5.89	6.19	6.74	7.86
Spectator entertainment	0.45	0.37	0.34	0.32	0.36	0.40
Performing arts	0.07	0.07	0.09	0.11	0.13	0.17
Motion pictures[a]	0.22	0.19	0.13	0.11	0.12	0.11
Spectator sports	0.13	0.12	0.12	0.11	0.10	0.11
	Subsector as a percentage of recreation spending					
Spectator entertainment	7.65	6.12	5.73	5.24	5.38	5.04
Performing arts	1.23	1.12	1.54	1.73	1.99	2.16
Motion pictures[a]	3.78	3.12	2.22	1.75	1.84	1.43
Spectator sports	2.64	1.89	1.97	1.76	1.55	1.45

SOURCE: U.S. Department of Commerce, *National Income and Product Accounts of the United States, Statistical Tables*, various years.
[a] In theaters only.

ter 1985 outlays for the latter far outran spending for the other two. It should be pointed out, however, that movie-going in the theater now has to compete with movies on television and videotape, and attending sporting events with watching on TV, while the live performing arts have faced less direct competition from the electronic media.[17]

Because the quantity of performing arts activity, as measured by number of performances, rose strongly from 1970 to 1975, it is something of a puzzle that the spending ratio fell over that same period. Bearing in mind the mathematical fact that the dollar amount of spending is necessarily the product of quantity times price, the key to the puzzle may be that in those years ticket prices in the arts failed to keep up with the pace of general inflation, which was then rapidly increasing. As "attendance maximizers," arts company managers were reluctant to raise prices, as to a lesser extent, they still are. Evidence from the early 1970s on this point is inconclusive.[18]

That the spending ratio for the performing arts continued to rise strongly from 1985 to 1996 also requires some explanation in view of the general tone of malaise that pervades the nonprofit arts industry these days. Our explanation is that after 1985 the physical level of activity in most arts sectors (productions, performances, attendance) leveled off or declined, but that ticket prices continued to rise, producing a more or less steady increase in aggregate consumer spending for admissions.

That higher ticket prices lead to a rise rather than a fall in revenue is consistent with the general finding that the demand for tickets is price inelastic.[19] Price elasticity measures the sensitivity of demand for a product to changes in its price. Mathematically it equals the ratio of the percentage change in quantity demanded to the percentage change in price that brings it about. If the value of that ratio is less than one, we call the case inelastic, meaning that quantity demanded is not very sensitive to changes in price. This would be the case, for example, if a 10 percent increase in the price of tickets led to a decline of only 3 percent in quantity purchased. When demand is inelastic an increase in price causes revenue to rise because the firm gains more from the increased price per unit sold than it loses from selling fewer units. In the case of the performing arts, of course, while higher ticket prices have brought increased revenue, they are also one of the reasons attendance has tended to level off or fall.

The Trend of "Real Output" in the Arts

Economists speak of physical indicators of activity as measuring "real" output, measured as number of performances or attendance, as distinct from output measured in money terms. In every nonprofit performing arts sector except dance, we now have quite good data not only on such money measures as revenues and expenditures, but also on real output. In this section we will examine recent trends in theater, opera, dance, and symphony concerts, by looking at both physical and money measures of activity.

Four clear trends emerge in those disciplines:

- Real output reached a peak in the late 1980s or early 1990s, then leveled off, or in the case of symphony orchestras, slightly declined.
- Total income increased more or less steadily, because ticket prices were rising.
- Earned income rose and contributed income fell, as a percentage of total income.
- Within the category of contributed income, the share of public support declined, while that of private contributions increased.

What can account for the slowdown in the growth of real arts activity after 1990? We posit that the answer is the increasingly powerful competition of popular culture.[20] The people who are not attending symphony concerts or the theater are doing something else instead.

Theater. Table 8.6 displays data for the nonprofit theater. Look first at the physical (nonmonetary) indicators. Under the heading of Actors' Equity Workweeks, the top panel shows the amount of work recorded for several major labor contracts. The most important of these, the LORT

Table 8.6. Nonprofit Theater

Actors' Equity workweeks	SEASON ENDING					PERCENT CHANGE,
	1980	1985	1990	1996	1997	1990–1997
LORT contract	42,910	53,529	58,550	50,841	49,054	−16.2
Off-Broadway contract	9,313	11,341	11,840	8,642	6,698	−43.4
Chicago area contract	2,093	3,183	5,344	5,358	5,488	2.7

Theatre Communications	1992	1993	1994	1995	1996	PERCENT CHANGE, 1992–1996
Group, 68 theaters						
Performances	21,615	21,756	21,682	22,373	22,252	2.9
Attendance (000)	8,366	8,270	8,098	8,307	8,130	−2.8
Total income ($000)	229,159	237,592	246,340	265,700	273,533	19.4
Earned income	139,281	144,140	146,152	164,759	166,497	19.5
Contributed income	89,878	93,452	100,188	100,950	107,036	19.1
Private, total[a]	72,441	77,594	83,145	83,182	90,659	25.1
Individuals	19,749	20,954	23,243	24,057	26,968	36.6
Foundations	14,113	16,825	19,460	18,320	18,320	29.8
Corporations	13,059	15,783	14,090	14,454	15,037	15.1
Other						
Government, total	17,437	15,858	17,043	17,768	16,377	−6.1
Federal	6,106	5,713	6,087	5,844	4,389	−28.2
State	6,379	5,805	6,190	6,733	6,310	−1.1
City/county	4,952	4,340	4,766	5,191	5,678	4.7

SOURCES: *Equity News*, December issues; Theatre Communications Group, *Theatre Facts 1996*.
[a] The implementation of new accounting rules for nonprofits promulgated by the financial Accounting Standards Board led to a bulge in reported private contributions in 1996 and produced a discontinuity in that data.

contract, covers work for the League of Resident Theatres, an organization of the principal nonprofit theaters in the United States. LORT workweeks reached a peak of 62,397 in 1989, slipped to 58,550 the next year and continued downward to 49,054 in 1997. Work under the Off-Broadway contract also peaked in the late 1980s and had fallen substantially by 1997.[21]

The second section of table 8.6 shows data gathered by the Theatre Communications Group (TCG) from a constant sample of 68 member companies for the five seasons 1991–1992 through 1995–1996. The first two lines, which are physical measures, show that over that five-year period total performances went up 3 percent, while total attendance fell by the same proportion.

That the LORT contract data show workweeks down 16 percent, while the TCG figures have the number of performances (for a subset of theaters, to be sure) rising 3 percent, is a curiosity. This anomaly is indirect evidence of an "artistic deficit": Theaters hold down their costs by putting on plays with smaller casts. A concrete example of that effect is provided by a 1997 article in the *New York Times*, which reported that in 1990–1991 there were 120 roles for actors at the Arena Stage. By 1996–1997 the number had fallen to just 70 (Weber 1997). Apparently the ideal production these days has one set and two characters. And why bother with a set? Shakespeare didn't.

The TCG sample data also cover the usual categories of income. Total income, earned income, and contributed income all increased substantially over the five-year span. The fact that earned income rose 20 percent while attendance was down 3 percent shows that average ticket prices must have risen substantially. Support from government fell 6.1 percent, but that loss was more than offset by increased gifts from individuals, foundations, and corporations, so that total contributed income rose 19.1 percent. By 1996 earned income had risen slightly and contributed income fallen slightly as a percent of total income. Earned revenue in 1996 accounted for 61 percent of total theatrical income, the highest proportion among the three sectors examined.

Opera. Table 8.7 displays data from Opera America, the organization of major U. S and Canadian professional opera companies.[22] The upper panel is based on data solicited from all member companies, but is not quite a consistent sample since not all companies report each year. Attendance rose more or less steadily from 1983 (earliest available data) to a peak of 4.304 million in 1991, after which it fluctuated slightly, with no discernible trend. The number of performances peaked in 1990 and has also fluctuated slightly since then. Box office receipts, of course, have climbed steadily, indicating a persistent increase in ticket prices.

The lower section of table 8.7 presents data for a constant sample of sixty-two companies from 1992 through 1996. Mainstage attendance fluctuated a bit, but reached its highest level in 1996. Opera is the only one of the live performing arts in which the physical level of activity appears still to be rising, however slowly. Money measures, of course, continue their rapid growth. Total income increased 39.6 percent from 1992 to 1996. Earned income rose 33.9 percent, while contributed income was up 45.7 percent. The jump in the latter category, as well as the sharp rise in total income, reflects a change in accounting rules imposed by the Financial Accounting Standards Board which introduced a temporary bulge in contributions reported in 1996.[23]

Symphony Orchestras. Table 8.8 is based on data from the American Symphony Orchestra League and shows two different sets of data. The

Table 8.7. Opera

OPERA America major companies	SEASON ENDING						PERCENT CHANGE, 1990–1997
	1983	1992	1993	1994	1995	1996	
Performances[a]	1,789	2,424	2,130	2,273	2,324	2,521	4.0
Attendance (millions)	2.46	4.30	3.90	4.06	4.29	4.34	1.0
Attendance per performance	1,375	1,774	1,830	1,738	1,848	1,723	−2.9
Constant sample group 62 companies Mainstage attendance (millions)		2.441	2.372	2.517	2.617	2.624	8.9
Total income ($millions)		233.6	239.4	251.0	273.1	326.0	39.6
Earned		121.6	128.5	134.1	148.2	162.8	33.9
Contributed		112.1	111.0	117.0	124.8	163.3	45.7
Total private[b]		97.9	96.7	101.2	111.0	148.9	52.1
Individuals		39.3	39.2	46.4	49.3	80.5	104.8
Foundations		19.4	19.5	19.0	21.1	24.1	24.2
Corporations		15.1	13.7	13.5	15.1	18.0	19.2
Other		24.1	24.4	22.3	25.5	26.3	9.7
Total government		14.2	14.4	15.9	13.8	14.4	1.4
Federal		4.42	4.94	5.25	3.19	3.50	−20.8
State		4.55	4.42	4.34	4.69	4.13	−9.2
City/county		5.21	5.01	6.27	5.92	6.74	29.4

SOURCES: OPERA America, Profile, various issues; OPERA America Annual Field Report, various years.
NOTES:
[a] Mainstage and festival performances, fully staged.
[b] See note (a) Nonprofit Theater tab. 8.4.

"old series" draws on information from 254 orchestras and ran from 1984 to 1995. The "new series" covering 1991 and all seasons from 1995 onward, includes 1,209 orchestras and is therefore more representative of the entire industry. The old series shows that the number of concerts and attendance both reached a peak in 1988. The former had declined 13 percent and the latter 15 percent by 1995. The new series shows much more moderate declines, but over a shorter time span. Symphony orchestras are the only one of the live performing arts in which the real level of activity has clearly declined. Total income rose from $776.7 million in 1991 to $976.6 million in 1997. The shares of concert income and of total contributed support changes little during that period, but the components of support changed substantially: government contributions fell from 8.6 to 5.6 percent of income, while private support rose from 32.7 to 35.5 percent (these latter percentages are not shown in the table).

Table 8.8. Symphony Orchestras

	SEASON ENDING						
OLD SERIES[a]	1985	1988	1990	1991	1995	1996	1997
Concerts	19,573	21,306	18,931		118,543		
Attendance (millions)	24.0	27.4	24.7		23.2		
New Series[b]							
Concerts				27,263	29,328	28,887	26,906
Attendance (millions)				33.1	30.9	31.1	31,9
Income ($ millions)				766.7	887.2	941.7	976.6
Concert income				310.9	368.6	383.7	390.6
Endowment income				61.9	76.2	79.9	91.4
Other earned income				77.6	91.4	95.3	93.5
Total support				316.3	351.0	382.8	401.1
Tax supported				65.9	55.5	57.6	54.5
Private sector				250.4	295.5	325.3	346.6

SOURCE: *American Symphony Orchestra League, U.S. Orchestra Profiles,* various years.
NOTES:
[a] Based on 254 orchestras.
[b] Based on 1209 orchestras.

Dance. Table 8.9 shows divergent patterns in funding between selected ballet and modern dance companies. For the former, earned income grew faster than contributions from 1983 to 1992, while for the latter earned income grew at a much slower pace than contributions. These few companies by no means constitute a representative sample of companies nationwide, yet we cannot resist a very tentative interpretation: Ballet, a more widely accepted high art form, may be less in need of subsidy than modern dance, which by its very nature is more experimental and challenging to conventional tastes. In light of the asymmetric information inherent in modern dance, the modern dance companies are more dependent upon subsidies for fiscal health.

The lower panel of table 8.9 offers some limited, but interesting, data on trends in the ballet sector. Limited because it is based on a sample of only four relatively large companies, interesting because it shows that real (inflation adjusted) expenditures of the group rose by an extraordinary 11.7 percent per year from 1972 through 1982 and 5.5 percent per year from 1982 through 1992. This occurred during a period when real GDP was growing only 2.5 percent annually! High as these numbers are, they do conform to the pattern of slower growth for the nonprofit performing arts after the mid 1980s.

Was There a Downturn?

Felton's studies of funding patterns in the nonprofit performing arts delineate a break in the upward trend of real activity

Table 8.9. Ballet and Modern Dance

| | PERCENTAGE CHANGE 1983–92 (FINANCIAL DATA IN CONSTANT DOLLARS) | |
	SEVEN BALLET COMPANIES	SIX MODERN DANCE COMPANIES
Total revenue	71.6	60.4
Earned income	78.2	23.6
Contributed income	60.2	109.1
	AVERAGE ANNUAL GROWTH RATE	
	1972–82	1982–92
Expenditures, four Ballet companies	11.7	5.5

SOURCES: Felton (1994); Bowen et al. (1994, fig. 10.2, p. 172).

during the 1980s. She looked not only at attendance but also at money measures in constant (deflated) dollars, which are equivalent to a physical measure of activity. Table 8.10 summarizes her results for samples of 24 opera companies, 25 large orchestras, and 39 theaters. For opera and orchestras she measures trends by calculating the compound annual rate of growth for a period of rapid growth in the 1970s and early to mid 1980s, and a period of much slower growth or decline from the late 1980s into the early 1990s.

It is interesting to note that the real level of total revenue continued to rise for both the opera companies and the orchestras even during the period of slower growth (see second column of tab. 8.10). For orchestras Felton found that real average subscription prices rose throughout the period studied. Although she does not supply real ticket prices for the opera companies, it seems likely that they followed a similar path, since real opera revenues rose even during the 1980s, when attendance was relatively flat (see tab. 8.11).

For the theater sample, table 8.10 shows that 1990 was at least a temporary peak: attendance rose substantially from 1980 to 1990, then declined to 1992, but was still almost 10 percent above its 1980 level. The sample data in table 8.6 suggest that the decline did not persist in the 1990s. Since 1992 was a recession year, later data (not yet available in Felton's study) may show that the 1992 number was not, in fact, the beginning of a downtrend.

Evidence from the SPPA

The 1982, 1992, and 1997 surveys of public participation in the arts (SPPAs) offer some additional evidence on trends. Table

Table 8.10.   Dating the Downturn in Activity

24 OPERA COMPANIES	COMPOUND REAL ANNUAL RATES OF GROWTH, PERCENTAGE (ALL FINANCIAL DATA ARE IN CONSTANT DOLLARS)	
	1981–1987	1987–1991
Total revenue	5.8	1.5
Earned income	6.5	1.8
Contributed income	5.1	1.2
25 LARGE ORCHESTRAS	**1983–86**	**1986–92**
Total attendance	8.4	−4.7
	1977-87	**1987-92**
Total revenue	5.9	0.6
Noncontributed income	6.2	0.8
39 TCG THEATERS	**1980** **1990**	**1992**
Total attendance (millions)	6.02 7.28	6.62

SOURCES: Felton (1994, 1996).

8.11 shows comparative participation rates in each of the three years for the seven "benchmark" arts listed at the outset of this essay. Respondents were asked whether they attended a performance or visited an art museum in the prior twelve-month period. Only in the case of art museums was there a statistically significant increase from 1982 to 1992. All of the other participation rates showed minimal change in either a positive or negative direction. But from 1992 to 1997, attendance rates rose for all seven art forms, and four were statistically significant increases. We hesitate to draw optimistic inferences just yet, as differences in survey methodology between the earlier years and 1997 dictate caution.[24] The larger populations in 1992 and 1997 mean, of course, that in any event the total number of attenders grew, but audiences for some of the high arts are aging, with uncertain implications for the future.[25]

The Response to Cutbacks in Government Support

Tables 8.6 and 8.7 show that during the 1990s federal support for the arts through the NEA was cut back sharply. State support fluctuated erratically. Support from local government rose substantially but, during the period covered here, not enough to offset fully the drop in federal support. Hence, aggregate public funding fell. An important question as we near the end of the 1990s, is how nonprofit

Table 8.11. Attendance Rates in the Arts, 1982–1997

	PERCENTAGE ATTENDING			CHANGE IN PERCENTAGE	
Arts Activity	1982 (n=17,254)	1992 (n=12,735)	1997 (n=12,349)	1982– 1992	1992– 1997
Jazz	9.6	10.6	11.9	+1.0	+1.3
Classical music	13.0	12.5	15.5	−0.5	+3.0[a]
Opera	3.0	3.3	4.7	+0.3	+1.4
Musicals	18.6	17.4	24.5	−1.2	+7.1[a]
Plays	11.9	13.5	15.8	+1.6	+2.3[a]
Ballet	4.2	4.7	5.8	+0.5	+1.1
Art museums	22.1	26.7	34.9	+4.6[a]	+12.2[a]

SOURCE: Robinson (1993), tab. 1.3; Robinson (1998), tab. 1.
[a] Statistically significant at .05 level.

firms in the arts are responding to this decline in government assistance. Table 8.12 focuses on that question. (We have not updated the numbers to 1996 because, while 1996 data are available, they are not fully comparable to earlier years, as with our discussion of opera.) The first two columns show the percentage breakdown between earned and contributed income in 1991 and 1995. In the three fields for which we have data, companies responded by increasing their reliance on earned income as a proportion of the total. Within the category of contributed income, the relative importance of support from private sources obviously rose as the level of government assistance fell. The third column of table 8.12 shows that while the dollar amount of government aid was declining, the amount of private support rose substantially: 20.5 percent for theater companies, 22.3 percent for operas, and 18.0 percent for symphony orchestras.

So the answer to the question: How have these organizations coped? is that they have slightly increased their reliance on earned income and greatly increased their dependence on private contributions. Those changes make them more sensitive to the predictable vagaries of the economy—since both attendance and corporate contributions respond to the business cycle—but, on the other hand, leave them less dependent on the unpredictable vagaries of politics.

The message here is mixed. The bad news is that quantity measures of activity in some of the live performing arts have leveled off or even begun to decline and that government is not going to come to the rescue anytime soon. Competition from popular culture probably contributes to that slowdown, and there is no reason to think such competition will abate. The good news is that some measures, especially participation

Table 8.12. Levels and Trends in Earned and Contributed Income

	PERCENTAGE BREAKDOWN OF TOTAL INCOME		PERCENTAGE CHANGE IN $ AMOUNT
	1991	1995	1991–1995
Theatre Communications Group, 66 theaters			
Earned income	60.8	62.3	23.2
Contributed income	39.2	37.8	15.7
Private	31.1	31.1	20.5
Government	8.1	6.5	−2.6
OPERA America, 65 companies			
Earned income	51.1	53.7	31.4
Contributed income	48.9	46.2	18.4
Private	42.0	41.0	22.3
Government	6.9	5.2	−5.3
American Symphony Orchestra League			
Earned income	58.7	60.4	19.0
Contributed income	41.3	39.6	11.0
Private	32.7	33.3	18.0
Government	8.6	6.3	−15.8

SOURCES: Tab. 8.6, 8.7, and 8.8.

levels, have increased, and in any event audiences are apparently willing to pay more. Most performing arts companies have managed to stay afloat by raising ticket prices faster than the overall inflation rate, so that their real income continues to increase even if their output—performances or ticket sales—does not. As economists we may well ask how long that can go on. One is tempted to argue that sooner or later nonprofit arts companies will reach the elastic range on their demand curves at which point ticket price increases will reduce rather than increase box office revenues. But that argument overlooks another factor: If real incomes in the United States continue their historical upward march, consumer demand for the arts will increase, and it may be possible to continue into the foreseeable future the strategy of boosting company revenue by raising ticket prices a little faster than the rate of inflation.[26] That may not sound like the best of all possible worlds, but it appears to be the one we will have for the foreseeable future.

Research and Policy Considerations

How can economists continue to contribute to our understanding of the sector and its efficacy in the future? Certainly we must continue to be able to track the size, growth, structure, and geographic distribution of the arts sector. But we must also explore other sector attributes more fully. More specifically, we recommend:

- Collection and publication of consistent and reliable data on the costs, revenues, and activity levels of arts organizations. Such data will support more sophisticated analyses of operating efficiency, interaction among funding sources, and related issues on national, state, and substate levels. The reader will surely have noted that we have had to gather organizational and sectoral data from a variety of sources, with consequent issues of noncomparability both across sectors and over time.

- Well-designed studies of organizational architecture in the nonprofit arts. These should include both statistical analyses and case studies of organizational structure decision making, and so on.[27]

- Contingent valuation studies of the arts at both the national and subnational levels. Such research, patterned after extant studies in other nations that elicit citizens' expression of willingness to pay, may provide much better estimates of the overall value of the arts, which in turn could influence issues of public support.

- Research on the best means of subsidizing the arts. For example, it is not clear whether the nonprofit arts, and society as a whole, are best served by subsidizing the organization, the consumer, the artist, or some combination of thereof. Nor is it clear which levels of government in a federal system are best suited to provide arts subsidies.

- More and better studies of the interactions among arts and other organizations in specific market areas. When, for example, are organizations and their publics better served by competition, and when by cooperation? How can nonprofit arts and commercial nonarts organizations work together for mutual benefit? (Kotler and Scheff 1997).

- Continued focus on arts education as a means of addressing the asymmetric information problem in arts markets. In addition to traditional arts education in the schools, community-organization partnerships may well explore the efficacy of lifelong-learning programming in the arts.[28]

We have learned a great deal about the economics of the nonprofit arts, but effective policy and management dictate that we learn a great deal more.

Notes

1. Vicky Felton and the Minnesota Council on Nonprofits generously provided some of the data used in this chapter.

2. This essay thus represents an extension in coverage and an update over time of our prior collaboration (Heilbrun and Gray 1993).
3. This calculation is described more fully below.
4. The time estimate derives from the 1979 initial meeting of the group, which eventually evolved into the Association for Cultural Economics, International. Cultural economists publish their work in the *Journal of Cultural Economics* and elsewhere, and are accorded a separate classification (Z1) in the *Journal of Economic Literature*.
5. These core arts are classical music, opera, jazz, theater, musicals, dance, and art museums. See Chartrand, chapter 2 in this volume, for a somewhat different economic classification of the arts.
6. Organizational architecture refers to the assignment of decision rights in the organization, the compensation structure, and evaluation systems.
7. The classic reference is Baumol and Bowen (1966). See Heilbrun and Gray (1993, ch. 8) for discussion and illustrations of this issue.
8. In his intermediate microeconomics text, Nicholson (1990) accords the entire nonprofit sector a single page as a special case, about half of which is based upon Gapinski (1986). The final (!) chapter of Petersen and Lewis (1990), entitled "Management of the Nonprofit Enterprise," mentions neither art nor culture.
9. Cyert and March (1990, 1). The original edition of this classic work appeared in 1963.
10. Early examples of such work, in addition to the earlier citation of Weisbrod (1988), are assembled in the edited works of Rose-Ackerman (1986) and DiMaggio (1986).
11. See Peterson (1986) for an interesting account of early principal-agent conflict at the Metropolitan Museum of Art in New York City.
12. Many of these studies assume that the arts are part of the "export base" sector, which, for most communities, is extremely unlikely. For a critical assessment, see Seaman (1987). Heilbrun and Gray (1993, ch. 15) offer a more complete survey.
13. Indeed, wags may argue that the arts are "credence goods," in that actual consumption fails to reveal total satisfaction or benefit. The next-morning newspaper's critical comments on a performance may reveal whether we actually enjoyed it! See also Cameron (1995).
14. See Weisbrod (1986) for an early and detailed treatment of the economics of NPOs.
15. Among the seminal references are Tirole (1988) and Fudenberg and Tirole (1991).
16. Netzer (1992, 174–206) estimated the income of the nonprofit arts sector at $4.71 billion in 1985. Even allowing for expansion between 1985 and 1990, that figure falls somewhat below our estimate.
17. For a more extensive examination, see Gray (1995).
18. See the discussion in Heilbrun (1984).
19. See Heilbrun and Gray (1993), table 5.3.
20. See Heilbrun (1997).
21. The Off-Broadway group is partly not-for-profit, partly commercial.
22. The Canadian data are included because they are difficult to separate out, and they constitute a minuscule component of the total.
23. A change in when gifts must be reported as income accounted for the temporary bulge (*Opera America* 1996 p. 25).
24. For example, during the first two years the SPPA was conducted as an addendum to the National Crime Survey, while it stood alone in 1997. It is not clear how this would influence respondent answers. Survey methodol-

ogy, including other differences between 1997 and the earlier SPPAs, is detailed in Robinson (1998) and Loomis and Collins (1998).
25. See the studies collected in Lehman (1996).
26. See Baumol (1993).
27. See, for example, Owen (1997).
28. See Bergonzi and Smith (1996).

HAROLD L. VOGEL

9 Flickering Images
The Business of Hollywood

An exploration of the economics of the arts is to many akin to a visit to a foreign country. We of the Wall Street contingent are steeped in notions of returns on capital, cash flows, hurdle rates, discounted present values—and profits. We're not fully comfortable with the nonprofit aspect of the arts, nor do we quite grasp the ways in which these arts manage to survive economically and sometimes even to prosper. Furthermore, unlike in the nonprofit arts, the complexity and diversity of the entertainment industry makes it impossible to view all the segments monolithically. Regulatory and operating conditions vary significantly across the subsectors. The only art we know is, as Donald Trump has so elegantly phrased it, "the art of the deal."

Actually, though, the art of the deal isn't too bad a place to start, because even in the nonprofit world, everything has to begin with a deal. And there is perhaps no better place to look at the intersection of art and commerce than in the business of Hollywood—a global twentieth-century art form that touches almost everyone.

The following excerpts, concerning the macroeconomics of the movie business, have been adapted from my text *Entertainment Industry Economics* (1998). The material reviews the historical context out of which filmmaking enterprises have evolved, and also provides a framework for analyzing the major economic forces that affect this art form. As such, the focus on filmed entertainment provides a solid platform for understanding the approach used in analyzing businesses that profit from making or distributing culturally driven products and services—such as music, theater, recordings, television productions.

Screenings

Snuggled comfortably in the seat of your local theater or, as is increasingly likely, in front of the screen attached to your home video-exhibition device, you are transported far away by your imagination as you watch—a movie. Of course, not all movies have the substance and style to accomplish this incredible feat of emotional transportation, but a surprising number of them do. In any case, what is seen on the screen is there because of a remarkable history of tumultuous development that is still largely in process.

Putting pictures on a strip of film that moved was not a unique or new idea among photographers of the late nineteenth century. As noted by Margolies and Gwathmey (1991, 9), it was by then already known that the way we see film move is an optical illusion based upon the eye's persistence of vision; an image is retained for a fraction of a second longer than it actually appears. But the man who synthesized it all into a workable invention was Thomas Edison. By the early 1890s, Edison and his assistant, William Dickson, had succeeded in perfecting a camera (Kinetograph) that was capable of photographing objects in motion. Soon thereafter, the first motion picture studio was formed to manufacture Kinetoscopes at Edison's laboratory in West Orange, New Jersey. These first primitive movies—filmstrips viewed through a peephole machine—were then shown at a Kinetoscope Parlor on lower Broadway in New York, where crowds formed to see this most amazing novelty.

The technological development of cameras, films, and projection equipment accelerated considerably at this stage, and the most astute of the business were quick to understand the money-making potential in showing films to the public. The early years, though, were marked by a series of patent infringement suits and attempts at monopolization that were to characterize the industry's internal relations for a long time. As Stanley (1978, 10) notes, "Movies were being shown in thousands of theaters around the country. . . . After years of patent disputes, the major movie companies realized it was to their mutual advantage to cooperate. . . . A complex natural monopoly over almost all phases of the nascent motion picture industry was organized in December 1908. It was called the Motion Picture Patents Company."

This company held pooled patents for films, cameras, and projectors, and apportioned royalties on the patents. It also attempted to control the industry by buying up most of the major film exchanges (distributors) then in existence, with the goal of organizing them into a massive rental exchange, the General Film Company.

The Patents Company and its distribution subsidiary (together known as the Trust) often engaged in crude and oppressive business practices that fostered great resentment and discontent. But eventually the Trust was overwhelmed by the growing numbers, and by the increasing market power, of the independents that sprang up in all areas of production, distribution, and exhibition (that is, theaters). The Trust's control of the industry, for example, was undermined by the many independent producers who would use the Patent Company's machines, without authorization, on film stock that was imported. Yet more significantly, it was from within the ranks of these very independents that there emerged the founders of companies that were later to become Hollywood's giants: Carl Laemmle, credited with starting the star system and founder of Universal; William Fox, founder of the Fox Film Company, which was combined in 1935 with Twentieth Century Pictures; Adolph Zukor, who came to dominate Paramount Pictures; and Marcus Loew, who in the early 1920s assembled two failing companies (Metro Pictures and Goldwyn Pictures) to form the core of MGM.

At around the same time, there began a distinct movement of production activity to the West Coast. Southern California was not only far for the Trust enforcers to reach, but it could also provide low-cost nonunion labor and advantageous climate and geography for filming. Thus, by the mid 1920s, most production had shifted to the West, although New York retained its importance as the industry's financial seat.

However, not long after, the industry was shaken by the introduction of motion pictures with sound, and by the onset of the Great Depression. In that time of economic collapse, the large amounts of capital required to convert to sound equipment could only be provided by the Eastern banking firms, which refinanced and reorganized the major companies. Ultimately, it was those companies with the most vertical integration—controlling production, distribution, and exhibition—that survived this period intact. Those companies were Warner Brothers, RKO, Twentieth Century Fox, Paramount, and MGM. On a lesser scale were Universal and Columbia, who were only producer-distributors, and United Artists, essentially a distributor. The Depression, moreover, also led to the formation of powerful unions of skilled craftsmen, talent guilds, and other institutions that now play an important role in the economics of filmmaking.

Except for their sometimes strained relations with the unions, the eight major companies came out of this period of restructuring with a degree of control over the business that the early Patents Company founders could envy, and the complaints of those harmed in such an environment began to be heard by the U.S. Department of Justice. After five years of intensive investigation, the government filed suit in 1938 against the eight companies and charged them with illegally conspiring to restrain trade by, among other things, causing an exhibitor who wanted any of a distributor's pictures to take all of them (that is, block booking them). Yet, by agreeing to a few relatively minor restrictions in a consent decree signed in 1940, the majors were able to settle the case without having to sever the link between distribution and exhibition. Because of this, five majors retained dominance in about 70 percent of the first-run theaters in the country.

Not surprisingly, complaints persisted, and the Justice Department found it necessary to reactivate its suit against Paramount in 1944. After several more years of legal wrangling, the defendants finally agreed in 1948 to sign a decree that separated production and distribution from exhibition. It was this decree—combined with the contemporaneous emergence of television—that ushered the movie business into the modern era. Figure 9.1 illustrates the film industry's milestones.

May the Forces Be With You
Evolutionary Elements
The major forces that continue to shape the structure of the movie industry include: (1 technological advances in the film-making process itself, in marketing and audience sampling methods, and in the development of distribution and data storage capabilities using television signals, cable, satellites video recorders, computers, and laser discs; (2) the need for ever larger pools of capital in order to launch motion picture projects; (3) the 1948 consent decree separating distribution from exhibition; (4) the emergence of large multiplex theater chains in new suburban locations; and (5) the constant evolution and growth of independent production and service organizations.

Technology
Unquestionably the most potent impetus for change over the long term has been, and will continue to be, the development of technology. As Fielding (1967, :v) has observed "If the artistic and historical development of film and television are to be understood, then so must the peculiar marriage of art and technology which prevails in their operation. It is the involvement of twentieth-century technology which renders these media so unlike the other, older arts."

In the filmmaking process itself, for instance, the impact of technological improvements has been phenomenal. To see how far we have come, we need only remember that "talkies" were the special-effects movies of the late 1920s; indeed, it was not until the 1970s that special effects began to be created with the help of advanced computer-aided designs and electronic editing and composition devices. *Titanic, Terminator*

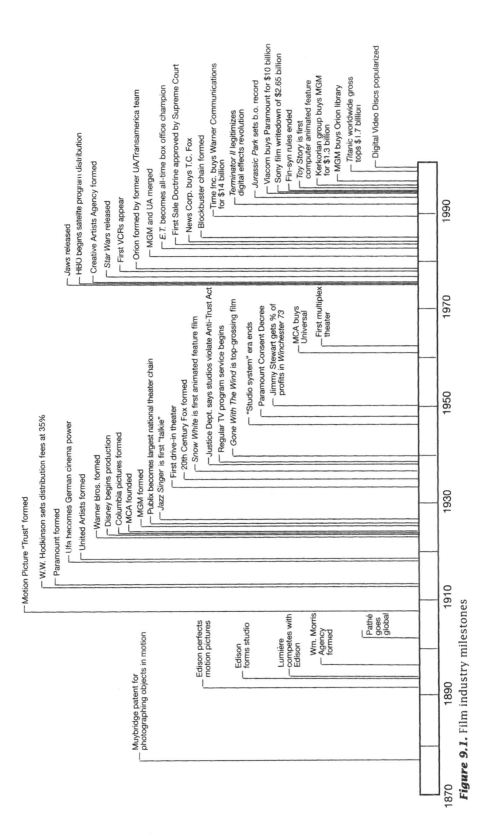

Figure 9.1. Film industry milestones

2, and *Independence Day* are examples of films that would not and could not have been made without the new machines and methods.

In addition, technological developments have enabled distributors to launch international marketing campaigns with much more speed and complexity than could have been imagined in the early years of the industry. And distributors and exhibitors now have the ability—using sophisticated sampling techniques and forecasting models—to closely estimate audience size and demographic responsiveness to a picture within a day or two of its release, and therefore to make quick adjustments.

Of course, the ready availability of television, cable, and other home video displays has also been important in changing the movie industry's economic and physical structure; film presentations on any of these media are competitive as well as supplementary to theatrical exhibitions—historically the core business. Indeed, advancements in program distribution and storage capabilities have made it possible to see a wide variety of films in the comfort of our homes and at our own discretion. Such unprecedented access to filmed entertainment, enabling viewers to control the time and place of viewing, has redirected the economic power of studios and distributors and opened the way for new enterprises to flourish. As the rate of change in signal distribution technology (Internet bandwidth, for example) begins to outpace the rate of change in production technology, filmed entertainment products and services are sure to become ever more personalized and adaptable.

Capital

After technology, the second most important long-term force for change has been the packaging and application of relatively large amounts of capital to the total process of production, distribution, and marketing. In this regard, financing innovations have played a leading role. Without the development of sophisticated financing methods and access to a broad and deep capital market, it is doubtful that the movie industry could have arrived at the position it occupies today.

From an economist's standpoint, it is also interesting to observe further that the feature-film business does not easily fit the usual molds. Industries requiring sizable capital investments can normally be expected to evolve into purely oligopolistic forms: steel and automobile manufacturing, for example. But because movies—each uniquely designed and packaged—are not stamped out on cookie-cutter assembly lines, the economic structure is somewhat different. Here, instead, we find a combination of large oligopolistic production/distribution/financing organizations regularly interfacing with and being highly dependent on a fragmented assortment of small, specialized service and production firms (see fig. 9.2).

At least in Hollywood, energetic little fish often can swim with great agility and success among the giant whales, assorted sharks, and hungry piranha.

Pecking orders

Exhibition. Back in the 1920s, a 65–cent movie ticket would buy a comfortable seat in the grandeur of a marbled and gilded theater palace in which complimentary coffee was graciously served while a string quartet played softly in the background. But those were the good old days.

The 1948 antitrust consent decree had considerable impact on movie industry structure because it disallowed control of the retail exhibition side of the business (local movie theaters) by the major production/distribution entities of that time. Disgruntled independent theater owners had initiated the action leading to issuance of the decree because they felt that studios were discriminating against them: Studios would book pictures into their captive outlets without public bidding.

However, the divestitures, ordered in the name of preserving competition, turned out to be a hollow victory for those independents. Soon after the distribution-exhibition split had been effected, studios realized that it was no longer necessary to supply a new picture every week, and they proceeded to substantially reduce production schedules. Competition for the best pictures out of a diminished supply then raised prices beyond what many owners of small theaters could afford. And by that time, television had begun to wean audiences away from big-screen entertainment; the number of movie admissions had begun a steep downward slide. The 1948 decree thus triggered and also hastened the arrival of a major structural change that would have eventually happened anyway.

In the United States, exhibition is dominated by several major theater chains, including those operated by AMC Entertainment (American Multi-Cinema), Carmike Cinemas, GC Companies (formerly General Cinema), Regal, Sony (Loews, Cineplex, Plitt, Walter Reade, and RKO), UA (formerly UA Theater Circuit), Redstone (National Amusements, Inc.), Commonwealth, and Marcus Corp. In aggregate, these companies operate approximately sixteen thousand of the best-located and most modern urban and suburban (for example, shopping mall) movie screens, with most of the other sixteen thousand or so older theaters still owned by individuals and small private companies. As such, the chains control 45 percent of the screens, but probably account for at least 80 percent of the total exhibition revenues generated.

In Canada, however, two chains, Loews Cineplex (Sony Corp.) and

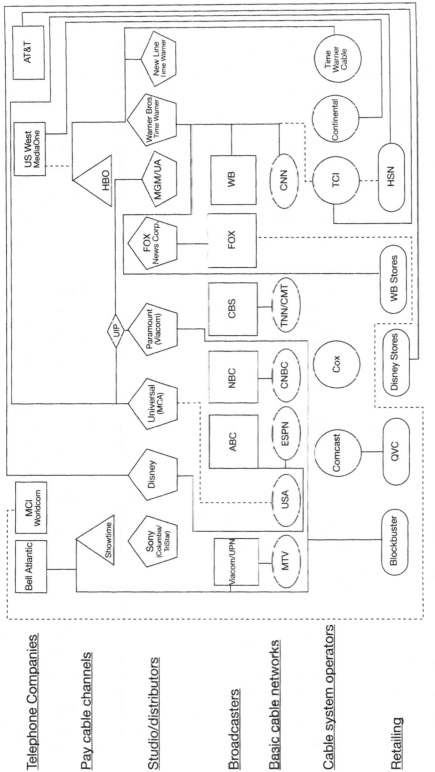

Telephone Companies

Pay cable channels

Studio/distributors

Broadcasters

Basic cable networks

Cable system operators

Retailing

Figure 9.2. Film Industry Relationships, 1998

Famous Players Ltd. (owned by Viacom Inc.), are estimated to control about 65 percent of annual theatrical revenues, which are roughly 10 percent of those in the United States.

In both the United States and Canada, construction of conveniently located multiple-screen (multiplexed) theaters in suburban areas by these large chains has more than offset the decline of older drive-in and inner-city locations and has accordingly helped to stave off competition from other forms of entertainment, including home video. The chains, moreover, have brought economies of scale to a business that used to be notoriously inefficient in its operating practices and procedures. As a result, control of exhibition is gradually being consolidated into fewer and financially stronger hands. Indeed, seven companies together account for over 50 percent of total industry dollar volume.

Production and Distribution. Theatrical film production and distribution have evolved into a multifaceted business, with many different sizes and types of organizations participating in some or all parts of the project development and marketing processes. However, companies with important and long-standing presences in both production and distribution, with substantial library assets, and with some studio production facilities (although nowadays this is not a necessity) have been collectively and historically known as "the majors."

As of the late 1990s, subsequent to many mergers and restructurings, there were six major theatrical film distributors (studios): The Walt Disney Company (Buena Vista, Touchstone, and Hollywood Pictures), Sony Pictures (formerly Columbia Pictures Entertainment, wholly owned by Sony and distributor of Columbia and TriStar films), Paramount (Viacom Inc.), Twentieth Century Fox (News Corp.), Warner Bros. (Time Warner Inc.), and Universal (80 percent owned by Seagram Co. as of 1995 and formerly MCA, Inc.). These companies produce, finance, and distribute their own films, but also finance and distribute pictures initiated by so-called independent filmmakers who either work directly for them or have projects picked up after progress toward completion has already been made.

Of considerably lesser size and scope in production and distribution activities are Metro-Goldwyn-Mayer Inc. (an oft-restructured, erstwhile major), and so-called mini-majors such as New Line Cinema (Time Warner), the recently formed DreamWorks, and the defunct Orion Pictures (whose library was bought by MGM). Many smaller production companies also often have distribution capabilites in specialized market segments (such as for art films). Generally, such smaller companies could not handle theatrical product lines that are as broad as those of the majors, nor do they have the considerable access to capital that a major would have. Nevertheless, these smaller companies may occasionally produce and nationally distribute pictures that generate box office revenues that are large enough to attract media attention.

Several smaller, independent producers also either feed their production into the established distribution pipelines of the larger companies or have mini-distribution organizations of their own. Many of these newer independents, formed in the late 1980s, largely finance their productions away from the majors and then, in effect, merely make distribution agreements with the larger studios (that is, they "rent" the studio's distribution apparatus). They thus retain much more control over a film's rights and can build a library of such rights. In addition, many executive project development firms do not produce films, but instead option existing literary properties and/or develop new properties for others to produce.

Small independent firms, sometimes called states'-righters, handle distributions in local and regional markets not well covered by the majors or submajors. They have counterparts in overseas markets, where distributors of various sizes operate.

Although at first it may be a bit startling to learn of the existence of so many different production and service organizations, their enduring presence underscores the entrepreneurial qualities of this business. The many independents have been a structural fact of life since the industry began; they add considerable variety and spice to the filmmaking process; and they help prevent stagnation.

Ups and Downs
Admission Cycles

There has long been a notion, derived from the depression-resistant performance of motion picture ticket sales, that the movie business has somewhat contracyclical characteristics. Indeed, it may be theorized that as the economy enters a recessionary phase, the leisure-time spending preferences of consumers shift toward lower-cost, closer-to-home entertainment activities than when the economy is robust and expansionary. If so, this would explain why ticket sales often remain steady during the early to middle stages of a recession, faltering only near the recession's end. By that stage, many people's budgets are apt to be severely stretched, and long-postponed purchases of essential goods (for example, new cars) and services (fixing leaky ceilings) will naturally take priority over spending on entertainment.

In fact, an important study of cycles in ticket demand (Nardone 1982) has indicated that the motion picture industry acts contracyclically to

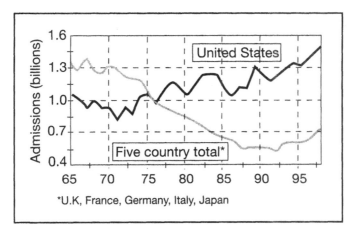

Figure 9.3. Ticket sales (admissions) in the U.S. and five leading countries, 1965–1997.

the economy 87.5 percent of the time in peaks and 69.3 percent of the time in troughs. Also, there are suggestions that both a four-year and a ten-year cycle in movie admissions may be present, but the statistical evidence in this regard is inconclusive. Ticket sales peaked in 1946 and troughed in 1971—a time when the economic survival of several major distributors was seriously in question. (See fig. 9.3.)

Seasonal demand patterns are, fortunately, much easier to discern and to interpret than are the long-wave cycles. Families find it most convenient to see films during vacation periods such as Thanksgiving, Christmas, and Easter, and children out of school during the summer months have time to frequent the box office. In the fall, however, school begins again, new television programs are introduced, and elections are held; people are busy with activities other than moviegoing. And in the period just prior to Christmas, shopping takes precedence. Thus the industry tends to concentrate most of its important film releases within just a few weeks of the year. This makes the competition for moviegoers' attention and time more expensive than it would be if audience attendance patterns were not as seasonally skewed. In all, since 1929, personal consumption expenditures on movies, in current and constant dollar terms, have traced the patterns shown in figure 9.4.

Prices and Elasticities

Ticket sales for new film releases normally are not very responsive to changes in box office prices per se, but there may be sensitivity to the total cost of moviegoing, which can include fees for baby-sitters, restaurant meals, and parking. Although demand for major-event movies, backed by strong word-of-mouth advertising and reviewer

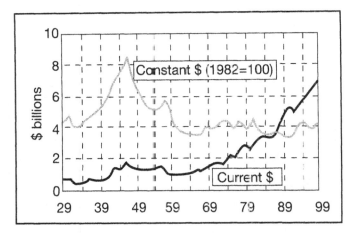

Figure 9.4. Personal consumption expenditures on movies, in current and constant dollars, 1929–1997.

support, is essentially price inelastic, exhibitors are often able to stimulate admissions by showing somewhat older features at very low prices during off-peak times (for example, Tuesday noon screenings when schools are in session). Many retired and unemployed people, and probably bored housewives and truants, like to take advantage of such bargains. There is, moreover, a widespread impression that ticket prices have risen inordinately. Yet movie ticket prices, as deflated by the consumer price index, remain below the peak of the early 1970s.

Primary and Secondary Markets

Theaters have historically been the primary retail outlet for movies, the place where most of the revenues have been collected and where most of the viewing has occurred. But since the mid 1980s, the total fees from the licensing of films for use in ancillary markets—network and syndicated television, pay cable, and home video—have collectively far overshadowed revenues derived from theatrical release.

Technological development, which has been the driving force behind the transition to dominance by so-called ancillary markets, has led to sharp decreases in the costs of distributing and storing the bits of information that are contained in entertainment software. But whether such unit-cost decreases are in themselves sufficient to sustain the industry's profitability is as yet an open question.

An individual seeing a newly released feature film in a theater would, for example, ordinarily generate revenue (rental or gross) to the distributor of anywhere between $1.50 and $4.00. However, viewing on pay television, or from a rented prerecorded disc or cassette, sometimes results

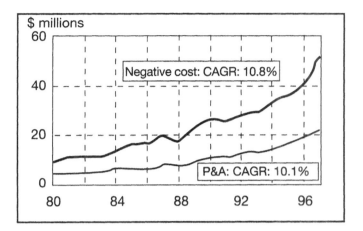

Figure 9.5. Costs of making and marketing movies, 1980–1997

in revenue per person-view of as little as 20 to 30 cents. That happens when several people in a household watch a film at the same time, or when one watches several times without incurring additional charges.

It may, of course, be argued that in recent years declining average unit costs at home have had no discernible effect on theater admissions and that, indeed, markets for filmed entertainment products have been broadened by attracting, at the margin, viewers who (because of age, infirmities, or poverty) would not pay the price of a ticket in any case. In addition, it seems that, no matter how low the price at home, people still enjoy going out to the movies.

But as sensible as this line of reasoning appears to be, there are several problems in accepting it without challenge. One of the most noticeable tendencies, for instance, has been the virtual dichotomization of the theatrical market into a relative handful of hits and a mass of also-rans. This can be seen from several recent peak-season box-office experiences, in which four out of perhaps a dozen major releases generated as much as 80 percent of total revenues.

Although must-see media-event films are as much in demand as ever, such dichotomization suggests that admissions to pictures requiring less immediate responsiveness are probably being replaced by home screenings that on average generate much less revenue per view. The new home-video options obviously allow people to become much more discriminating as to when and where they spend an evening out.

In other words, what is gained in one market may be at least partially lost in another. Indeed, in the aggregate, ancillary market cash flow is often largely substitutional and thus not necessarily a net increment to total revenues. Extensive exposures on pay cable prior to showings

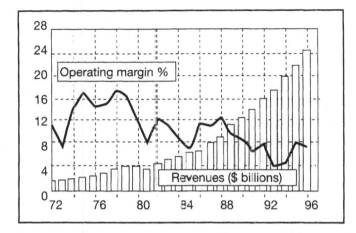

Figure 9.6. Revenues and operating margins for major filmed entertainment companies, 1972–1996.

on network television have sharply reduced network ratings garnered by feature film broadcasts. And the networks, on the average, now generally pay much less than they used to for feature-film exhibition rights.

The development of ancillary markets has, of course, been widely heralded as a boon to movie industry profitability. But despite the effective quadrupling of industry revenues since 1980—with much of the gain derived from the growth of new media sources—aggregate industry profits have not kept pace, and industry operating margins have also remained well below the peaks of the late 1970s.

As can be seen in figure 9.5, costs of production (negative costs) and marketing (prints and advertising) have, since 1980, been rising at compound annual rates of approximately 10 percent, or well over twice the inflation rate in the economy. Indeed, the cost of the average picture made by a major studio has risen from $9.4 million in 1980 to $53 million in 1998, and marketing costs have, over this span, more than quadrupled to $25 million: The return on revenues (operating margins), meanwhile, have fallen by at least one-third (see fig. 9.6).

Just as significantly, however, the existence of ancillary markets has enabled many independent producers to finance their films through so-called presales of rights. Presales, which may be in the form of funds, guarantees, or commitments that may be used to obtain funds, often support projects that perhaps could not and should not have otherwise been made. Indeed, many projects financed in this manner, typically through sale of foreign rights, are unable to generate cash flows in excess of the amounts required to cover the costs of both production and release (marketing and prints).

Companies generally relying on presale strategies manage to cushion, but not eliminate, their downside risks while giving away much of the substantial upside profit and cash flow potential from hits. Such companies will also inevitably have a relatively high cost of capital compared to that of a major studio if only because presale cash commitments (from downstream distributors) are generally relayed to the producer in installments. The producer will still usually need interim (and relatively costly) loans to cover cash outlays during the period of production and perhaps up until well after theatrical release. Thus, over the longer run, the relatively few hits such firms might produce are often insufficient in number or in degree of success to cover their many losing or break-even projects.

In all, ancillary market development has not as yet been (and may never be) fully translated into enhanced profitability. In essence, weak cost constraints (especially in regard to the hiring of top talent), fragmentation of markets and audiences, and increased competition for talent resources have capped profit margins.

Yet there is no denying that the new media have forever changed the income structure of the film business at large. As recently as 1980, theatrical sources accounted for over half of all industry revenues. Eighteen years later, theatrical sources accounted for less than a fourth of all such revenues. Also, as of 1998, consumers spent approximately $52 billion on direct purchases of entertainment services ($7 billion in tickets, $30 billion on cable, and $15 billion for home video), whereas advertisers spent about $45 billion to sponsor "free" programming.

For the most part, the inherent uncertainties have instead created a constantly shifting jumble of corporate cross-ownership and joint-venture arrangements (see fig. 9.2) that—in a scramble for control of "content" and distribution power—more often resemble hedged bets than bold and insightful strategic maneuvers.

New technology, now very visibly emerging in the form of what has come to be broadly known as interactive multimedia, will indeed provide the viewer with unprecedented control over when and where entertainment may be enjoyed. Technology has already also significantly lowered the price per view and established important new revenue sources, thus generally diffusing the economic power of the more traditional suppliers of programming. Still, new viewing options almost invariably displace older ones. And marketing costs rise as both the old and the new compete for the attention of wide-ranging, yet fickle, audiences.

Bridges

Despite the industry's unrelenting pressures for profit, however, there is an unmistakable link to the world of nonprofit arts that has been largely ignored by most observers of the cinema scene. The nonprofit component is largely influential in support of film festivals and other special corporate and foundation sponsorships that provide a platform for new talent that might not otherwise be noticed. Support of this kind allows new creative elements to be showcased and refined without the great financial pressures that attend most commercial enterprises.

The major studios, as well as producers, agents, directors, writers, and actors, are also all interested in sustaining independent venues for new productions and in discovering and nurturing talent at the top film schools. These nonprofit relationships and activities thus, in effect, function as the commercial industry's research and development laboratories and are equivalent in many respects to the farm clubs of major-league baseball teams.

However, perhaps the biggest bridge of all, including both profit and nonprofit segments of the movie business, is the cultural bridge that extends into virtually every country in the world. Although each continent seems to have at least a few indigenous film production and distribution organizations of significance, it is the globally dominant American industry that has attracted the envy and also the criticism if not outright scorn of self-appointed guardians of local cultures.

These guardians, brimming with righteous indignation and nationalistic rhetoric, seem to be greatly concerned that their sacred cultures will be overwhelmed by American values and ideals transmitted either directly or subliminally through the American movie distribution pipeline. And many trade disagreements and limitations (quotas) on imports such as those coming out of the GATT (General Agreements on Tariffs and Trade) negotiations of the early 1990s (Putnam 1997) have been rooted in such populist and popular delusions.

Yet, given that the traditions of other cultures, especially of the major European, Asian, and Latin American countries have proven rather robust for a long time, the concerns of the culture guardians seem misdirected and overblown. In fact, it might be argued that the new film distribution technologies now make it possible for more people to be exposed to many more different cultures at a lower cost than ever before. This view is consistent with that of Cowen (1998), who suggests that culture and commerce are complementary and that culture benefits greatly from the decentralization, innovation, and feedback mechanisms of the commercial market. After all is said and done, great works of art and great tales have always transcended generations and national boundaries by stimulating our emotions with their enduring universal appeal.

Indeed, it is those very enduring and endearing qualities that have led American filmmakers to often base their projects on stories that have been adapted from other cultures. For instance, in almost all of the highly successful Disney animated films such as *Beauty and the Beast* (1991), *The Lion King* (1994), or *Hercules* (1997), there is a remarkable reliance on old-culture stories repackaged into the modern American idiom. And a similar reliance is seen in live-action features, for which the effects of a well-executed drama, comedy, action-adventure, or musical are the same in terms of emotional impact no matter where the viewing audience resides: *Titanic* (1997) earned over $1.7 billion in worldwide theatrical release, with more than half generated outside the United States.

In fact, the cultural bridge from Hollywood to the rest of the world and from the rest of the world back to Hollywood has heavy traffic in both directions, with many foreign-born star directors, writers, producers, and actors making their marks in what appear ostensibly to be American films, but that are actually financed and distributed by several major companies such as Sony (Columbia/TriStar, Japan), Seagram (Universal, Canada), and News Corp. (Fox, Australia) that are largely owned, controlled, or affliliated with shareholders and managements based offshore.

Full Circle

With the costs of production soaring to new heights, it has become necessary to find new ways to amortize the costs by exposing a film's creative elements in as many revenue-enhancing positions as possible: Exposure through books, television, cable, home video, theater, theme park rides, music albums, and foreign markets has become imperative. The capital barriers to entry are higher than ever, and global distribution capability is crucial to success. All of this, combined with recent regulatory changes that have included termination of the Financial Interest and Syndication rules and passage of the Telecommunications Act of 1996, has resulted in a wave of entertainment company consolidations. Ironically, we've come full circle back to a situation similar to the early days of the business, when one corporation (or lone entrepreneur) controlled production, distribution, marketing, and exhibition.

This, it might be readily argued, is a restoration of the natural order of things. It is not, however, the end of the world for the artist: Giant media companies can only prosper over the long term by attracting early on the best and most promising talent and by encouraging—indeed, incubating—creative activity through significant financial support of development projects.

Moreover, technology, is likely to keep the monopolistic instincts of the giant companies at bay. The Internet now allows the supply of content to grow exponentially while at the same time opening a new, low-cost form of program distribution. In only a few years, Internet broadcasting of films and television shows could seriously challenge the traditional economic model of broadcast and cable networks. Already, broadcast network viewership has declined as audience share is lost to Internet surfing and to other computer-related activities.

Yet even with all of this change, people will still go to the movies. The competition for time and money is fierce. But new cinema complexes are opening with great success in Europe and elsewhere around the world, and a construction boom in so-called location-based entertainment theaters featuring ride-simulator and special-effects films is currently spreading throughout the United States. Hollywood's art form is secure. Its flickering images still attract audiences. The show goes on.

Bibliography

Alliance of Artists' Communities. 1996. *National Directory of Artist Communities*. St. Paul, Minn.: Allworth Press.

Almond, G. A., and S. Verba. 1965. *The Civic Culture: Political Attitudes and Democracy in Five Nations*. Boston: Little, Brown.

Alper, N., S. Butcher, H. Chartrand, R. Greenblatt, J. Jeffri, A. Kay, and G. Wassall. 1996. *Artists in the Workforce: Employment and Earnings, 1970–1990*. Santa Ana, Calif.: National Endowment for the Arts/Seven Locks Press.

Alper, N., and G. Wassall.1994. *The Write Stuff: Employment and Earnings of Authors, 1970 to 1990*. Washington, D.C.: National Endowment for the Arts (ERIC:ED385856).

Alsop, J. 1982. *The Rare Art Traditions*. New York: Harper and Row.

American Assembly. 1997. *The Arts and the Public Purpose: Final Report of the Ninety-Second American Assembly*. Arden House, Harriman, New York: The American Assembly, Columbia University, 29 May–1 June 1997.

Americans and the Arts. 1980. Survey of public opinion conducted for the American Council for the Arts and sponsored by Philip Morris, Inc., and the National Endowment for the Arts. Conducted by the National Research Center of the Arts., Inc., an affiliate of Louis Harris and Associates, Inc.; project director: Louis Harris. New York: American Council for the Arts.

Americans and the Arts. October 1984. Survey of public opinion conducted for Philip Morris, Inc. Conducted by the National Research Center of the Arts, Inc., an affiliate of Louis Harris and Associates, Inc., project director: Louis Harris. New York: Louis Harris and Associates, Inc.

Americans and the Arts: A Survey of Public Opinion. 1975. Research conducted by the National Research Center of the Arts, Inc., an affiliate of Louis Harris and Associates, Inc. New York: Associated Councils of the Arts.

Americans and the Arts: A Survey of the Attitudes Toward and Participation in the Arts and Culture of the United States Public. 1976. Conducted for the

National Committee for Cultural Resources, Amyas Ames, chairman, by the National Research Center of the Arts, an affiliate of Louis Harris and Associated, Inc. August 1975. New York: Associated Councils of the Arts.

Americans and the Arts V. 1988. Conducted by the National Research Center of the Arts, an affiliate of Louis Harris and Associates. Project Director: Louis Harris. New York: Philip Morris Companies, Inc.

Americans and the Arts VI: Nationwide Survey of Public Opinion. March 1992. Prepared for the American Council for the Arts. Conducted by LH Research, directed by Louis Harris. Sponsored by Philip Morris.

Americans for the Arts. 1998. *Local Arts Agency Facts.* Washington, D.C.: AFTA.

American Symphony Orchestra League. *U.S. Orchestra Profiles,* various years. Washington, D.C.: ASOL.

Andrault, M., and P. Dressayre. 1987. "Government and the Arts in France." In *The Patron State,* edited by M. C. Cummings, Jr., and R. S. Katz. New York: Oxford University Press.

Andrews, E. L. 5 August 1990. "When Imitation Isn't the Sincerest Form of Flattery." *New York Times,* E20.

The Arts as an Industry: Their Economic Importance to the New York–New Jersey Metropolitan Region. 1993. New York: Port Authority of New York and New Jersey.

Bain, J. S. 1968. *Industrial Organization.* 2nd ed. New York: John Wiley.

Bakke, M. 1994. "Centralized Decentralization in Norwegian Cultural Policy." *The Journal of Arts Management Law and Society,* 24:111–127.

Balfe, J. H., ed. 1993. *Paying the Piper: Causes and Consequences of Art Patronage.* Champaign-Urbana: University of Illinois Press.

Banfield, E. 1984. *The Democratic Muse: The Visual Arts and the Public Interest.* New York: Basic Books (A Twentieth Century Fund Essay).

Barber, B. 1996. "Serving Democracy by Serving the Arts" (unpublished essay prepared for the President's Committee on the Arts and the Humanities).

Barsdate, K. J./NASAA. November 1996. *A State Arts Agency Performance Measurement Toolkit.* Washington, D.C.: National Assembly of State Arts Agencies.

Barzun, J. 1965. "Art-by-act-of-Congress." *The Public Interest,* no. 1 (fall).

Baumgartner, F. R., and B. D. Jones. 1993. *Agendas and Instability in American Politics.* Chicago: University of Chicago Press.

Baumol, W. J. 1993. "Good News? Health and Education Costs are Rising Rapidly!" *CV Starr Newsletter,* New York University, 11: 26–29.

Baumol, W. J., and H. Baumol. 1984. "The Mass Media and the Cost Disease." In *The Economics of Cultural Industries,* edited by W. Hendon, N. Grant, and D. Shaw. Akron, Ohio: Association for Cultural Economics, University of Akron.

Baumol, W. J., and W. G. Bowen. 1966. *Performing Arts: The Economic Dilemma.* New York: Twentieth Century.

Baumol, W. J., and M. I. Oates. 1976. "Comment: The Economics of Theatre in Renaissance London." *Scandinavian Journal of Economics* 78.

———. 1974. "The Economics of Theatre in Renaissance London." *Swedish Journal of Economics* 76, 3: 369.

———. 1972. "The Economics of Theatre in Renaissance London." *Swedish Journal of Economics* 74: 136–180.

Bell, D. 1976. *The Cultural Contradictions of Capitalism*. New York City: Basic Books.

———. 1981. "Models and Reality in Economic Discourse." In *The Crisis in Economic Theory*, edited by D. Bell and I. Kristol. New York City: Basic Books.

Bellah, R. J., R. Madsen, W. M. Sullivan, A. Swidler, and S. M. Tipton. 1985. *Habits of the Heart: Individualism and Commitment in American Life*. New York: Harper and Row.

Ben-Ner, A. 1986. "Nonprofit Organizations: Why Do They Exist in Market Economies?" Chapter 5 in *The Economics of Nonprofit Institutions*, edited by S. Rose-Ackerman. New York: Oxford University Press.

Bennett, W. J. 1992. *The De-Valuing of America: The Fight for Our Culture and Our Children*. New York: Touchstone.

Berg, M. 1987. "Government Policy and the Arts in Norway." In *The Patron State*, edited by M. C. Cummings Jr. and R. S. Katz. New York: Oxford University Press.

Bergonzi, L., and J. Smith. 1996. *Effects of Arts Education on Participation in the Arts*. National Endowment for the Arts, Research Division Report #36. Santa Ana, Calif.: Seven Locks Press.

Biddle, L. 1988. *Our Government and the Arts: A Perspective from the Inside*. New York: American Council for the Arts.

Billington, J. H. February 1991. *The Intellectual and Cultural Dimensions of International Relations*. Washington, D.C.: President's Committee on the Arts and Humanities.

Blau, J. R. 1989. *The Shape of Culture: A Study of Contemporary Cultural Patterns in the United States*. New York: Cambridge University Press.

Boulding, K. E. 1973. *The Economy of Love and Fear: A Preface to Grant Economics*. Belmont, Calif.: Wadsworth.

———. September 1972. "Toward the Development of a Cultural Economics." *Social Science Quarterly* 53(2).

Bourdieu, P. 1984. *Distinctions*. Cambridge, Mass.: Harvard University Press.

Bowen, W. G., et al. 1994. *The Charitable Nonprofits*. San Francisco: Jossey-Bass.

Breslauer, J. 16 March 1997. "The NEA's Real Offense." *Washington Post*, G1.

Brown, P. L. 6 February 1997. "Reading the Message in the Bottles." *New York Times*, C1.

Bryson, B. 1996. "Symbolic Exclusion and Musical Dislikes." *American Sociological Review* 16(5): 884–899.

Bureau of Economic Analysis. 1991. *Baseline 1982 Input/Ouput Matrix*. Washington, D.C.: Department of Commerce.

Burns, J. S. 1975. *The Awkward Embrace: The Creative Artist and the Institution in America*. New York: Alfred A. Knopf.

Busch, W. vom, ed. 1985. *Art Education and Artists' Training in the Federal Republic of Germany*. Bonn: Inter Nationes, No. 7–8e.

Business Week. 21 March 1984. "Industry Outlook Scoreboard," 236.

Bygren, L. O., B.B.K. Knolaan, and S. E. Johansson. 21 December 1996. "Attendance at Cultural Events, Reading Books or Periodicals, and Making Music or Singing in a Choir as Determinants for Survival: Swedish Interview Survey of Living Conditions." *British Medical Journal* 7072: 313.

Cameron, S. 1995. "On the Role of Critics in the Culture Industry." *Journal of Cultural Economics*, 19(4): 321–351.

Cantor, N. F. 1969. *Medieval History: The Life and Death of a Civilization.* 2nd ed. New York City: Macmillan.

Chafee, Z., Jr. 1984. "Reflections on the Law of Copyright: I & II." In *Columbia Law Review,* vol. 45, nos. 4 and 5, July and September 1945, in *Great American Law Reviews,* edited by R. C. Berrings. Birmingham, Ala.: Legal Classics Library.

Chartrand, H. H. 1992a. *The American Arts Industry: Size and Significance.* Saskatchewan, Alberta: Kultural Econometrics International.

———. 1996. *Architecture & Design Occupations in America: 1940 to 1990.* Washington, D.C.: National Endowments for the Arts Research Division (ERIC).

———. Spring 1992b. "Art, Culture and Global Business: Snapshots from the World Economic Forum." *Journal of Arts Management, Law and Society* 22(1).

———. Summer 1998. "The Arts and the Public Purpose—The Economic of It All." Journal of Arts Management, Law and Society 28(2).

———. 1987. "The Arts: Consumption Skills in the Post-Modern Economy." *Journal of Art and Design Education* 6(1).

———. Summer 1991. "Context and Continuity: Philistines, Pharisees and Art in English Culture." *Journal of Arts Management, Law and Society* 21(2).

———. 1989. "The Contribution of Art to National Income." In *Cultural Economics: A Canadian Perspective '88,* edited by H. H. Chartrand, W. Hendon, and C. McCaughey. Akron, Ohio: University of Akron.

———. 1990. "The Hard Facts: Perspectives of Cultural Economics." In *Transactions of the Royal Society of Canada 1989.* Fifth Series, vol. IV. Ontario, Canada: University of Toronto Press.

———. Winter 1996. "Intellectual Property in the Post-Modern World." *Journal of Arts Management Law and Society* 25(4).

Chartrand, H. H., and C. McCaughey. 1989. "The Arm's Length Principle and the Arts: An International Perspective—Past, Present and Future." In *Who's to Pay for the Arts?* edited by M. C. Cummings and J. M. Davidson Schuster. New York: American Council for the Arts.

Cherbo, J. M. 1992. "A Department of Cultural Resources: A Perspective on the Arts." *Journal of Arts Management Law and Society* 22: 44–62.

Cherbo, J. M., and M. Peters. 1995. *American Participation in Opera and Musical Theater, 1992.* Santa Ana, Calif.: Seven Locks Press.

Christopherson, S. 1996. "Flexibility and Adaptation in Industrial Relations: The Exceptional Case of the U.S. Media Entertainment Industries." In *Under the Stars: Essays on Labor Relations in Arts and Entertainment,* edited by L. Gray and R. Seeber. Ithaca, N.Y.: ILR Press.

Clotfelter, C. T. 1992. "The Distributional Consequences of Nonprofit Activities." In *Who Benefits from the Nonprofit Sector?* edited by C. T. Clotfelter. Chicago: University of Chicago Press.

Coase, R. 1937. "The Nature of the Firm." *Economica* 4: 386–405.

Cobb, R. W., and C. D. Elder. 1983. *Participation in American Politics: The Dynamics of Agenda-Building.* Baltimore: Johns Hopkins University Press.

Cohen, S. F. 1991. *Study of Health Coverage and Health-Care Needs of Orienting Artists in the United States.* New York: American Council for the Arts.

Cole, J. 1995. *The UCLA Television Violence Monitoring Report* (Los Angeles: UCLA Center for Communication Policy).

Commons, J. R. 1957. *The Legal Foundations of Capitalism.* Originally published 1926. Madison: University of Wisconsin Press.

Communications Industry Forecast. 1996. New York: Veronis, Suhler and Associates.

Coombs, P. H. 1964. *The Fourth Dimension of Foreign Policy: Educational and Cultural Affairs.* New York: Harper and Row.

Cornwell, T. L. 1985. "Party Platforms and the Arts." In *Art, Ideology and Politics*, edited by J. H. Balfe and M. J. Wyszomirski. New York: Praeger.

Couto, R. 1997. *Measuring Social Capital and the Democratic Prospect*, presented at the 20–21 March 1997 Independent Sector Spring Research Forum, Alexandria, Va.

Cowen, Tyler. 1998. *In Praise of Commercial Culture.* Cambridge, Mass.: Harvard University Press.

Cremin. L. 1969. *The Transformation of the School: Progressivism in American Education, 1876–1957.* New York: Alfred A. Knopf.

Csikszentmihalyi. M. 1996. *Creativity: Flow and the Psychology of Discovery and Invention.* New York: HarperCollins Publishers.

Cummings, M. C., Jr., 1991. "Government and the Arts: An Overview." In *Public Money and the Muse*, edited by Stephen Benedict. New York: W. W. Norton.

———. 1982. "To Change a Nation's Cultural Policy." In *Public Policy and the Arts*, edited by K. V. Mulcahy and C. R. Swarn. Boulder, Colo.: Westview Press.

———. 1995. "To Change a Nation's Cultural Policy." In *America's Commitment to Culture: Government and the Arts*, edited by K. Mulcahy and M. Wyszomirski. Boulder: Westview Press.

Cummings, M. C., Jr., and R. S. Katz 1987. *The Patron State.* New York: Oxford University Press.

Cwi, D. 1982. "Merit Good or Market Failure: Justifying and Analyzing Public Support for the Arts." In *Public Policy and the Arts* edited by R. Swaim and K. V. Mulcahy. Boulder: Westview Press.

Cyert, R. M., and J. G. March. 1992. *A Behavioral Theory of the Firm*, 2nd ed. Cambridge, Mass.: Blackwell.

The Data Report from the 1989 National Museum Survey. 1992. Washington, D.C.: American Association of Museums.

DiMaggio, P. 1982. "Cultural Entrepreneurship in Nineteenth Century Boston, I and II." *Media, Culture and Society* 4(33–50): 303–322.

———, ed. 1986. *Nonprofit Enterprise in the Arts: Studies in Mission and Constraint.* New York: Oxford University Press.

DiMaggio, P., and B. Pettit. Fall 1993. "Surveys of Public Attitudes toward the Arts: What Surveys Tell Us about the Arts' Political Trials—and How They Might Tell Us Even More." *Grantmakers in the Arts* 9(2) Fall: 26–30.

Dorian, F. 1964. *Commitment to Culture.* Pittsburgh: University of Pittsburgh Press.

Dorn, C. M. 1995. "Privatization of the Arts and the Public Interest: An Issue for Local Arts for Local Arts Agencies." *Journal of Arts Management, Law and Society* 25: 82–91.

Easley, D., and M. O'Hara. 1986. "Optimal Nonprofit Firms." Chapter 4 in *The Economics of Nonprofit Institutions*, edited by S. Rose-Ackerman. New York: Oxford University Press.

The Economist. 1 July 1989. "Economic and Financial Indicators."

The Economist. 11 March 1989. "Meet the New Media Monsters." 65–66.

The Economist. 22 December 1990. "Survey of the World Art Market."

Ellis, D., and J. Beresford. 1994. *Trends in Artist Occupations: 1970–1990.* Washington, D.C.: National Endowment for the Arts Research Division.

Epstein, J. 3 June 1996. "W. C. Fields Was Wrong: Why, Despite Everything, Republicans Should Not Abandon the Arts." *Weekly Standard*, 29–36.

Executive Office of the President, 1987. *Standard Industrial Classification Manual*. Springfield, Va.: U.S.G.P.O.

Farhi, P. 16 February 1997. "NAB: Their Reception's Great." *Washington Post*, H1, 5.

Farrer, C. Winter 1994. "Who Owns the Words? An Anthropological Perspective of Public Law 101–601." *Journal of Arts Management Law and Society*, 317–326.

Felton, M. V. 1994/95. "Evidence of the Existence of the Cost Disease in the Performing Arts." *Journal of Cultural Economics* 18(4): 301–312.

———. 1996. *Historical Funding Patterns in Nonprofit Theaters, 1980–1992*. Paper presented at the Ninth International Conference on Cultural Economics, Boston, 8–12 May.

———. Spring 1994. "Historical Funding Patterns in Symphony Orchestras, Dance, and Opera Companies." *Journal of Arts Management Law and Society*, 8–31.

Fielding, R., ed. 1967. "A Technological History of Motion Pictures and Television: An Anthology." *Journal of the Society of Motion Pictures and Television Engineers*. Los Angeles: University of California Press.

Filer, R. 1986. "The 'Starving Artist'—Myth or Reality? Earnings of Artists in the United States." *Journal of Political Economy*, 94.

Filicko, T. Fall 1996. "In What Spirit Do Americans Cultivate the Arts? A Review of Survey Questions on the Arts." *Journal of Arts Management Law and Society* 26(3):221–246.

———. 1997. "What Do We Need to Know About Culture?" Prepared for the 23rd Annual Conference on Social Theory, Politics and the Arts, 2–4 October. Cocoa Beach, Fla.

Focke, A. 1996. *Financial Support for Artists: A Study of Past and Current Support, with Reflections on the Findings and Recommendations for Future Action*. Seattle: Grantmakers in the Arts.

Frank, R., and P. Cook. 1995. *Winner-Take-All Society*. New York: Free Press.

Frankel, C. 1966. *The Neglected Aspect of Foreign Affairs: Educational and Cultural Policy Abroad*. Washington, D.C.: The Brookings Institution.

Frey, B. S., and W. W. Pommerehne. 1989. *Muses & Markets: Explorations in the Economics of the Arts*. London: Basil Blackwell.

Fudenberg, D., and J. Tirole. 1991. *Game Theory*. Cambridge: MIT Press.

Galbraith, J. K. 18 February 1983. "The Artist and the Economist: Why the Twain Must Meet." *The Times Higher Education Supplement*.

———. 1973. "The Market System and the Arts." In *Economics and the Public Purpose*. Scarborough: New American Library.

———. 1968. *The New Industrial State*. New York: Signet.

Galligan, A. 1993. "The Politicization of Panels of Peer-Review Panels at the NEA." In *Paying the Piper: Causes and Consequences of Arts Patronage*, edited by J. Balfe. Chicago: University of Illinois Press.

Galligan, A., and T. Brown. Winter 1992. "Warning Labels on Records and Tapes: The Mapping of Two Conflicting Policy Positions." *Journal of Arts Management and Law* 21(4): 355–372.

Galligan, A., and N. Alper. Summer 1998. "Characteristics of Performing Artists: A Baseline Profile." *Journal of Arts Management Law and Society* 29(2).

Gans, H. 1985. "American Popular Culture and High Culture in a Changing Class Structure." In *Art, Ideology and Politics*, edited by J. H. Balfe and M. J. Wyszomirski. New York: Praeger.

Gapinski, James H. May 1986. "The Lively Arts as Substitutes for the Lively Arts." *American Economic Review* 76(2).

General Social Surveys, 1972–1994: Cumulative Codebook. November 1994. Conducted for The National Data Program for the Social Sciences at National Opinion Research Center, University of Chicago.

Gildea, R. 1996. *France Since 1945.* New York: University of Oxford Press.

Goodwin, C. D. and M. Nacht. 1991. *Missing the Boat: The Failure to Internationalize American Higher Education.* New York and Cambridge, U.K.: Cambridge University Press.

Gray, C. M. 1995. *Turning On and Tuning In: Media Participation in the Arts.* National Endowment for the Arts, Research Division Report #33. Carson, Calif.: Seven Locks Press.

Gray, L., and R. Seeber, eds. 1996. *Under the Stars: Essays on Labor Relations in Arts and Entertainment.* Ithaca, N.Y.: ILR Press.

Greene, M. 1995. *Releasing the Imagination: Essays on Education, the Arts, and Social Change.* San Francisco: Jossey-Bass.

Habib, M. S. 1998. "Copyrights Under Islamic Law." Private correspondence with H. H. Chartrand.

Hall, M., and E. Metcalf, Jr., eds. 1994. *The Artist Outsider: Creativity and the Boundaries of Culture.* Washington, D.C.: Smithsonian Institution Press.

Hamilton, R. 1991. "Work and Leisure: On the Reporting of Poll Results." *Public Opinion Quarterly* 55: 347–356.

Handy, F. Winter 1995. "Reputation as Collateral: An Economic Analysis of the Role of Trustees of Nonprofits." *Nonprofit and Voluntary Sector Quarterly* 24(4): 293–306.

Hansmann, H. B. 1986a. "Nonprofit Enterprise in the Performing Arts." Chapter 1 in *Nonprofit Enterprise in the Arts: Studies in Mission and Constraint*, edited by P. DiMaggio. New York: Oxford University Press.

———. 1986b. "The Role of Nonprofit Enterprise" Chapter 3 in *The Economics of Nonprofit Institutions*, edited by S. Rose-Ackerman. New York: Oxford University Press.

Hanson, A. 1973. *Omnibus Copyright Revision: Comparative Analysis of the Issues.* Washington D.C.: American Society for Information Science.

Harris, Neil. Spring 1996. "Public Subsidies and American Art." *Newsletter of Grantmakers in the Arts.* 5–9, 25.

Heikkinen, M. 1989. " Situational Portrait of Writers: A Study of the Position of Authors in Finland (English summary). Helsinki, Finland: The Arts Council of Finland.

Heilbrun, J. "The Competition Between High Culture and Popular Culture as Seen in the New York Times." *Journal of Cultural Economics* (forthcoming).

———. 1984. "Once More, with Feeling: the Arts Boom Revisited." In *The Economics of Cultural Industries*, edited by William S. Hendon, et al. Akron: Association for Cultural Economics.

Heilbrun, J., and C. Gray. 1993. *The Economics of Art and Culture: An American Perspective.* New York: Cambridge University Press.

Henderson, J. L. 1984. *Cultural Attitudes in Psychological Perspective.* Toronto: Inner City Books.

Hendon, William S., et al., eds. 1984. *The Economics of Cultural Industries*. Akron, Ohio: Association for Cultural Economics.

Heyne, P. 1997. *The Economic Way of Thinking*. 8th ed. Upper Saddle River, N.J.: Prentice Hall.

Hillman, G. 1996. *Artists in the Community: Training Artists to Work in Alternative Settings*. New York: Americans for the Arts and the Institute for Community Development and the Arts.

Hillman, J. 1981. *The Thoughts of the Heart*. Eranos Lectures 2. Dallas, Tex.: Spring Publications Inc.

Hirsch, E. D. 1988. *Cultural Literacy*. New York: Vintage Books.

Hirschman, A. O. 1984. "Against Parsimony: Three Easy Ways of Complicating Some Categories of Economic Discourse." *American Economic Association Papers and Proceedings* 74(2): 89–96.

Holbrook, M. B. 1987. "Progress and Problems in Research on Consumer Esthetics." In *Artists and Cultural Consumers*, edited by D. Shaw, W. Hendon, and C. Richard Waits. Akron, Ohio: Association for Cultural Economics, University of Akron.

Holbrook, M. B. and E. C. Hirschman. September 1982. "The Experiential Aspects of Consumption: Consumer Fantasies, Feeling, and Fun." *Journal of Consumer Research*.

House Republican Conference (HRP). 9 April 1997. *Talking Points: No More Federal Funds for the NEA!* Press release.

Hughes, R. October 1984. "Art and Money Part I." *New Art Examiner*.

Hunter, J. D. 1991. *Culture Wars: The Struggle to Define America*. New York: Basic Books.

Huntington, S. Summer 1993. "The Clash of Civilizations?" *Foreign Affairs*.

Independent Commission on the NEA. 1990. *A Report to Congress on the National Endowment for the Arts*. Washington, D.C.: Independent Commission.

Jeffri, J. 1991. "The Artist in an Integrated Society." In *Public Money and the Muse*. New York: The American Assembly and W. W. Norton Press.

_____. Fall 1982. "Making Money: Real Estate Strategies for the Arts." *Journal of Arts Management Law and Society*.

Jeffri, J., J. Hosie, and R. Greenblat. Fall 1987. "The Artist Alone: Work-Related, Human and Social Service Needs—Select Findings." *Journal of Arts Management Law and Society* 17(3).

Kangas, A., and J. Onsér-Franzén. 1996. "Is There a Need for a New Cultural Policy Strategy in the Nordic Welfare State?" *International Journal of Cultural Policy*. 3: 15–26.

Keynes, J. M. 1949. *The General Theory of Employment, Interest and Money*. London: Macmillan.

Kimball, R. Spring 1997. "Art Without Beauty." *Public Interest*, 127: 44–59.

Kingston, P., and J. Cole. 1986. *The Wages of Writing: Per Word, Per Piece, or Perhaps*. New York: Columbia University Press.

Kleberg, C. J. 1987. "Cultural Policy in Sweden." In *The Patron State*, edited by M. C. Cummings, Jr., and R. S. Katz. New York: Oxford University Press.

Kolbert, E. 20 August 1995. "Americans Despair of Popular Culture." *New York Times*, II, 1, 23.

Konig, H. December 1995. "A French Mirror." *Atlantic Monthly*.

Kotler, P., and J. Scheff. 1997. *Standing Room Only: Strategies for Marketing the Performing Arts*. Boston: Harvard Business School Press.

Kushner, R., and A. E. King. 1994. "Performing Arts as a Club Good: Evidence from a Nonprofit Organization." *Journal of Cultural Economics* 13(1): 5–28.

Kushner, R., and P. P. Poole. Winter 1996. "Exploring Structure—Effectiveness Relationships in Nonprofit Arts Organizations." *Nonprofit Management and Leadership* 7(2): 119–136.

Kreidler, J. Summer 1996. "Leverage Lost: The Nonprofit Arts in the Post-Ford Era." *Journal of Arts Management, Law, and Society* 26(2): 79–100.

Lang, G. E., and K. Lang. 1991. "Public Opinion and the Helms Amendment." *Journal of Arts Management and Law* 21: 127–140.

Larson, G. O. 1983. *The Reluctant Patron: The United States Government and the Arts, 1943–1965*. Philadelphia: University of Pennsylvania Press.

Lehman, C., and L. Merrill. 1986. "Transforming the Technocrat: Redefining Business Survival." In *Corporations at Risk: Liberal Learning and Private Enterprise*. Cambridge, Mass.: Harvard University Press.

Lehman, E.V., ed. 1996. *Art and Arts Participation: With a Focus on the Baby Boom Cohort*. National Endowment for the Arts, Research Division Report #34. Santa Ana, Calif.: Seven Locks Press.

Leroy, D. 1980. *Economics of the Live Performing Arts—Essays on the Relation Between Economics and Aesthetics*. Amiens, France: Groupe de recherches en economie de la culture, University of Amiens.

Levine, L. W. 1986. *Highbrow/Lowbrow: The Emergence of Cultural Hierarchy in America*. Cambridge: Harvard University Press.

Liebenstein, H. June 1966. "Allocative Efficiency vs. X-Efficiency." *American Economic Review*.

———. 1981. "Microeconomis and X-Efficiency Theory: If There is No Crisis There Ought to Be." In *The Crisis in Economic Theory*, edited by D. Bell and I. Kristol. New York City: Basic Books.

Lijphart, A. 1977. *Democracy in Plural Societies: A Comparative Exploration*. New Haven: Yale University Press.

Lippman, W. 1992. *Public Opinion*. New York: Macmillan.

Lipset, S. M. 1990. *Continental Divide: The Values and Institutions of the United States and Canada*. New York: Routledge.

Litt, P. 1992. *The Muses, the Masses, and the Massey Commission*. Toronto: University of Toronto Press.

Lowi, T. J. 1964. "American Business, Public Policy, Case Studies and Political Theory." *World Politics* 16: 677–693.

MacDonald, B. 1971. *Copyright in Context: The Challenge of Change*. Ottawa, Canada: Economic Council of Canada.

MacNeil, R. April 1997. "Who Needs Artists?" *American Theatre*, 11–14.

Mangset, P. 1995. "Risks and Benefits of Decentralisation: The Development of Local Cultural Administration in Norway." *International Journal of Cultural Policy* 2: 67–86.

Margolies, J., and Gwathmey, E. 1991. *Tickets to Paradise: American Movie Theaters and How We Had Fun*. Boston: Little, Brown (Bullfinch Press).

Marquis, A. G. 1995. *Art Lessons: Learning from the Rise and Fall of Public Arts Funding*. New York: Basic Books.

Marshall, A. 1969. *Principles of Economics* 8th ed., 1920. London: English Language Book Society.

Martin, D., ed. 1995. *The Guide to Arts Administration, Training and Research, 1995–97*. San Francisco: American Association of Arts Administrators.

Mayor's Office of Cultural Affairs. 1994. *Artists' Health Care Task Force: A Report to Congress*. Boston: Artists' Foundation, and Boston Health Care for the Homeless.

McCracken, G. 1988. *Culture and Consumption: New Approaches to the Symbolic Character of Consumer Goods and Services*. Bloomington: Indiana University Press.

McWilliams, W. C. 1985. "The Arts and the American Political Tradition." In *Art, Ideology and Politics*, edited by J. H. Balfe and M. J. Wyszomirski. New York: Praeger.

Meisel, John. 1989. "Government and the Arts in Canada." In *Who's to Pay for the Arts?* edited by M. C. Cummings, Jr., and J. M. Davidson Schuster. New York: American Council for the Arts.

Meisel, J., and J. Van Loon. 1987. "Cultivating the Bushgarden: Cultural Policy in Canada." In *The Patron State*, edited by M. C. Cummings, Jr., and R. S. Katz. New York: Oxford University Press.

Mencher, S. January–February 1997. "Jazz Meets the Classics." *Symphony Magazine*, 19–65.

Meyersohn, R. 1990. "Culture in the Bronx: Minority Participation in the Arts." In *The Future of the Arts: Public Policy and Arts Research*, edited by D. B. Pankratz and V. B. Morris. New York: Praeger.

Milgrom, P., and J. Roberts. 1992. *Economics, Organization, and Management*. Englewood Cliffs, N.J.: Prentice-Hall.

Morin, A. J. 1993. *Science Policy and Politics*. Boston: Little Brown.

Morone, J. A. 1990. *The Democratic Wish: Popular Participation and the Limits of American Government*. New York: Basic Books.

Morris, D. 1982. "Art and Religion." In *The Human Race*. U.K.: Thames Television.

Mulcahy, K. V. 1982. "Cultural Diplomacy: Foreign Policy and the Exchange Programs." In *Public Policy and the Arts*. Boulder, Colo.: Westview Press.

———. 1992a. "Government and the Arts in the United States." In *Public Policy and the Aesthetic Interest*, edited by R. A. Smith and R. Berman. Urbana, Ill.: University of Illinois.

———. 1985. "The NEA as Public Patron of the Arts." In *Art, Ideology, and Politics*, edited by J. H. Balfe and M. J. Wyszomirski. New York: Praeger.

———. 1995a. "Public Culture and Political Culture." In *Québec Under Free Trade: Making Public Policy in America*, edited by G. Lachapelle. Québec: Presses de l'Université du Québec.

———. 1995b. "The Public Interest and Arts Policy," in *America's Commitment to Culture: Government and the Arts*, edited by K. Mulcahy and M. Wyszomirski. Boulder: Westview Press.

———. 1991. "The Public Interest in Public Culture." *Journal of Arts Management, Law, and Society* 21: 5–25.

———. 1992b. "The Structure and Politics of Local Support for the Arts in the United States." In *Décentralisation, régionalisation, et action culturelle municipale*, edited by M. Beaulac and F. Colbert. Montréal: École des Hautes Études Commerciales de Montréal.

Mulcahy, K. V., and C. R. Swaim. 1982. *Public Policy and the Arts*. Boulder: Westview Press.

Mulcahy, K. V., and M. J. Wyszomirski. 1995. *America's Commitment to Culture*. Boulder: Westview Press.

Nardone, J. M. April 1982. "Is the Movie Industry Contracyclical." *Cycles* 33(3).

National Assembly of State Arts Agencies. 1992. State Arts Agencies Legislative Appropriations—Annual Survey, fiscal years 1992 and 1993.

National Assembly of State Arts Agencies. 1992, 1991. *State Arts Agency Profile.*

National Assembly of State Arts Agencies. 1992. *The State of the State Arts Agencies.*

National Association of Local Arts Agencies. 1992. *Art Start: Funding Innovations for Local Arts Agencies.*

National Association of Local Arts Agencies. 1994. 'Local Arts Agency Facts."

National Association of Local Arts Agencies. 1995. *Resource Development Handbook: Untapped Public Funding for the Arts.*

National Endowment for the Arts (NEA). September 1998. *Research Division Report #39, 1997 Survey of Public Participation in the Art: Summary Report.* Washington D.C.: NEA.

———. September 1998. *Research Division Report #70, 1997 Survey of Public Participation in the Art: Half of U.S. Adults Attended Arts Performances or Exhibitions.* Washington D.C.: NEA.

———. 1982 and 1992. *Survey of Public Participation in the Arts.* Washington, D.C.: NEA.

National Telecommunications and Information Administration. 1990. *Comprehensive Study on the Globalization of Mass Medic Firms: Notice of Inquiry and Request for Comments.* Washington, D.C.

Nemmers, E. E. 1974. *Dictionary of Economics and Business.* Totowa, N.J.: Littlefield-Adams.

Netzer, D. 1992. "Arts and Culture.' In *Who Benefits from the Nonprofit Sector?* edited by C. T. Clotfelter. Chicago: University of Chicago Press.

Netzer, D. 1978. *The Subsidized Muse: Public Support for the Arts in the United States.* New York: Cambridge University Press.

Netzer, D., and E. Parker. 1993. *Dancemakers.* National Endowment for the Arts Research Report # 28 NEA.

Nicholson, W. 1990. *Intermediate Microeconomics*, 5th ed. Orlando: Dryden Press.

Norrander, Barbara, and Clyde Wilcox. 1997. *Understanding Public Opinion.* Washington, D.C.: CQ Press.

Opera America. *Profile*, various issues.

Opera America Annual Field Report. 1995 and 1996. Washington, D.C.: Opera America, Inc.

Orren, G. R. 1988. "Beyond Self-Interest." In *The Power of Public Ideas*, edited by R. B. Reich. Cambridge, Mass : Ballinger Publishing Co.

Ortmann, A. December 1996. "Modern Economic Theory and the Study of Nonprofit Organizations: Why the Twain Shall Meet." *Nonprofit and Voluntary Sector Quarterly* 25(4): 470–484.

Owen, V. L. March 1997. *Reconciling the Conflict Between Revenue Maximization and Audience Size*, unpublished manuscript presented at Midwest Economics Association, Kansas City

Page, B. I., and R. Y. Shapiro. 1993. *The Rational Public: Fifty Years of Trends in Americans' Policy Preferences.* Chicago: University of Chicago.

Park, M., and G. F. Markowitz. 1992. "New Deal for Public Art." In *Critical Issues in Public Art*, edited by H. F. Senie and S. Webster. New York: HarperCollins Publishers.

Pearlstein, S. November 1995. "Reshaped Economy Exacts Tough Toll." *Washington Post*, 12: A-14.

People for the American Way (PAW). 1994. *Artistic Freedom Under Attack*. Washington, D.C.: PAW.

Perret, J., and G. Saez. 1996. *Institutions et vie culturelles*. Paris: La Documentation Française.

Peters, M., and J. M. Cherbo. 1994. *Americans' Personal Participation in the Arts: 1992*. Washington, D.C.: Report to the Research Division of the NEA.

Petersen, H. C., and W. C. Lewis. 1990. *Managerial Economics*. 2nd ed. New York: Macmillan.

Peterson, R.A. 1986. "From Impresario to Arts Administrator: Formal Accountability in Nonprofit Cultural Organizations." Chapter 7 in *Nonprofit Enterprise in the Arts: Studies in Mission and Constraint*, edited by P. DiMaggio. New York: Oxford University Press.

Peterson, R. A. and R. M. Kern. 1996. "Changing Highbrow Taste: From Snob to Omnivore." *American Sociological Review* 61(5): 900–907.

Peterson, R. A., D. E. Sherkat, J. H. Balfe, and R. Meyersohn. 1996. *Age and Arts Participation with a Focus on the Baby Boom Cohort*. Santa Ana, Calif.: Seven Locks Press.

Peterson, R. A. and A. Simkus. 1992. "How Musical Taste Groups Mark Occupational Status Groups." In *Cultivating Differences Symbolic Boundaries and the Making of Inequality*, edited by M. Lamont and M. Fournier. Chicago: University of Chicago Press.

President's Committee on the Arts and Humanities (PCAH). 1992. *The Value of the Arts*. Washington, D.C.: President's Committee.

President's Committee on the Arts and Humanities (PCAH). February 1997. *Creative America*. Washington, D.C.: President's Committee.

Public Law 89–209. 1965. Congressional Declaration of Purpose Establishing the National Endowment for the Humanities and the National Endowment for the Arts; National Foundation on the Arts and Humanities Act of 1965. Washington, D.C.: U.S. Government Printing Office.

Public Law 101-512. 1990. National Foundation for the Arts and Humanities Act as Amended Through November 1990.

Putnam, D. 1997. *The Undeclared War. The Struggle for Control of the World's Film Industry*. London: HarperCollins.

Putnam, R. D. 1993. *Making Democracy Work: Civic Traditions in Modern Italy*. Princeton: Princeton University Press.

———. December 1995. "Tuning In, Tuning Out: The Strange Disappearance of Social Capital in America." *PS: Political Science and Politics*, 664–683.

Radich, A., ed. 1987. *Economic Impact of the Arts: A Sourcebook*. Denver: National Conference of State Legislatures.

Rafool, M., and L. Loyacono. 1995. *Creative Solutions for Funding the Arts*. Denver: National Conference of State Legislatures.

Research & Forecasts. 1990. "The American Public's Perspective on Federal Support for the Arts, and the Controversy over Funding for the National Endowment for the Arts." Prepared for the People for the American Way Action Fund. New York: Research & Forecasts.

Ripley, R. B., and G. A. Franklin. 1991. *Congress, the Bureaucracy, and Public Policy*. 5th ed. Pacific Grove, Calif.: Brooks-Cole.

Robinson, J. 1994. "The Arts Hold Steady in Hard Times." *American Demographics*. Ithaca, N.Y.: American Demographics Inc.

———. 1993. *Arts Participation in America: 1982–1992*. Research Division Report #27 for the NEA. Washington, D.C.: Jack Faucett Associates.

———. Fall 1989. "The Polls—A Review: Survey Organization Differences in Estimating Public Participation in the Arts." *Public Opinion Quarterly* 53: 397–414.

Robinson, J., and J. Fleishman. 1984. "Trends in Ideological Identification in the American Public." *Annals of Political and Social Science*, 50–60.

Robinson, J., and G. Godbey. 1997. *Time for Life: The Surprising Ways Americans Use Their Time*. University Park: Pennsylvania State University Press.

Robinson, J., and N. Zill. 1994. "Name That Tune." *American Demographics*. Ithaca, N.Y.: American Demographics, Inc.

Robinson, K., ed. 1982. *The Arts and Higher Education*. Guildford, U.K.: Society for Research into Higher Education.

Rose-Ackerman, S., ed. 1986. *The Economics of Nonprofit Institutions*. New York: Oxford University Press.

Rouet, F., and X. Dupin. 1991. *Le Soutien aux Industries Culturelles*. Paris: Département des Etudes et de la Prospective.

Rushefsky, M. E. 1995. *Public Policy in the United States*. 2nd ed. Belmont, Calif.: Wadsworth Publishing Co.

Ruttenberg, F., Kilgallon, Gutchess & Associates, Inc. 1978. *Survey of Employment, Underemployment in the Performing Arts*. Washington, D.C.: Human Resources Development

Ruttenberg, F., Kilgallon, Gutchess & Associates, Inc. 1981. *Working and Notworking in the Performing Arts: Survey of Employment, Underemployment, and Underemployment Among Performing Artists in 1980*. Washington, D.C.: Labor Institute for Human Enrichment, AFL-CIO.

Saez, G. 1996. "Les politiques culturelles des villes." In *Institutions et vie culturelles*, edited by J. Perret and G. Saez. Paris: La documentation française.

Salamon, L. M. 1989. *Beyond Privatization: The Tools of Government Action*. Washington, D.C.: Urban Institute Press.

———. 1993. *The Nonprofit Sector and Democracy: Prerequisite, Impediment, or Irrelevance?* Paper presented at the symposium Democracy and the Nonprofit Sector. Washington, D.C.: Aspen Institute Nonprofit Sector Research Fund.

Samuels, S., and A. Tonsic. 1995. *Theatre Facts*. N.Y.: TCG Theatre Communications Group.

Samuelson, P. A. 1961. *Economics*. New York: McGraw-Hill.

Scherer, F. M. 1971. *Industrial Market Structure and Economic Performance*. Chicago: Rand McNally.

Schumpeter, J. A. 1968. *History of Economic Analysis*. New York: Oxford University Press.

Schuster, J. M. Davidson. 1989. "The Search for International Models: Results from Recent Comparative Research in Arts Policy." In *Who's to Pay for the Arts?*, edited by M. C. Cummings Jr. and J. M. Davidson Schuster. New York: American Council for the Arts.

Scitovsky, T. 1989. "Culture Is a Good Thing: A Welfare-Economic Judgment." In *Cultural Economics: An American Perspective '88*. Akron, Ohio: Association for Cultural Economics, University of Akron.

————. 1976. *The Joyless Economy.* London: Oxford University Press.

————. May 1972. "What's Wrong with the Arts Is What's Wrong with Society." *American Economic Review.*

Seaman, B. A. 1987. "Economic Impact Studies: A Fashionable Excess." In *Economic Impact of the Arts: A Sourcebook,* edited by A. J. Radich and S. K. Foss. Denver: National Conference of State Legislatures.

Shapiro, E. 1970. *Macroeconomic Analysis.* New York: Harcourt, Brace and World.

Shiva, V. 21 September 1993. *Monocultures of the Mind: Understanding the Threats to Biological and Cultural Diversity.* Centre of International Programs, University of Guelph.

Siwek, S. E. and H. W. Furchtgott-Roth. 1990. *Copyright Industries in the U.S. Economy.* Washington, D.C.: Economists Inc.

Smith, A. 1961. *An Inquiry into the Wealth of Nations.* London: Methuen.

Spencer, M. J. 1997. *Live Arts Experiences: Their Impact on Health and Wellness.* New York: Hospital Audiences, Inc.

Stanley, R. 1978. *The Celluloid Empire: A History of the American Motion Picture Industry.* New York: Hastings House.

Stevens, L. Summer 1996. "The Earnings Shift: The New Bottom Line Paradigm for the Arts Industry in a Market-Driven Era." *Journal of Arts Management, Law and Society* 26(2): 101–114.

Stevens, Louise. 1997. Report, Study of Participation in the Arts. Commission and sponsored by the Arts Council of Indianapolis and by the Indianapolis Foundation.

Stigler, G., and G. Becker. 1977. "De Gustibus non est Disputandum." *American Economic Review.* Nashville, Tenn.: American Economic Association.

Stone, D. A. 1988. *Policy Paradox and Political Reason.* Glenview, Ill: Scotts, Foresman and Company.

Sullivan, J. E. Spring 1996. "Copyright for Visual Art in the Digital Age: A Modern Adventure in Wonderland." *Journal of Arts Management, Law, and Society* 26(1).

Swords, P. DeL. 1985. "Introductory Statements: Symposium on the Public Benefits of the Arts and Humanities." *Columbia-VLA Art & the Law* 9(2): 127–131.

Sykes, J. B. 1976. *The Concise Oxford Dictionary of Current English,* 6th ed. Oxford, U.K.: Clarendon Press.

Throsby, D. 1996. "Economic Circumstances of the Performing Artist: Baumol and Bowen Thirty Years On." *Journal of Cultural Economics* 20(3): 225–240.

Throsby, D., and D. Mills. 1989. *When Are You Going to Get a Real Job?* Sydney, Australia: Australia Council.

Throsby, D., and G. Withers. 1983. "Measuring the Demand for the Arts as a Public Good: Theory and Evidence." In *Economic Support for the Arts,* edited by J. L. Shanahan et al. Akron, Ohio: Association for Cultural Economics.

Tirole, J. 1988. *The Theory of Industrial Organization.* Cambridge: MIT Press.

Tocqueville, A. de. 1969. *Democracy in America,* edited by J. P. Mayer (a new translation by G. Lawrence). Garden City, N.Y.: Doubleday and Co./Anchor Books.

Traugott, M. W. and P. J. Lavrakas. 1996. *The Voter's Guide to Election Polls.* Chatham, N.J.: Chatham House.

Tullock, G. 1976. "Comment: The Economics of Theatre in Renaissance London." *Scandinavian Journal of Economics* 78: 115.

———. 1974. "Economics of Theatre in Renaissance London and Gay Ninties Eldora." *Swedish Journal of Economics* 76(3): 366–368.

UNESCO. 1996. *Our Creative Diversity: Report of the World Commission on Culture and Development.* New York: UNESCO.

UNESCO. 1980. *Recommendations Concerning the Status of the Artist.* Paris: UNESCO.

U.S. Department of Commerce. *National Income and Product Accounts of the United States*, statistical tables, various years. Washington, D.C.: GPO.

van Hemel, Annemoon, H. Mommaas, and C. Smithuijsen. 1996. *Trading Culture: GATT, European Cultural Policies and the Transatlantic Market.* Amsterdam: Boekman Foundation.

Vaver, D. March 1987. "Copyright in Foreign Works: Canada's International Obligations." *Canadian Bar Review* 66(1).

Vessilier-Ressi, M. 1994. *The Author's Trade.* New York: Center for the Arts, Columbia University School of Law.

Vogel, H. L. 1998. *Entertainment Industry Economics*, 4th ed. New York and Cambridge, U.K.: Cambridge University Press.

Wassall, G., and N. Alper. 1984. "Determinants of Artists Earnings." In *The Economics of Cultural Industries*, edited by W. Hendon et al. Akron, Ohio: Association of Cultural Economics.

———. June 1985. "Occupational Characteristics of Artists: A Statistical Analysis." *Journal of Cultural Economics.*

———. 1992. "Toward a Unified Theory of the Determinants of the Earnings of Artists." In *Cultural Economics*, edited by R. Towse and A. Khakee. Berlin/Heidelberg: Springer-Verlag.

———. Winter 1990. "When Is an Artist an Artist?: An Analysis of Factors Related to Claiming Membership in This Profession " *Journal of Arts Management, Law and Society.*

Wassall, G., N. Alper, and R. Davison. 1983. *Art Work: Artists in the New England Labor Market.* Cambridge, Mass.: New England Foundation for the Arts.

Wax, L., and NASSA. 1995. *1994 State Arts Agency Profile.* Washington, D.C.: National Assembly of State Arts Agencies.

Weber, B. 27 February 1997. "Birth of a Salesman." *New York Times*, C-13.

Weisbrod, B. A. 1988. *The Nonprofit Economy.* Cambridge, Mass.: Harvard University Press.

———. 1986. "Toward a Theory of the Voluntary Nonprofit Sector in a Three-Sector Economy." Chapter 1 in *The Economics of Nonprofit Institutions*, edited by S. Rose-Ackerman. New York: Oxford University Press.

Williamson, O. 1989. "Transaction Cost Economics. ' chapter 3 in *Handbook of Industrial Economics*, edited by R. Schmalensee and R. Willig. New York: North-Holland.

Winner, E. 1996. *Gifted Children: Myths and Realities.* New York: Basic Books.

Wolfe, T. 1974. *The Painted Word.* New York: Bantam Books.

Wollheim, R. A. 1985. "Remarks at a Panel Discussion on the Arts, the Humanities, and Their Institutions." *Art and the Law* 9(2): 179–186 (A Symposium on the Public Benefits of the Arts and Humanities, 30 April–1 May 1984).

Wriston, W. B. 1985. "Gnomons, Words and Politics." *The Executive Club.* Chicago.

Wyszomirski, M. J. 1995a. "Core Ideas, Policy Agendas, and Advocacy Coalitions:

Preliminary Observations from Cases in the Arts, Sciences, and Public Television." Paper presented at the Independent Sector Spring Research Forum. Alexandria, Va., 23–24 March.

————. 1995b. "Federal Cultural Support: Toward A New Paradigm?" *Journal of Arts Management, Law, and Society* 25: 69–83.

————. 1995c. "From Accord to Discord: Arts Policy During and After the Culture Wars." In *America's Commitment to Culture*, edited by K. V. Mulcahy and M. J. Wyszomirski. Boulder: Westview Press.

————. 1997a. "From Nancy Hanks to Jane Alexander: Generating Support for Art's Sake at the National Endowment for the Arts." In *Leadership for the Public Service*, edited by R. A. Loverd. Upper Saddle River, N.J.: Prentice Hall.

————. 1987. "Philanthropy, the Arts and Public Policy." *Journal of Arts Management, Law, and Society* 16(4): 5–30.

————. Autumn 1996. "Policy Communities and Policy Influence." *Newsletter of Grantmakers in the Arts* 6(2): 10–13, 33–34.

————. 1995d. "The Politics of Arts Policy: Subgovernment to Issue Network." In *America's Commitment to Culture*, edited by K. V. Mulcahy and M. J. Wyszomirski. Boulder: Westview Press.

————. 1997b. "Revealing the Implicit: Searching for Measures of the Impact of the Arts." In *Measuring the Impact of the Nonprofit Sector on Society*, edited by V. Hodgkinson and P. Flynn. San Francisco: Jossey-Bass.

Yudice, G. 1995. "Civil Society, Consumption, and Govermentality in an Age of Global Restructuring." *Social Text* 45: 1–26.

Zeigler, J. W. 1994. *Arts in Crisis: The National Endowment for the Arts versus America*. Chicago: Cappella Books.

————. 30 December 1996. *U.S. World and News Report*.

Zill, N., and J. Robinson. April 1995. "The Generation X Difference." *American Demographics* 17: 32–39.

Zimmer, A., and S. Toeppler. 1996. "Cultural Policies and the Welfare State: The Cases of Sweden, Germany and the United States." *Journal of Arts Management, Law and Society* 26(3): 167–194.

Zolberg, V., and J. M. Cherbo. 1997. *Outsider Art: Contesting Boundaries in Contemporary Culture*. New York: Cambridge University Press.

Biographical Notes

About the Editors

JONI M. CHERBO holds a Ph.D. in sociology from New York University and has taught at Hunter College, Columbia Presbyterian Hospital, SUNY-Purchase, and New York University. She was the research director for the American Assembly's 1997 meeting, "The Arts and the Public Purpose." She has also served on committees and boards of cultural institutions like American Ballet Theater, the International Center of Photography, Musical Theatre Works, and America for the Arts. Her publications include two studies for the NEA Arts, American Participation in Opera and Musical Theatre, 1992 (1994), and American Participation in the Arts, 1992 (1994). She coauthored *Outsider Art: Contesting Boundaries in Contemporary Culture* (1997) and was the editor for the *Journal of Arts Management and Law*, summer 1998, The Arts Sector, to which she contributed two articles "Creative Synergy: Commercial and Not for Profit Live Theater in America" and "The Missing Sector: The Unincorporated Arts."

MARGARET J. WYSZOMIRSKI is director of the graduate Arts Policy and Management Program at The Ohio State University with faculty appointments in both the art education and public policy departments. In addition to faculty positions at Dickinson College, as well as Rutgers, Georgetown, and Case Western Reserve Universities, she served as staff director for the 1990 Independent Commission on the NEA and as the director of the Office of Policy Planning, Research and Budget at the NEA from 1991 to 1993. She chaired the Steering Committee for the 1997 American Assembly on "The Arts and the Public Purpose." She holds a B.A. in history from SUNY-Binghamton, M.A.s in political science from SUNY-Binghamton and Cornell University, and a Ph.D. from Cornell University in government.

About the Contributors

NEIL O. ALPER is an associate professor in the economics department at Northeastern University. He received his bachelor's degree in economics from the State University of New York at Stony Brook, and master's and doctorate degrees in economics from the University of Pittsburgh. His teaching and research interests are in the area of applied microeconomics. He has published a number of articles, books, and reports, and has presented professional papers on cultural economics, the economics of crime, and labor economics. His research has involved primary data collection through large-scale surveys, including a survey of individual artists in New England and a current survey of Rhode Island artists with Ann M. Galligan. His publications include "Characteristics of Performing Artists: A Baseline Profile of Sectoral Crossovers," *Journal of Arts Management Law and Society* (summer 1998) with Galligan; and *Artists in the Work Force: Employment and Earnings, 1970–1990*, with G. Wassall et al. (1996).

JUDITH HUGGINS BALFE is professor of sociology at the City University of New York: College of Staten Island and Graduate Center. She is coauthor of *Age and Arts Participation with a Focus on the Baby Boom* (1996); editor and contributor to *Paying the Piper: Causes and Consequences of Art Patronage* (1993); coeditor and contributor to *Art, Ideology and Politics* (1985); and author of numerous articles on the sociology of the arts. She was an executive editor of *The Journal of Arts Management Law and Society* from 1990 to 1998.

HARRY HILLMAN CHARTRAND is a cultural economist and publisher of Compiler Press in Saskatoon, Saskatchewan, Canada. He has written extensively about cultural economic policy, planning, and evaluation. He has served as research director for the Canada Council for the Arts and is past vice president of the Association for Cultural Economics. He has been a consulting editor for the *Journal of Arts Management, Law and Society* since 1991. He has published *The Compleat Canadian Copyright Act 1921 to 1997–Current, Past and Proposed Provisions of the Act* and *The Compleat International Copyright and Related Conventions '98*.

THERESE FILICKO is the research director for the National and Local Profiles of Cultural Support project in the Arts Policy and Administration Program at Ohio State University. She has published work exploring the available survey questions on art and culture, the link between public opinion and public policy on the arts, and the state of public opinion research on arts policy. Her other research interests include the study of how individuals think about citizenship and political efficacy; presidential approval ratings and their link to how individuals think about the role of president; and how attention to politics is related to trust in government. Prior to her work on the Profiles Project, she was on the faculty at Case Western Reserve University in Cleveland, Ohio, where she taught courses in American politics, public opinion, political psychology, legislative politics, women and politics, and political theory.

ANN M. GALLIGAN is an associate professor and fine arts coordinator in the Department of Cooperative Education, and former fellow in the Northeastern University Center for the Arts. She holds a bachelor's degree in English from Brown University and a master's in communication and a doctorate in the history of education from Columbia University. Her teaching and research interests are in the area of arts policy and education. She has acted as a consultant and project assessor for a number of arts and community organizations, including the New York City Ballet, the Metropolitan Museum, Dance Umbrella, and WNET. Currently, she is the research director for the Rhode Island State Council on the Arts/Department of Education Arts Policy Task Force. In addition to the works coauthored with Neil O. Alper, she has written on the subject of arts funding and policy and has authored a chapter on peer-review panels at the National Endowment for the Arts in *Paying the Piper: Causes and Consequences of Art Patronage* (1993). She has written about experiential and multicultural arts education, and has served as book review editor (1994–98) and as an executive editor for *The Journal of Arts Management Law and Society*.

CHARLES M. GRAY is professor of economics in the Graduate School of Business, University of St. Thomas, where he also serves as research coordinator for the Center for Nonprofit Management. He has previously been a research economist at the Federal Reserve Banks of St. Louis and Minneapolis, and he has been staff economist for a Minnesota state agency. He has been teaching and studying the economics of the arts for nearly twenty years, is a consultant to the National Endowment for the Arts, and is coauthor with James Heilbrun of *The Economics of Art and Culture*.

JAMES HEILBRUN is professor of economics at Fordham University, where he has taught the economics of the arts since 1984. He is coauthor, with Charles M. Gray, of *The Economics of Art and Culture: An American Perspective* (1993), and has published *Real Estate Taxes and Urban Housing* (1966), and *Urban Ecomonics and Public Policy* (1987). He serves on the executive board of the Association of Cultural Economics International and on the editorial board of the *Journal of Cultural Economics*.

KEVIN V. MULCAHY is a professor of political science and the humanities at Louisiana State University. He received his Ph.D. from Brown University. He is the coauthor or coeditor of six books including *Public Policy and the Arts* and *America's Commitment to Culture*, and is currently an executive editor of the *Journal of Arts Management Law and Society*. He was cultural advisor to the speaker of the Louisiana House of Representatives and has served frequently as a panelist for state and local arts councils. In 1990 he testified as an expert witness before the Independent Commission on the Arts. He was the 1996 exchange professor at the Université de Provence in Aix-en-Provence and has lectured at the Observatoire des politiques culturelles in Grenoble, the École des Hautes Études Commerciales de Montréal, the Royal Institute of Technology in Stockholm, and the University of Jyväskylä, Finland. He has been the recipient of a National Endowment for the Humanities Summer Fellowship in Paris, the Manship Humanities Fellowship, and the Amoco Foundation Award for Distinguished Undergraduate Teaching.

MONNIE PETERS is a management consultant and researcher in the nonprofit sector, specializing in arts and culture. Her areas of expertise include long-range planning and feasibility studies, financial consulting, and date collection and research. Her recent publications include "The Missing Sector: The Unincorporated Arts," with Joni Maya Cherbo in the *Journal of Arts Management Law and Society* (summer 1998) and *Counting Arts Organizations Using the 1992 Census of Service Industries*, a report to the Research Division of the National Endowment for the Arts, 1998 (with related articles and notes available on the National Endowment for the Arts website: http:/www.arts.gov).

JOHN ROBINSON is a professor of sociology and directs the "Americans' Use of Time" project at the University of Maryland. His areas of specialization include social science methodology, attitude and behavior measurement, social change, and the impact of mass communication and other home technology. He founded and directed the Survey Research Center at the University of Maryland and the Communication

Research Center at Cleveland State University. He is the senior author of *Measures of Personality and Social Psychological Attitudes* (1991), *Polls Apart* (1993), and *How Americans Use Time* (1977). He has published more than one hundred articles in professional journals and books and is a contributing author to *American Demographics* magazine, in which he has published more than twenty-five articles related to social trends and the use of time.

HAROLD VOGEL was a managing director at SG Cowen Securities in New York and prior to that was first vice president and senior entertainment industry analyst at Merrill Lynch for seventeen years. Vogel holds an M.B.A. degree in finance from the Columbia University Graduate School of Business, and an M.A. in economics from New York University, and is a Chartered Financial Analyst. He serves on the New York State Governor's Advisory Board for Motion Pictures and Television, and is the author of *Entertainment Industry Economics* (1998). He also serves as adjunct professor of media economics at the Columbia University Graduate School of Business.

Index

CPSIA information can be obtained at www.ICGtesting.com
Printed in the USA
BVOW06s2033140915

417950BV00002B/4/P